Herbert Sussman's book explores ideas of manhood and masculinity as they emerged in the early Victorian period, and traces these through diverse formations in the literature and art of the time. Concentrating on representative major figures – Thomas Carlyle, Robert Browning, the Pre-Raphaelite Brotherhood, and Walter Pater – Sussman focuses on areas of conflict and contradiction within their formulation of the masculine. He identifies the development of "masculine poetics" as a project which was for the Victorians, and continues to be, crucial to an industrial and commercial age. The book reveals manhood as an unstable equilibrium, and is responsive to the complex ways in which the early Victorians' masculine poetics simultaneously subvert and maintain patriarchal power.

CAMBRIDGE STUDIES IN NINETEENTH-CENTURY
LITERATURE AND CULTURE 3

VICTORIAN MASCULINITIES

CAMBRIDGE STUDIES IN NINETEENTH-CENTURY
LITERATURE AND CULTURE

General editors
Gillian Beer, *University of Cambridge*
Catherine Gallagher, *University of California, Berkeley*

Editorial board
Isobel Armstrong, *Birkbeck College, London*
Terry Eagleton, *University of Oxford*
Leonore Davidoff, *University of Essex*
D. A. Miller, *Harvard University*
J. Hillis Miller, *University of California, Irvine*
Mary Poovey, *The Johns Hopkins University*
Elaine Showalter, *Princeton University*

Nineteenth-century British literature and culture have been a rich field for interdisciplinary studies. Since the turn of the twentieth century, scholars and critics have tracked the intersections between Victorian literature and the visual arts, politics, social organizations, economic life, technical innovations, scientific thought – in short, culture, in its broadest sense. In recent years, theoretical challenges and historiographical shifts have unsettled the assumptions of previous scholarly syntheses and called into question the terms of older debates. Whereas the tendency in much past literary critical interpretation was to use the metaphor of culture as "background," feminist, Foucauldian, and other analyses have employed more dynamic models that raise questions of power and of circulation. Such developments have re-animated the field.

This new series aims to accommodate and promote the most interesting work being undertaken on the frontiers of the field of nineteenth-century literary studies: work which intersects fruitfully with other fields of study such as history, or literary theory, or the history of science. Comparative as well as interdisciplinary approaches are welcomed.

Titles published
The Sickroom in Victorian Fiction
The Art of Being Ill
by Miriam Bailin, *Washington University*

Muscular Christianity
Embodying the Victorian Age
edited by Donald E. Hall, *California State University, Northbridge*

VICTORIAN MASCULINITIES

Manhood and Masculine Poetics in Early Victorian Literature and Art

HERBERT SUSSMAN

Northeastern University

CAMBRIDGE UNIVERSITY PRESS
Cambridge, New York, Melbourne, Madrid, Cape Town, Singapore, São Paulo

Cambridge University Press
The Edinburgh Building, Cambridge CB2 8RU, UK

Published in the United States of America by Cambridge University Press, New York

www.cambridge.org
Information on this title: www.cambridge.org/9780521465717

© Cambridge University Press 1995

This publication is in copyright. Subject to statutory exception
and to the provisions of relevant collective licensing agreements,
no reproduction of any part may take place without the written
permission of Cambridge University Press.

First published 1995
This digitally printed version 2008

A catalogue record for this publication is available from the British Library

Library of Congress Cataloguing in Publication data
Sussman, Herbert L.
Victorian masculinities: manhood and masculine poetics in early Victorian literature and art / Herbert Sussman.
p. cm. – (Cambridge studies in nineteenth-century literature and culture; 3)
Includes bibliographical references and index.
ISBN 0 521 46571 0
1. English literature – 19th century – History and criticism.   2. Masculinity (Psychology) in literature.   3. English literature – Men authors – History and criticism.   4. Men authors, English – 19th century – Psychology.   5. Art, Modern – 19th century – Great Britain.   6. Art and literature – Great Britain.   7. Preraphaelitism.   8. Poetics.   I. Title.
II. Series.
PR468.M38S87   1995
820.9′353–dc20   94-10268   CIP

ISBN 978-0-521-46571-7 hardback
ISBN 978-0-521-05466-9 paperback

To
Elisabeth Sacks Sussman, Charlotte Sacks Sussman,
Lucas George Sussman

Contents

List of plates		*page* x
Acknowledgments		xii
	Introduction	1
1	The condition of manliness question: Thomas Carlyle and industrial manhood	16
2	The problematic of a masculine poetic: Robert Browning	73
3	Artistic manhood: the Pre-Raphaelite Brotherhood	111
4	Masculinity transformed: appropriation in Walter Pater's early writing	173
Notes		203
Bibliography		214
Index		222

Plates

1 Ford Madox Brown, *Work*. Manchester City Art Galleries. *page* 40
2 J. E. Millais, *Christ in the House of His Parents (The Carpenter's Shop)*. Tate Gallery, London. 113
3 D. G. Rossetti, *The Passover in the Holy Family: Gathering Bitter Herbs*. Tate Gallery, London 122
4 J. E. Millais, Study for *Christ in the House of His Parents*. Fitzwilliam Museum, Cambridge. 123
5 Holman Hunt, *The Light of the World*. By permission of the Warden and Fellows of Keble College, Oxford. 124
6 D. G. Rossetti, *Mary Magdalene at the Door of Simon the Pharisee*. Fitzwilliam Museum, Cambridge. 127
7 J. E. Millais, *Mariana*. Makins Collection. 134
8 J. E. Millais, *The Disentombment of Queen Matilda*. Tate Gallery, London. 135
9 Holman Hunt, *Claudio and Isabella*. Tate Gallery, London. 136
10 Charles Collins, *Convent Thoughts*. Ashmolean Museum, Oxford. 138
11 D. G. Rossetti, *The Story of St. George and the Dragon: St. George and the Dragon*. Birmingham Museums and Art Gallery. 142
12 J. E. Millais, *The Rescue*. Felton Bequest 1924, National Gallery of Victoria, Melbourne, Australia. 145
13 J. E. Millais, *The Knight Errant*. Tate Gallery, London. 147
14 J. E. Millais, *The Order of Release, 1746*. Tate Gallery, London. 149
15 J. E. Millais, *Lorenzo and Isabella*. The Board of Trustees of the National Museums and Galleries on Merseyside (Walker Art Gallery, Liverpool). 151

16	J. E. Millais at Dalguise, Scotland. Private Collection.	154
17	J. E. Millais in his studio at Palace Gate. Private Collection.	156
18	Carte-de-visite of Holman Hunt. Jeremy Maas.	159
19	Carte-de-visite of Thomas Carlyle. Jeremy Maas.	159
20	Holman Hunt reenacting the painting of *The Scapegoat*. Jeremy Maas.	165
21	D. G. Rossetti. Delaware Art Museum, Samuel and Mary R. Bancroft Memorial.	167
22	D. G. Rossetti, *The Beloved*. Tate Gallery, London.	170

Acknowledgments

I would like to thank the many colleagues who have generously read portions of this work in manuscript and have shared with me ideas about masculinity that have shaped this text: Jim Adams, Julie Codell, Fred Kaplan, Mary Loeffelholz, John Maynard, Thaïs Morgan, Adrienne Munich, Michael Ryan, Carole Silver, Carolyn Williams. I would also like to thank the anonymous readers of *Victorian Studies* for their careful and helpful comments about Robert Browning, the members of the Victorian Seminar of CUNY for their observations on Carlyle, and the graduate students at Northeastern who have shared with me their valued observations about nineteenth-century masculinities.

My thanks, also, to the College of Arts and Sciences of Northeastern University for the sabbatical leave that enabled me to complete this project.

I would also like to thank the Trustees of Indiana University for permission to reprint material that appeared in *Victorian Studies* and the Editors for permission to reprint material published in *Victorian Literature and Culture*.

My gratitude, of course, to Elisabeth, who encouraged me in this task.

Introduction

This work is a study of masculinities, more specifically of the varied masculinities, masculine poetics, and constructions of artistic manhood that emerged in the early Victorian period, as well as an examination of the inscription of these diverse formations of the masculine in the high literature and visual art of this time. I have limited this study to the period extending from the early 1830s through the later 1860s, a relatively unexamined moment in the history of masculinities whose beginning is marked by the drive to construct a new form of manhood and a new masculine poetic for the industrial age, an enterprise exemplified in Thomas Carlyle's *Sartor Resartus* (1833–34) and his *Past and Present* (1843), and whose dissolution is seen in the emergence of a gay or homosexual discourse, represented here by such early critical essays of Walter Pater as "Poems by William Morris" (1868), that destabilize early Victorian formations of manhood and of the masculine in literature and in art. Keeping within this period, the study concentrates on representative figures – Carlyle, Robert Browning, the Pre-Raphaelite Brothers, Pater – as a way of exploring problematics within the construction of Victorian masculinities as well as within the efforts of Victorian men to fashion manly poetics and new styles of artistic manhood for their time.

OF MONKS AND MASCULINITIES

Readers who finish this study might well say, in Carlyle's words of the 1840s, "We have heard so much of Monks; everywhere, in real and fictitious History" (*Past* 48). The figures in "real" Victorian history include the Tractarians who established celibate male religious communities in the 1840s, the female celibates of the new Puseyite sisterhoods of the same decade, the secular Brotherhood of the Pre-Raphaelites, and William Morris, who for the early Pater appeared to manifest in contemporary life the medieval "mood of the cloister" ("Morris" 144). And since for the Victorians the line between "real and fictitious History" was notably blurred, we can also include Abbot Samson and the monks of St. Edmundsbury, the speaker of the "Soliloquy of a Spanish Cloister" as well as Pictor Ignotus and Fra Lippo Lippi, and Pater's imagined monk who "escapes from the sombre legend of his cloister to that true light" ("Morris" 147). To these must be added the cloistered females who in varied ways serve as surrogates for the celibate male – the nun of Charles Collins' *Convent Thoughts*, the nun-like Mariana of Tennyson and Millais.

For early Victorian writers and artists facing the need to refashion the notion of manliness and of artistic manhood in a world transformed by industrialization and by *embourgoisement*, the figures of the monk and of monasticism, energized by contemporary fears about the revival of celibate religious communities, provided a rich, malleable, and available metaphorics through which to register male anxieties. This discourse of monasticism, then, became the code through which the early Victorians debated what might be called, following Carlyle, the "Condition of Manliness question." Without a psychological vocabulary, debate about practices of the male self was conducted through the historicist formulation and reformulation, the valuing and revaluing of the monk as celibate male. Concerns about relationships among men in the present were posed as historical accounts of these all-male religious communities of the past.

The intensity with which male writers and artists fixed on the monk and monasticism – Carlyle's often embarrassing obeisance to Abbot Samson, Browning's nostalgic heroicizing of Lippo, Kingsley's hysterical reactions to Tractarian religious communities, the young Pre-Raphaelites' zeal to establish a secular Brotherhood devoted to art, Pater's account of Morris as modern-day monk – the disproportionate emotional energy expended on an anachronistic or, in its contemporary manifestation, a socially marginal topic provides insight into the male anxieties of this time. In Foucauldian terms, that debate centered on the all-male world of the monastery and the monk as celibate male enables us to identify points of problematization in the early Victorian formation of a male identity. And the variousness and incompatibility of these representations, the protean quality of the monk and of the monastery within this monastic discourse shows early Victorian masculinity not as a consensual or unitary formation, but rather as fluid and shifting, a set of

Introduction

contradictions and anxieties so irreconcilable within male life in the present as to be harmonized only through fictive projections into the past, the future, or even the afterlife.

For the Victorians, then, the monk and the monastery provided particularly labile and particularly suitable figures for the problematics and the contradictory possibilities of manhood in these decades.

As celibate male, the monk becomes the extreme or limit case of the central problematic in the Victorian practice of masculinity, the proper regulation of an innate male energy.[1] At the center of the early Victorian occupation with the technology of the self as the management of energy, particularly of sexualized desire, lies a crucial problematic. While psychic discipline defines what the Victorians term manliness, if such discipline becomes too rigorous the extreme constraint of male desire will distort the male psyche and deform the very energy that powers and empowers men. Setting the intensity of discipline, then, becomes the crucial issue within the practice of the self. The formations of Victorian manhood may be set along a continuum of degrees of self-regulation, and along this continuum the monk, the celibate male safely displaced into the past, becomes the test or limit case. In exemplifying the extreme position in the Victorian practice of manliness as reserve, the monk becomes the figure through whom Victorian men in a mode of historicized psychology could argue their widely varied views about self-discipline, the management of male sexuality, and the function of repression.[2] Thus we see great variations in the Victorian valuing of monkish celibacy, encompassing Carlyle's heroicizing of sexual abstinence as the desexualization of desire, Browning's representation of the psychic distortions generated by sexual repression in the cloister as the historicist analogue for the contemporary deformation of male creative potency through puritanical repression, the Pre-Raphaelite fixation upon the sexual longings of immured women, and Pater's vision of the medieval cloister as prefiguring the practice of intensifying homoerotic desire through internalization. A rich Victorian history of male sexuality, these historicist codings of the monk center on monasticism not as a devotional, but as a psychosexual practice.

Not only as celibate male, but as celibate male artist, and more specifically as celibate male painter, the monk provides the limit case for another crucial problematic of early Victorian artistic manhood, the relation of sexual to artistic potency. The monastic artist becomes the variously valued exemplar in the debate about finding the most efficient technology for turning male energy, more particularly sexualized male energy, to the production of art. From Carlyle through Pater the practice of masculine art is consistently theorized as being grounded in the regulation of male sexual energy and its history written as change within the practice of sexual self-discipline. There even develops in the 1840s and 1850s a psycho-sexual theory of mimesis that argues for the dependence of representational accuracy on the proper management of male sexuality and whose touchstone is medieval monastic painting. Within the assumption that the creative prowess of men depends upon the appropriate regulation of their sexuality, the views about the relation of artistic to sexual potency as coded within monastic discourse vary widely. For Carlyle the heroism of sublimation exemplified by Abbot Samson in the twelfth century is to be emulated by the heroic Man of Letters in the nineteenth. For the Pre-Raphaelite Brothers such Carlylean sublimation provides a model, albeit ambivalently practiced, for contemporary artists. Browning's artist-monks, Pictor Ignotus and Fra Lippo Lippi, exemplify as extreme cases the necessity of fleshly sexual life to artistic achievement. And to Pater the erotics of repression in the monastery provides a typological figure for a refashioned discipline of the "aesthetic" in the present. Even the oft-repeated narrative of the monk escaping the cloister that encodes the relation of artistic to sexual liberation takes on varied signification, from Browning's ambivalence to Pater's later subversion of the received liberationist narrative.

In living a celibate life within an enclosed all-male society, the monk provides an equally resonant and diversely valued figure for yet another problematic of normative bourgeois masculinity, the uneasy relation between the male sphere and the domestic sphere, the opposition of bonds within the all-male world of work to the heterosexual ties of marriage. Bourgeois industrial manhood defines manliness as success within the male sphere, the new arena of commerce and technology in which sexual energy is transmuted into constructive labor. And for this wholly male zone of energy made productive by being desexualized, for this homosocial sphere cemented by chaste affective bonds between men, the monastery provides an historicist coding. And yet, if normative bourgeois manliness is defined as success within the world of work inhabited solely by other man, bourgeois masculinity is also defined in relation to the domestic

Introduction 5

sphere within criteria that value the role of breadwinner for a domestic establishment and that situate affectionate as well as sexual life within marriage. In short, normative bourgeois masculinity enforces compulsory heterosexuality and compulsory matrimony.

It is this tension in bourgeois masculinity between the homosocial and the heterosexual that energizes the Victorian idealization of monasticism. For those middle-class male writers dissatisfied with the demands of this hegemonic valorization of domesticity, marriage, and even heterosexuality, the monastery as a sacralized, celibate all-male society safely distanced in time provides a figure through which they could express in covert form, or as an open secret, their attraction to a world of chaste masculine bonding from which the female has been magically eliminated, an attraction that clearly resonated with the longings of their middle-class male readers. For some writers, notably Carlyle, the all-male society of the cloister becomes intensely attractive as the safely distanced locus, as in early Victorian manly tales of shipboard life or imperialist quest, of a life of productive work from which the demands of marriage and even of heterosexuality have been eliminated, the utopian site that Herman Melville in idealizing the Inns of Court calls "The Paradise of Bachelors." And even in writers who present the all-male world of the monastery not as a utopia, but as a prison, notably Browning and the Pre-Raphaelites, we see a deep if often covert apprehension about a life lived outside a self-engendering male community, a barely concealed apprehension about bourgeois marriage sapping male energy and domesticity vitiating male creative potency.[3]

Furthermore, as the early Victorian signifier for affective life between men, the monastery becomes an imaginative zone in which male writers negotiate the troubled boundary between the homosocial and the homosexual. Again, the widely disparate representations of historical monasticism, drawing upon anxieties about the contemporary emergence of both male and female celibate religious communities, indicate both the intensity of homophobic feeling in the 1840s and 1850s as well as the varied practices for engaging the tension about male–male desire built into normative bourgeois masculinity. If to Carlyle and his many male readers in the early 1840s the monastery presented an ideal world of brotherhood as chaste male affection, to the critics of the Pre-Raphaelites at the end of the decade even a Brotherhood of male artists appeared to move beyond the bounds of the homosocial into the dangerous zone of feminization and even effeminacy. This troubled, edgy response in the late 1840s to communal masculine bonding, seen also in Kingsley's attack on contemporary religious communities of celibate men, marks the moment at which such bonds become problematized, the point at which monastic discourse comes to express the tension between the homosocial and the homophobic that becomes the central problematic in the formation of artistic manhood in the later Victorian period.

If the monastic life provided the limit case for affective life among men, it also provided the extreme case, valued along an equally wide range, for the relation of the male artist and poet to the economic basis of his practice, a problematic most frequently coded within monastic discourse as historicist retellings of the encounter of the poet/artist as monk with an emerging capitalism. In keeping with the ambivalence of early Victorian male artists to the art market, within these economic narratives the artist-monk and the monastery bear two wholly contradictory significations. In the Carlylean narrative, as a community organized not by seasonal rhythms, but by the mechanized scheduling of the clock,[4] the medieval monastery becomes a proto-factory prefiguring the historically inevitable coming of the factory system and the monk anticipates the factory worker sublimating his sexual energy into productive work. Within this narrative of monasticism, the artist as modern-day monk, the Hero as Man of Letters or the Pre-Raphaelite Brother, attains artistic manhood as a worker channeling desexualized desire into art production.

In the other, more widespread narrative the monastic artist represents in pure and unrealizable form the dream of the male artist existing outside the art market. As pre-capitalist art-workers, such artist-monks figure the irreconcilable contradictions of early Victorian artistic manhood, the intense ambivalence of the male poet and artist toward the commercial pressure of the male sphere. Artistic practice fantasized as existing beyond the demands of the market retains a purity from the commodification of male energy, yet in its distancing from the locus of aggressive competitive masculinity in the male sphere this isolated life is also figured as impotent, unmanly. Browning's Unknown Painter, the prototype of a gallery of isolated, imprisoned monks, such as those of the Grande Chartreuse, is an emasculated man. The artist-monk thus figures the paradox of artistic manhood – the domain of literature and art must be reserved for men, yet in being situated outside the male sphere, such activity unmans the male writer and artist.[5] And yet, the monk and the celibate male society of the monastery also come to represent early Victorian ways of resolving this paradox, becoming figures for a masculine poetic situated within a community of men and grounded in the values and the activities of normative bourgeois masculinity.

VICTORIAN MASCULINITIES

Several years ago, I went to Wordsworth, a state-of-the-art academic bookstore in Harvard Square, to buy a copy of Ehrenreich's *The Hearts of Men*, a wonderful account of the relocation of manliness from suburban split-level to *Playboy* pad in 1950s America. Unsure of where such a book would be shelved, I asked the clerk, whose computer told us that it was to be found in Women's Studies. When I suggested that it might be less than appropriate to set a book about men in a section devoted to women, I was told, "That's the way we do it."

That might have been the way Wordsworth did it only a few years ago, but when I went back recently to buy Leverenz's *Manhood and the American Renaissance*, a fine study of the conflicted self-fashionings of manhood in such nineteenth-century American figures as Emerson, Thoreau, Douglass, and Hawthorne, I found that Wordsworth had added between Women's Studies and Gay and Lesbian Studies three shelves devoted to what was now called "Men's Issues," a section containing not only Bly's *Iron John*, but also Leverenz' study as well as Ehrenreich's *The Hearts of Men*.

This anecdote of reshelving illustrates, in brief, the history, the current condition, and the problematics of the project that may be called the study of masculinities. Shelving scholarly works about men to follow scholarly works in Women's Studies suggests the theoretical source of such studies of masculinity in the feminist scholarship of our time, particularly in the awareness of gender as a social construction, multiform and historically specific. That studies of masculinity now have shelves of their own suggests that examination of the social construction of the masculine now constitutes a demarcated field of study, while the position between Women's Studies and Gay and Lesbian Studies indicates the inextricable connection of such inquiry with the study of other formations of gender and sexuality. And that these studies of masculinity in history take up only three shelves, as opposed to many times that number for books about women and about gay and lesbian life indicates the relatively small scale of this project at the present moment. Finally, that in these few shelves devoted to Men's Issues the psychoanalytic writing of Leverenz and the politically astute high popularization of Ehrenreich rub book jackets with the cult of Bly indicates the connection of highly theorized and historicized study of the formations of masculinity to the "Issues" or tensions in the lives of Wordsworth's customers.

Rather than "Men's Issues," I would employ for this field and for the methodology of this book the term the "study of masculinities," a name that foregrounds the major concerns of this volume. "Masculinities," in distinction to Men's Studies, emphasizes not the biological determinants but the social construction of what at any historical moment is marked as "masculine." The plural, "masculinities," stresses the multiple possibilities of such social formations, the variability in the gendering of the biological male, and the range of such constructions over time and within any specific historical moment, and especially within the early Victorian period. This emphasis on the multiplicity, the plurality of male gender formations is crucial not only to counter the still pervasive essentialist view of maleness, but also to deconstruct the monolithic view of masculinity, the unitary vision of the "masculine" that, with seeming disregard to the success of feminism in exploding such essentialist and monolithic thinking about women, still pervades and even structures discussion of men, particularly of men in the nineteenth century. Only a sense of the plurality of formations of the masculine among the Victorians can productively open the discussion of manhood in the nineteenth century to the issue of competition among multiple possibilities of masculinity, to the instability in the configuration of male identity shaped from among these competing formations by specific individuals and specific groups of men, and to the ways in which such tensions are inscribed in the literature and the art of the time.

Yet any study of masculinities and particularly of Victorian masculinities faces several crucial issues that must be confronted at the outset. One of the chief difficulties lies, quite simply, in the question of power. If Women's Studies as well as Gay and Lesbian Studies derive their energy and purpose from engaging a history of oppression and thereby liberating the self from that oppression, a study of masculinities examines the history of the oppressors, of the hegemonic discourse, of the patriarchy. This justifiable anxiety about

Introduction 9

the study of the masculine must be acknowledged, and may be addressed in several ways. For one, the emphasis on the constructed rather than the innate, and on the multiple rather than the unitary view of the masculine calls attention to the historical contingency of such formations of manliness and of male power itself, thus questioning male dominance and supporting the possibility of altering the configuration of what is marked as masculine. Furthermore, for the writer on Victorian masculinities the problem of power and patriarchy calls for a double awareness, a sensitivity both to the ways in which these social formations of the masculine created conflict, anxiety, tension in men while acknowledging that, in spite of the stress, men accepted these formations as a form of self-policing crucial to patriarchal domination. As Munich notes at the beginning of her fine study *Andromeda's Chains: Gender and Interpretation in Victorian Art and Literature*, "Men used the Andromeda myth not only to celebrate the rewards of a patriarchal system, but also to record their discomforts with it" (2).

A second major issue for the study of masculinities in the nineteenth century lies in the relation of this enterprise to the field of gender study currently so productive within Victorian studies – Gay Studies. Like any student of Victorian masculinities I am indebted to the work done within the project of Gay Studies. My inquiry has been invigorated by the model, associated with the work of Sedgwick, describing male–male relationships along a continuum of male desire (*Between Men* Introduction), a model that I employ throughout this study. Sedgwick's work has enabled Victorianists to see conflict between male–male desire and its social interdiction as an important reason for the instability of male identity in Victorian male writers, an issue defended against by the Victorian writers themselves, by their contemporary readers and by the modern male (?) critical tradition. Indeed, one of the dismaying pleasures of reading Sedgwick on *The Princess* or critics such as Craft ("Descend") and Sinfield on the Tennyson/Hallam relation is realizing how much I, like other Victorianists, have resisted seeing the intensity of male–male desire in this poet. Similarly, to see homophobic tensions in Dickens' novels (Sedgwick *Between Men* chs. 9, 10) or in Stoker's *Dracula* (Craft "Kiss Me") is to see the fault lines within what had traditionally been seen as a monolithic Victorian male consciousness.

Yet here, as with the issue of power, a doubleness of vision is needed, a negotiation that acknowledges male–male desire as crucial to the construction of and the problematics of male identity in the nineteenth century, but does not see such desire as the single or necessarily primary constitutive force in the formation of and conflicts within Victorian masculinities. Rather, my own study of the social construction of Victorian manliness considers the homoerotic as one among the many psychological and social forces that troubled Victorian manhood, among them industrialization, the development of bourgeois hegemony, class conflict, the feminization of culture.

Furthermore, if students of Victorian masculinities must be attentive to conflict between male–male desire and the normative formation of the masculine as one important cause, among many, for the instability of manhood in writers and artists, Sedgwick's description of male–male relationships as a continuum rather than a simple binary of straight/gay suggests that important work is to be done at the troubled boundaries between the developing gay discourse and hegemonic forms of masculinity. In the concluding chapter of this study I focus on a crucial moment of this intersection, the early critical writing of Pater, in order to examine this complex process of appropriation, transformation and even acceptance of normative formations of heterosexual masculinity within the emergent gay discourse.[6]

Like most recent work on Victorian masculinities, this study is grounded in the work of Foucault, most specifically in *The History of Sexuality*. Indeed, writing the history of Victorian masculinities along the lines of a Foucauldian history of sexuality is particularly pertinent since Victorian men themselves wrote the history of literature and of art as the history of techniques of managing male desire. If, following Foucault, we look to the history of masculinities as "a history of ethical problematizations" (II: 13), then for the early Victorians the problematization of sexuality and of manliness are conjoined. To state briefly here what will be developed at length in this study, the early Victorians defined maleness as the possession of an innate, distinctively male energy that, in contrast to Freud, they did not represent as necessarily sexualized, but as an inchoate force that could be expressed in a variety of ways, only one of which is sexual.[7] This interior energy was consistently imagined or fantasized in a metaphorics of fluid, suggestively seminal, and in an imagery of flame. The point of problematization for manhood or what the Victorian middle-class termed "manliness" was situated in developing what Foucault calls "practices of the self" (II: 13) for properly

Introduction

regulating or managing this internal, natural energy, "technologies of the self" (II: 11) that were consistently identified with the technologies of an industrializing society obsessed with harnessing the natural energy of water and fire. This definition of manhood as self-discipline, as the ability to control male energy and to deploy this power not for sexual but for productive purposes was clearly specific to bourgeois man. For the industrialist as for the Pre-Raphaelite artist manliness as control validated the hegemony of the bourgeoisie by valorizing manliness as self-regulation over what was seen through middle-class eyes as the libertinism and idleness of the gentry and the irregularity and sexual license of the working class.

In seeing Victorian cultural products as inscriptions of varied male practices of the self, I have also drawn on another rich theoretical model for the study of masculinities and particularly of Victorian masculinities, Theweleit's *Male Fantasies*, volume I: *Women, Floods, Bodies, History* and volume II: *Male Bodies: Psychoanalyzing the White Terror*. In these fascinating volumes, Theweleit uses published materials such as novels and letters to present the configuration of the psychic life of men in the fascist para-military Freikorps in Germany between the wars. What is theoretically productive is that he does not posit a hidden explanatory ground, such as male–male desire or even a Freudian unconscious or libido that these fantasies express, does not theorize the shared fantasies of this specific group of males about the body, about women, about violence, and about the structure of society at a specific historical moment within a specific culture as signs of something else. As he states,

> Most centrally, we will look at... the language of the soldier males. The question here is not so much what such language "expresses" or "signifies," as how it functions, its role in the man's relationship to external reality, and its bodily location. The relationship of human bodies to the larger world of objective reality grows out of one's relationship to one's own body and to other human bodies. The relationship to the larger world in turn determines the way in which these bodies speak of themselves, of objects, and of relationships to objects. (1: 24)

Beyond the specific analogues of the twentieth-century fantasies he describes with certain early Victorian male fantasies, in its historical specificity and focus on a clearly defined group, in using sources beyond the high literary, and in its special attention to the image of the body, Theweleit provides a model for describing the psychic lives of specific Victorian men and groups of men as varied forms of male fantasies.

As Foucault and Theweleit demonstrate, the construction of male consciousness must be seen as specific to individuals and to groups or classes of men at any given historical moment. Any study of the inscriptions of the masculine must, then, be grounded in the history of these social formations of masculinity, in their variousness, their contradictions, their instabilities, and their transformations over time. Such social histories of Victorian masculinities have been remarkably rare, but recently there has been, if not a flood, a fruitful stream of studies of particular value to Victorianists and my own work draws upon these studies. The oldest, and still the best general study of "manhood as an evolving social construct reflecting some continuities but many more changes" (3) from the beginnings to the present moment is Stearns' *Be a Man! Males in Modern Society*. Stearns' discussion of the nineteenth century in Europe and America is particularly useful for its concern with the effects of industrialism on the shape of manhood, and the inflection of industrial manhood by class. His distinction between working-class and middle-class manhood in the nineteenth century provides a valuable corrective to the continuing tendency of Victorianists to conflate certain specifically bourgeois forms of manliness with Victorian manliness in general. For example, Vance's *The Sinews of the Spirit: The Ideal of Christian Manliness in Victorian Literature and Religious Thought*, although it offers a useful account of muscular Christianity, exemplifies this tendency to generalize bourgeois Christian manliness into Victorian manliness. Indeed, most historical accounts of Victorian masculinities, such as the valuable historical work of Davidoff and Hall, *Family Fortunes: Men and Women of the English Middle Class, 1780–1850*, focus, albeit self-consciously, on the bourgeoisie. Here I have tried to be attentive to the bourgeois class-position of the writers and artists I discuss, and particularly aware of their complex mix of repulsion and envy for what they saw as the relaxed and undisciplined physicality of working-class manliness.

In this study I have tried to employ a critical vocabulary that represents not only the constructed nature of the male self, but also the multiplicity of the formations of the masculine within the Victorian period. I use the term "male" only in the biological sense and the term "maleness" for fantasies about the essential nature of the "male," for that which the Victorians thought of as innate in

Introduction 13

men. I reserve the terms "masculinity" and "manliness" for those multifarious social constructions of the male current within the society. Thus, using "masculine bonding" rather than "male bonding" or "masculine poetic" rather than "male poetic" suggests the constructed rather than the essentialist, the diverse rather than the monolithic nature of these formations. Such a distinction is especially important for the Victorians for whom the hegemonic bourgeois view defined "manliness" as the control and discipline of an essential "maleness" fantasized as a potent yet dangerous energy.

Furthermore, I reserve the term "manhood" for the achievement of manliness, a state of being that is not innate, but the result of arduous public or private ritual and, for the Victorian bourgeois, of continued demanding self-discipline.[8] Furthermore, "manhood" as achieved manliness, the goal of the process of "masculinization," is a condition not achieved by all males and that once reached is for the Victorians exceedingly difficult to maintain. For nineteenth-century men, manhood was conceived as an unstable equilibrium of barely controlled energy that may collapse back into the inchoate flood or fire that limns the innate energy of maleness, into the gender-specific mental pathology that the Victorian saw as male hysteria or male madness. For the Victorians manhood is not an essence but a plot, a condition whose achievement and whose maintenance forms a narrative over time. It is this narrative of manhood achieved and manhood lost, what I term the "masculine plot," that structures the writing of such representative Victorian men as Carlyle and Browning, that informs the work and the careers of the Pre-Raphaelite Brotherhood, and that shapes Pater's early writing, including what now we know as the "Conclusion" to *The Renaissance*.

An historicist approach to masculinities opens up such Victorian terms as manliness, masculinity, manhood, so often identified with a single formation such as muscular Christianity or bourgeois paternalism, so that we can see the early Victorian decades as encompassing a variety of competing formations of the masculine. For example, following Stearns, we may recognize an emerging "industrial manhood" while being attentive to his distinction within this category between "working-class" and "aggressive middle-class" masculinity. I also find useful the opposition described by Davidoff and Hall of the "gentry" style to "the construction of a new subject – the Christian middle-class man" (*Family Fortunes* 110). Leverenz's paradigms of nineteenth-century American manhood as "patrician," "artisan," and "entrepreneurial" (ch. 3) may also be fruitfully applied to Victorian England. To these I have added such terms for artistic manhood as the "gentleman," the "prophet-sage," the "professional man," and the "Bohemian."

Applying such typologies of Victorian manliness to artists and to writers productively complicates the pervasive academic model that situates nineteenth-century gender conflicts solely within the binary of masculine/feminine. Early Victorian male poets and painters sought to differentiate themselves from the feminine, but to do so each male poet, novelist, painter had to shape from the varied possibilities of manly self-fashioning available in that historical moment a personal configuration of artistic manhood that was often at odds with the normative model of manliness in a bourgeois industrial society.[9] These individual formations of masculinity often failed to resolve their own internal contradictions, an instability that manifests larger strains within the culture's constructions of the masculine. This study will focus on the ways that such psychic tension is inscribed, often as inconsistencies of form, within the writing and visual art of the period.

This study, then, will focus on conflict and contradiction *within* literary and artistic formations of the masculine.[10] The emphasis will fall on what was for the Victorians and continues to be in our day an enormously important project, the development of "masculine poetics," of styles and practices that locate the sources of poetry and art in those various and often contradictory qualities marked by the age as masculine – in chaste masculine bonding as well as phallic sexuality; in emotional control and clear-eyed scientific objectivity as well as in prophetic vision; in the equation of artistic enterprise with the progress of British industrialism and the identification of artistic potency and sexual potency with England's commercial energy; and in the identification of artistic quest with the forward movement of British imperialism.

The goals of this study, then, are to see masculinity as an historical construction rather than an essentialist given; to present early Victorian masculinity not as monolithic but as varied and multiform; to be attentive to the way each male artist and writer shapes the possibilities of manliness available to him within his cultural moment into a very personal configuration that necessarily participates within the more general discourse of the masculine; to consider male identity within the individual not as a stable achievement but as an unstable equilibrium, so that the governing terms of Victorian manhood become contradiction, conflict, anxiety; and, finally, to remain responsive to the complex ways that these unstable and conflicted forms of literary and artistic manhood simultaneously subvert and maintain patriarchal power.

CHAPTER I

The condition of manliness question: Thomas Carlyle and industrial manhood

Within the historicist rhetoric of the early Victorian decades, the monk – the celibate male working and praying within an enclosed all-male community – becomes the central figure through which the contradictions and anxieties about manliness are registered. And the range of values attached to this figure by the male writers and artists of these decades indicates the multiple possibilities for the shape of masculinity in these formative years of the industrial system. If by the latter 1840s the life of the medieval monk came to represent for Browning, for Kingsley, for the Pre-Raphaelites, and for their critics, those qualities of passivity, sexual repression, isolation from the male sphere, even unmanly male–male attachments that threaten true manliness, earlier in the 1840s and even in the 1830s the monk and monasticism became for Thomas Carlyle the very model of a new form of manhood for the worker, the mill-owner, and the Man of Letters.

Sartor Resartus (1833–34), "The Hero as Man of Letters" in *On Heroes, Hero Worship, and the Heroic in History* (1841), and *Past and Present* (1843) become crucial texts in the debate within the early Victorian period on the Condition of Manliness. Carlyle's works quite self-consciously seek to establish a foundation myth of manliness for an industrial society. And yet their most striking quality is that the Carlylean male heroism figured within an historicist monastic discourse apparently contradicts several basic attributes of the newly emerging and soon to be hegemonic bourgeois model of manliness. There is, after all, a sharp difference between patience before marriage and a life of celibacy. The lives of Teufelsdröckh, of the Man of Letters as lived within a "Priesthood" (*Heroes* 385), and of Samson and his monks clearly run counter to the bourgeois script for achieving manhood, that is, to heterosexual fulfillment within marriage and to success as breadwinner for a domestic establishment.

And yet, the qualities of Carlyle's writing – the abhorrence of heterosexuality, the self-conscious rejection of the marriage plot in men's lives, the valorizing of male–male affective ties – that later in the century Pater would employ to subvert an established bourgeois manliness are here employed to model a new industrial manliness for writer and for worker, the transgressive potential seemingly invisible to early Victorian male readers.

This seeming paradox, the popularity of works that in many ways oppose hegemonic manhood, becomes less paradoxical if we see *Sartor Resartus*, "The Hero as Man of Letters," and *Past and Present* functioning less as realist modellings of the new industrial man than as male fantasies that figure certain acceptable qualities of industrial manhood while also representing certain oppositional feelings not permitted overt expression within the dominant model of manliness.[1] Shaped within a self-consciously masculine poetic, the achieved manhood of Teufelsdröckh, the utopian vision of an all-male society in *Past and Present*, and the ideal of the contemporary male author as taking his place within a "perpetual Priesthood, from age to age" (*Heroes* 385) provide, given the acute male anxieties of the 1840s, a safe resolution of several crucial problematics of male identity. Carlyle's Man of Letters as priest, as well as the figures of Abbot Samson and Teufelsdröckh, exemplify a technology of the self that resolves felt oppositions in the internal organization of male identity in the early industrial period, in particular the need to control the inward, specifically male energy that is seen by Carlyle as the very source of and yet the greatest danger to the integrity of manliness.

In Carlyle's vision of an all-male space beyond the society of the present day and of a literary terrain occupied only by *Men* of Letters the pollution of sexuality is controlled by excluding the female; the deep ambivalence toward male sexuality itself is resolved by an imaginatively distanced celibacy; virility is divorced from sexuality; potentially dangerous psychic energy channeled to productive work and contained by dissolving the individual ego in affective submission to a stronger male within a bonded male society. The historical distancing in *Past and Present* of this self-engendering male society devoted to sacralized labor prevents this fantasy of male–male affective bonds within a wholly male community from crossing the homophobic boundary into homoeroticism and thus models a social life that resolves the perilous erotic tensions for men created by patriarchy. Carlyle's life of Teufelsdröckh and his tale of monastic reform act out in imagination what is not so easily found in the lives of his male readers, the achievement of an integrated manhood.

Then, too, in their very form *Sartor Resartus* and *Past and Present* self-consciously exemplify the new masculine poetic set forth in "The Hero as Man of Letters," realizing for the industrial age the Wordsworthian project of becoming as writer "a man speaking to men."[2] John Sterling wrote to Carlyle of *Sartor Resartus*, "Something of this state of mind [of Teufelsdröckh] I may say that I understand; for I have myself experienced it. And the root of the matter appears to me: A want of sympathy with the great body of those who are now endeavouring to guide and help onward their fellow-men" (Seigel *Carlyle* 32). The male readers of *Past and Present* also responded enthusiastically to the male fantasies articulated by Carlyle as the new hero as Man of Letters. Like Sterling, and like modern followers of Robert Bly, these men felt Carlyle's words resonating with their own anxieties about male identity. The reviewer for *Blackwood's*, William Henry Smith, saw *Past and Present* as one of Carlyle's "appeals to the individual heart" (Seigel 212). Quite specifically, he responded to Carlyle's positive vision of "communities of men" (212), to the vision of an all-male society or brotherhood: "[*Past and Present* is] an appeal to the consciousness of each man, and to the high and eternal laws of justice and of charity – lo, ye are brethren!" (212).

Writing in America, Ralph Waldo Emerson also perceived the book within the terms of a masculine poetic as the circulation of wisdom among men: "It grapples honestly with the facts lying before all men" (Seigel 219). Like the *Blackwood's* reviewer, he also responds to the work as a mode of personal communication among men, as coming from the "heart." And, like the *Blackwood's* reviewer, he is particularly drawn to the major emotional quality of the book, the aura of deep affective bonds between man and man, the ideal of intense male–male ties, of brotherhood: "[Carlyle] offers his best counsel to his brothers" (219). To Emerson, Carlyle speaks with "a heart full of manly tenderness" (219).

But *Sartor Resartus* and *Past and Present*, as well as *The French Revolution* and "The Hero as Man of Letters," also exemplify the instability and the strains in the Carlylean construction of masculinity, strains that resonate with those of normative early Victorian masculinity. In these works we see inscribed the inability of Carlyle as well as of his age to resolve fully the contradictions of male identity.

In seeking a psychic armor to contain the inchoate, fluid energy within, Carlyle presents a particularly fragile and unstable model of the male psyche always at the edge of eruption, of dissolution, of madness, an instability registered in what Emerson calls the "lurid stormlights" (222) of his prose. And as attractive as the vision of a wholly male society of workers and of writers was to Carlyle and to his male readers, this fantasy depends upon psychically erasing women from the society of the past as well as of the present, on displacing the inner chaos and physical pollution that men feel within themselves onto the female, and on creating the compensatory fantasy of male self-engenderment. Indeed, Carlyle's fantasies became compelling to his readers as displaced resolutions of problematics within normative bourgeois masculinity – maintaining the fragile psychic stability attained by continuously transforming desire into productivity, negotiating a homosocial world of labor and of letters imbued with chaste yet perilously intense masculine bonding.

THE HYDRAULIC BODY

Reading *Sartor Resartus*, *The French Revolution*, *Past and Present*, and "The Hero as Man of Letters" as male fantasy and seeing the connection of this fantasy to crucial issues of early Victorian masculinity can best begin with Carlyle's imagining of the male body. For Carlyle, the interior space of the male body or, more accurately, of the male self since Carlyle's language consistently conflates the physical and the psychological, is characterized by unstable fluidity. In their primal being men appear as "little red-coloured pulpy infants" (*Past* 129); the newborn, without clothing, is "a watery, pulpy, slobbery freshman and new-comer in this Planet" (*Sartor* 43). The inner self is formless; the interior is "foam itself" (*Past* 128). Even "bodies, that took shape...will lose it, melting into air" (*Sartor* 15). Like Freud, Carlyle sees psychic action in hydraulic images. A "free-flowing channel" may be torn "through the sour mud-swamp of one's existence...making, instead of pestilential swamp, a green fruitful meadow with its clear-flowing stream" (*Past* 197).

Toward this restless, fluid, indeed seminal energy, "the Life-fountain within you" (*Past* 29), Carlyle, like other early Victorian males, is deeply ambivalent.[3] At times he sees the achievement of manliness as releasing this fluid energy from restraint, from imprisonment. Speaking to his male readers in *Past and Present*, much like a Victorian Robert Bly, he assumes an evangelical rhetoric, echoing the Wordsworthian trope of poetic creation as the overflow of internal energy:

There will a radical universal alteration of your regimen and way of life take place; there will a most agonising divorce between you and your chimeras, luxuries and falsities, take place ... so the inner fountains of life may again begin, like eternal Light-fountains, to irradiate and purify your bloated, swollen, foul existence ... But the Life-fountain within you once again set flowing, what innumerable "things,"... year after year, and decade after decade, and century after century, will then be doable and done! (28–29)

Such unrestricted and purified flow of inner energy is exemplified in "Great Men" who appear as "a flowing light-fountain ... of native original insight, of manhood and heroic nobleness" (*Heroes* 239).

And yet, like many other early Victorian men, Carlyle felt that this fluid energy within that powers and empowers masculinity is dangerous, that the very source of male identity is unclean, diseased. His fantasies of the male body turn upon a liquid interior whose touch is polluting. The representation of male identity in hydraulic terms, the occupation with flood and constraint, and with the unclean quality of the expressed fluid suggests the connection of these fantasies to anxieties about masturbation, nocturnal emissions, and, more generally, spermatorrhea as the unproductive discharge of seminal fluid, a locus of male sexual panic throughout the Victorian period.[4] But Carlyle's own continued warnings against contact with this interior fluidity registers an apprehension of physical contagion moralized by his Old Testament division of the clean and the unclean: "Religion is not a diseased self-introspection, an agonising inquiry ... never so morbid" (*Past* 66). Instead, as an emotional practice for the male a proper religion is limned as "the way of supreme good plain, indisputable, and they are travelling on it" (66). The topographical image represents Carlyle's characteristic sense of the male body as a hard surface or "plain" beneath which is "pestilential swamp" (*Past* 197) and mental life as a perilous passage over a surface that may at any time collapse into the miasmic waters beneath.[5]

To protect against this sense that the fluid, seminal energy that defines maleness is diseased, Carlyle consistently displaces interior sickness or disorder and its overflow or flood from the male self, more particularly the Anglo-Saxon male self, onto the Other, most notably onto the female.[6] In Carlyle's vision, male is to female as order is to chaos, external hardness to internal fluidity, boundedness to dissolution, containment to eruption, health to disease. The unclean, disruptive quality of the female in Carlyle's writing is overdetermined, powered by intense misogyny, by the fear of female sexuality, and the threatening power of the new women of letters.[7] In his political and historical writing, particularly in *The French Revolution*, insurrectionary women represent the chief threat to the patriarchal order of society.[8] But here I wish to emphasize the ways that women are charged with Carlyle's own sexual and psychological anxiety about male identity. His fixation with diseased and disruptive women works within a coherent male fantasy that displaces onto the female Carlyle's own dis-ease, his own anxieties about the inherently diseased male self, and his own fear of the eruption of the interior fluid energy with the consequent dissolution of psychic control. As projections of the male self, these disruptive women become a violent Other, woman as an anti-muse that figures the unhealthful, potentially uncontrollable energy that defines the male body and the male psyche. These monstrous diseased females act out Carlyle's deepest psycho-social anxiety in an apocalyptic vision of the destructive release of the pestilential fluid energy in eruption and flood. The fantasy of an all-male society and the ideal of male celibacy for Carlyle, then, functions not only as a defense against women, but also as a defense against the unclean essence of maleness.

In *Past and Present* Carlyle clearly transfers his own revulsion at the male body to the female. The female consistently represents the sickness, the excremental quality Carlyle envisions at the center of the male self: "Our larders are reduced to leanness, Jew Harpies and unclean creatures our purveyors; in our basket is no bread" (91). The Jew, the unmanly outsider, is merged with the Harpy, the monstrous female, and both with the "unclean," with pollution expressed through the Harpy's traditional association with excrement.

Even the celebrated "Irish Widow" (*Past* 150), although traditionally read as Carlyle's figure for human community, continues into the present the fantasy of the female Other as diseased and disruptive body and figures the same potential within the male. Her interpolated story recapitulates a central Carlylean trope, the need for rigid order to control the contagion within. In this emblematic incident, disease spreads once such control is loosened. As a widow, she "went forth" only after her husband died, after the dissolution of the rigid discipline that defines patriarchal manhood. Moving beyond social enclosure or boundary, in Carlyle's fantasy she inevitably becomes death personified: "She sank down in typhus-fever; died" (151). This wandering opens the flood of interior uncleanliness to pollute the society. Personal death becomes social death. She "infected her Lane with fever, so that 'seventeen other persons' died of fever there in consequence... her typhus-fever kills *them*: they actually were her brothers" (151). The verbal drift here from the ungendered words "persons" and "them" to males, "brothers," suggests that although projected onto the female, this interior sickness is primarily a threat to "brothers," to the male community.

The Irish widow, then, becomes one of a number of female surrogates who act out not only in images of contagion, but also in images of eruption and flood the male fear of losing control over male energy in both individual and social terms. In the twelfth century, it is not a rebellious peasantry, but women who manifest social disorder, social dissolution: "Old women with their distaffs rush out on a distressed Cellarer in shrill Chartism" (*Past* 91). Typically, the imagery combines uncontrolled fluidity or "rush" and the dissolving of gender boundaries as the women brandish their now phallicized "distaffs." The French Revolution becomes "The Insurrection of Women" (Book 7), women limned in images of internal energy, overwhelming yet formless, as "Insurrectionary Chaos" (*French* 1: 276), as diseased madness, "rabid" (1: 278). The fluidity of the inner life overflows its channels, "wild-surging" (1: 279), "like snowbreak from the mountains, for every staircase is a melted brook" (1: 252).

Carlyle displaces the unmanly not only onto women, but also onto the male Other of the white Anglo-Saxon male, as in the conflation of the Jew and the female as "Jew Harpies," and at mid-century to the non-white males or, to employ Carlyle's terminology, the "Nigger." In "The Nigger Question,"[9] Carlyle equates the "indolent" (327) "Black Quashee" (325) of the West Indies with the primeval unclean fluidity of swamp to figure his sense of the Black as the fluid, diseased essence of maleness not yet formed into the "manful industrious men" (327) of Europe. Since the islands first mounted oozy, on the back of earthquakes, from their dark bed in the Ocean deeps, and reeking saluted the tropical Sun, and ever onwards till the European white man first saw them some three short centuries ago, those Islands had produced mere jungle, savagery, poison-reptiles and swamp-malaria: till the white European first saw them, they were as if not yet created... Swamps, fever-jungles, man-eating Caribs, rattlesnakes, and reeking waste and putrefaction, this has been the produce of them under the incompetent Caribal (what we call Cannibal) possessors. (325–26)

Here, a racially charged colonialism becomes justified in the tropes used to valorize industrial labor in *Past and Present* as the divinely ordained manly work of making productive the swampy waste land. Furthermore, in Carlyle's male fantasies such exploitative colonialism, even the brutal repression of Black rebellion by Governor Eyre, becomes justified as the natural domination of the formed or white "manful industrious men" (327) over the unformed or primitive male, and resonates as an external enactment of the psychic formation or plot of manhood as the rigorous process of controlling and thereby cleansing the unclean mire of essential maleness, the miasmic fluid energy that for Carlyle lies within European and Black man alike.[10]

In Carlyle's psycho-social imagination, then, sickness is associated with the slackening of psychic control, as in the Irish Widow and the Jamaican Black. At the other extreme, and Carlyle's imaginings run to sets of extremes, too rigid control of the fluid interior results in eruption or "wasteful volcanoism" (*Past* 96). Associating extreme repression with the intensification and thus the corruption of internal energy, he consistently turns to the organic metaphor of fermentation; Abbot Samson will "educe organic method out of lazily fermenting wreck" (94). In *The French Revolution*, "Unshaped raw material of a thought, ferments universally under the female nightcap ... fermenting all night, universally in the female head" (1: 250–51). For Carlyle a too-strict control of inner space will only strengthen the indwelling disease, generate noxious gases that "on slight hint, will explode" (*French* 1: 250) destroying the fragile construction of masculine selfhood and of society.[11]

If Carlyle manifests an almost obsessive attraction/repulsion to fantasies of women acting out the destructive eruption of a projected male energy, he is equally transfixed by the opposing fantasy, the loss of this potency as emasculation, again displaced onto the agency of the female. Carlyle's male fantasies obsessively turn to the figure of the castrating woman. In *The French Revolution*, his gaze is mesmerized by the female dismembering of the male body. His mythic associations for the women of France turn to "Bacchantes" (1: 255) and in the chapter titled "The Menads" center on fantasies of emasculation: "Menads storm behind. If such hewed off the melodious head of Orpheus, and hurled it into the Peneus waters, what may they not make of thee" (1: 256). "Women snatch their cutlasses, or any other weapon, and storm-in Menadic: – other women lift the corpse of shot Jerôme; lay it down on the Marble steps; there shall the livid face and smashed head, dumb forever, *speak*" (1: 278). The biblical type of the castrating female, Judith, also appears, the anti-type of the generative female erased from Carlyle's fantasies of self-engendering male societies: "Descend, O mothers; descend, ye Judiths, to food and revenge!" (1: 252).

That Carlyle's fantasies oscillate between scenes of eruptive destruction acted out by female surrogates and scenes of emasculation by maddened women points to his occupation with the central problematic of early Victorian masculinity. Like other men of his time, Carlyle believed that the essence of maleness, of the male body, and of the male psyche lies in a seminal potency that energizes patriarchy, that is the source of national industrial power and of male literary power. Thus, Carlyle fears the weakening and the total loss of this potency as the loss of manliness itself, as castration, emasculation. But maleness, potentially progressive, is also innately diseased. The very spring of male identity is also potentially the source of its destruction as dissolution. Repelled by the male body, by male sexuality, by what he sees as the miasmic swamp of the male psyche, Carlyle imagines the interior of the male as polluted, unclean. Masculine energy may power the engine of industrial society but it may also disrupt it in a power surge, an overflow of the diseased fluid interior in a flood that would dissolve the ego boundaries of the male self and the patriarchal bounds of the social system.

MANLINESS AND MALENESS

With manliness threatened at one extreme by emasculation and at the other by social eruption and individual dissolution, the central problematic in achieving true manhood becomes the mediation of these opposing dangers. Carlyle's definition of such manhood depends upon the crucial early Victorian distinction between manliness and maleness. Maleness is defined in essentialist terms as the possession of innate potency or "untutored energy" (*Sartor* 21). Manliness is defined not as this essence but as a hard-won achievement, a continuous process of maintaining a perilous psychic balance characterized by regulation of this potentially destructive male energy.

Manliness as the management of internal fluid energy was an assumption Carlyle shared with his male readers. Writing to Carlyle of *Sartor*, John Sterling expresses within these same metaphorics of control his own identification with Teufelsdröckh's quest for manhood:

How evident is the strong inward unrest, the Titanic heaving of mountain on mountain; the storm-like rushing over land and sea in search of peace... He feels that duty is the highest law of his own being; and knowing how it bids the waves be stilled into an icy fixedness and grandeur, he trusts... that there is a principle of order which will reduce all confusion to shape and clearness. (Seigel 31–32)

Sterling concludes with the characteristic early Victorian paradox of contained force: "I find that I have not nearly done justice to my own sense of the genius and *moral energy* of the book" (33 emphasis added).

Much of the appeal of *Past and Present* lay in its presenting within the safe and appealing form of monastic coding the lineaments of the psychic and social management of maleness. The figure of regulated energy runs throughout the laudatory *Blackwood's* review, "We regard the chief *value* of Mr. Carlyle's writings to consist in the *tone of mind* which the individual reader acquires from their perusal; – manly, energetic, enduring, with high resolves and self-forgetting effort" (Seigel *Carlyle* 218). The reviewer sees as the central appeal of the book "an indisputable morality – precepts of charity, and self-denial, and strenuous effort" (209) and the essence of a moralized manliness in the combination of energy and restraint within "a stern, manly, energetic, self-denying character" (212). For the Victorian male readers, Abbot Samson, then, exemplifies a manliness that reconciles "self-denial, and strenuous effort," that becomes "energetic" by being "self-denying," "self-forgetting."

That Carlyle can transform this celibate medieval monk into the pattern of self-discipline in industrial man depends upon his adroit use of typological rhetoric in *Past and Present*. In this new Bible for the industrial age, Abbot Samson becomes the anti-type in the middle ages of the biblical Samson; the Captain of Industry becomes the fulfillment of this eternal type of the heroic male in the emerging industrial world.[12] This pattern of timeless forms realized or figured in historical time allows Carlyle to present Abbot Samson as simultaneously historical fact and divine incarnation, with historical distance and with contemporary relevance.

Furthermore, Carlyle's sacralized typological form in *Past and Present* resolves the troubling Victorian question of whether the shape of manliness exists as an unchanging aspect of the divine plan or merely as an historically relative construction. In seeing heroic manhood as a timeless, divinely sanctioned pattern manifested through human history, in the past as in the present, the text naturalizes, even sacralizes, male superiority and presents patriarchy itself as the realization through time of divine Will. Yet, since within the typological scheme the transcendental is figured in the historical, by showing masculinity as manifested in different forms through history, much as Browning does in his artist-poems, and even as prophesying a new shape for heroic manliness in future time, much as Pater does in his evocation of an emergent homoerotic manliness, Carlyle suggests the malleability and historical specificity of male identity, and thus the possibility of constructing manliness anew at each historical moment.

Carlyle's typological form also enables him to represent the specifically early Victorian problematic of regulating sexualized male energy as a transhistorical issue in manhood. The biblical Samson figures the contradictory and multiple threats to male identity that Carlyle saw in his own time. The cutting of his hair by Delilah traditionally represents castration by the destructive female, the loss of male power. Samson's pulling down the temple, much like the revolutionary activity represented by female surrogates in both *The French Revolution* and *Past and Present*, figures the eruption of male energy that is psychologically and socially liberating, yet destructive of both the self and the social order. Abbot Samson, then, is the anti-type of the biblical Samson in avoiding the twin dangers of impotence and of explosive rage by turning male desire from the temptations of sexuality to productive work within the all-male worlds of the monastery and, proleptically, the new mills of the industrial world. Carlyle looks to the "elect of the world; the born champions, strong men, and liberatory Samsons of this poor world: whom the poor Delilah-world will not always shear of their strength and eyesight, and set to grind in darkness at *its* poor gin-wheel!" (*Past* 286).

This turn from the "Delilah-world," the move from sexual activity to monastic celibacy, from the biblical Samson to Abbot Samson does not signify for Carlyle the severe threat to manliness that it does for other early Victorian writers and artists. Celibacy does not here signify feminized enervation as it does, for example, in "Pictor Ignotus." Nor does the cloistered life figure the bodily and psychic distortion induced by sexual repression, so feared by Browning and the Pre-Raphaelites, and so attractive to Pater. Rather, for Carlyle celibacy, the binding of male desire is "liberatory" in this Samson, a quality of "strong men." Safely distanced by history and moralized within the typological scheme, in *Past and Present* monastic celibacy as the limit case of the manly practice of the self figures at its most heroic the turning of the fluid energy within from unproductive benighted use, to "grind in darkness at *its* poor gin-wheel," into productive work, the new "gin-wheel[s]," with "gin" an allusion to the cotton gin, to cotton-spinning in the present. If in the terms of religious discourse celibacy becomes valorized as "virtuoso" religious practice,[13] in Carlyle's secular and psycho-sexual terms celibacy models a kind of virtuoso manliness, the highest and finest instance of that discipline of desire, that turn from pleasure to productivity that defines industrial manhood. Furthermore, given Carlyle's imagining of male sexuality as polluted or unclean, this male fantasy of an asexual life, particularly one not demanded in the nineteenth century but safely displaced to the middle ages and moralized by the discourse of monasticism, becomes an attractive, if extreme, mode of coping imaginatively with the attraction/repulsion toward heterosexuality he shared with his readers. For the men of the 1840s, Abbot Samson, like the Sterling Hayden figure in *Dr. Strangelove*, models the male fantasy of preserving "purity of essence."

That Carlyle can fashion the medieval monk into what the reviewers saw as the exemplar of all that is "manly" (Seigel *Carlyle* 212) suggests at the very least that heterosexual prowess was not the defining quality of manliness for the early Victorians. Rather, the manly heroism attributed to the celibate Abbot Samson, as well as to the celibate Teufelsdröckh, suggests that manliness lies in the technique of productive repression, a practice of energetic action directed to useful social ends that avoids the female qualities of passivity, interiority, isolation. Abbot Samson, then, exemplifies manliness by exemplifying reserve, the ability to forge an external restraint sufficiently strong to control and to channel powerful internal energies.

For Carlyle, then, manliness is not an essence, but a process, the achievement and the maintenance of a tense psychic equilibrium. This manliness or achieved manhood is consistently represented through the figure of balanced oppositions, as constrained power, "cautious energy" (94), "iron energy" (95). For Carlyle the mature male body and psyche exhibit a firm exterior containing a soft, fluid, protoplasmic interior. In *Past and Present* he envisions a "miscellany of men," for women do not appear in this imaginative pattern, as blood-like formless flesh, as "little red-coloured pulpy infants" who have now been "baked into any social form you choose" (129–30).

This same imaginative sense of male personality as perpetually engaged in the productive constraint of energy also underlies the occupation with clothing in *Sartor Resartus*. In this trope we can see, too, the ambivalence, the opposing psychic impulses that define Carlyle's vision of manhood. At one extreme, Carlyle employs clothing to figure the need for a psychic armor to hold within the uncleanliness of maleness and to prevent the eruption of male desire. In the characteristic Carlylean equation of the excremental or "soil" with the sexual and the metaphorics of male energy as fire or "stithy-sparks," Teufelsdröckh asks, "Rightly considered, what is your whole Military and Police Establishment, charged at uncalculated millions, but a huge scarlet-coloured, iron-fastened Apron, wherein Society works (uneasily enough); guarding itself from some soil and stithy-sparks, in this Devil's-smithy (*Teufelsschmiede*) of a world?" (32).

This social policing as body armor is literalized in *Sartor Resartus* in George Fox's "suit of Leather" (157). Here, in a condensed masculine narrative of initiation, Fox is shown seeking to become a "Man" (157). He renounces the flow of desire, specifically of sexualized desire, in rejecting the advice of his elders to "drink beer and dance with the girls" (158). Instead, he works as an artisan within that industrious self-discipline advocated by Samuel Smiles to stitch "one perennial suit of Leather" (158). Within the characteristic metaphorics of manliness, this binding of the body operates as a protection from watery dissolution, a defense against the "Chaotic

Night that threatened to engulf him in its hindrances and its horrors" (158–59). Paradoxically, for Carlyle self-constraint provides the means of liberation from the imprisonment that haunts the early Victorian male imagination, "Thy elbows jerk, and in strong swimmer-strokes, and every stroke is bearing thee across the Prison-ditch, within which Vanity holds her Work-house and Ragfair, into lands of true Liberty; were the work done, there is in broad Europe one Free Man, and thou art he!" (159). Finally, within this "Leather Hull" (159) that insulates him from the fluid of desire, Fox "stands on the adamantine basis of his Manhood" (159). Within Carlyle's typological mode, George Fox's leather coat, the emblem of manhood as control over the energies of maleness prefigures manhood as reserve, whose emblem is the buttoned frock coat of the Victorian gentleman.

But *Sartor Resartus* is, of course, highly ironized, and in its oscillation between extremes embodies the unresolved conflicts about manhood for the early Carlyle. Along with the desire for a paradoxical freedom through bondage, the trope of clothing also represents the opposing impulse to disrobe, to shatter reserve. "Adamitism" (43), casting off clothing as the rejection of class distinctions, represents for Carlyle and for his age the longing to allow male desire to flow freely, to return to the primal or even the animal state: "Nevertheless there is something great in the moment when a man first strips himself of adventitious wrappages; and sees indeed that he is naked, and, as Swift has it, 'a forked straddling animal with bandy legs'; yet also a Spirit, and unutterable Mystery of Mysteries" (42).

And yet even in this momentary vision of reversion to the Adamic condition, Carlyle's sense of the body, like that of other early Victorian men, cannot move from what Kristeva in her theorizing of horror terms "abjection" – terror at the dissolution of the boundaries of the body, fear of its unspeakable excremental and fluid nature.[14] In a typical passage on clothing as concealing the body, Teufelsdröckh says,

While I – good Heaven! – have thatched myself over with the dead fleeces of sheep, the bark of vegetables, the entrails of worms, the hides of oxen or seals, the felt of furred beasts; and walk abroad a moving Rag-screen, overheaped with shreds and tatters raked from the Charnel-house of Nature, where they would have rotted, to rot on me more slowly!... For my own part, these considerations, of our Clothes-thatch, and how, reaching inwards even to our heart of hearts, it tailorises and demoralises us, fill me with a certain horror at myself and mankind. (41-42)

Here we see displaced onto clothing imagined as a congeries of dead body parts – "dead fleeces of sheep...entrails of worms" – Carlyle's own sense of inhabiting a dissolving body that resides within the "Charnel-house of Nature."

As potentially dangerous to Carlyle as "Adamitism," the dissolution of control and the momentary horrific glimpse of the liquefying body, is the paralyzing power of constraint, the possibility that psychic armor may become so rigid, so mechanical or machine-like as to paralyze desire. The "very *skin* and *muscular tissue* of a Man's Life [are] a most blessed indispensable thing, so long as they have *vitality* withal, and are a *living* skin and tissue to him!" (*Past* 128). In the most extreme form of this fantasy, the male resembles nothing so much as an oyster: "Foam itself, and this is worth thinking of, can harden into oyster-shell; all living objects do by necessity form to themselves a skin" (*Past* 128). But when the skin or clothing has become "mere adscititious leather and callosity...mere calcified oyster-shell," then it must be cast off (128). At its extreme, the figure of psychic containment segues for Carlyle into the figure of incarceration, a trope that informs the male as well as the female literary imagination in the nineteenth century.[15] Men may begin as "little red-coloured pulpy infants," yet they have been "baked into any social form you choose...fixed and hardened, – into artisans, artists, clergy, gentry, learned sergeants, unlearned dandies" (*Past* 129-30). By inhabiting these male occupational and class roles, "the red pulpy infant has been baked and fashioned *so*" as to live in a perpetual mental "imprisonment" (130). For the English men of the present, "the element of Shakespearian melody does lie imprisoned in their nature" (*Past* 159). On the national scale, the figure for this stifling of energy by psychic armor is the literalized body armor of the anachronistic "Champion of England, cased in iron or tin" (*Past* 143). This figure of the prison house links Carlyle's men "cased in iron" to Lippo locked in the Medici palace, to the female surrogates for the male artist/poet in Tennyson and the Pre-Raphaelites caged in palaces of art, and, more generally, to the fear of early Victorian men about the destructive effects of repressing male sexual and artistic energy.

For Carlyle the equilibrium of manhood is particularly hard-won, particularly difficult to maintain for he is drawn toward each limit in this dichotomy of constraint/eruption. Intensely attracted to personal and political violence, he is equally drawn toward an almost masochistic personal abasement and to rigid social as well as psychic order. His images suggest the difficulty of such balance, even undermine the possibility of achieving the stability of manliness. In the monastery the "Spirit of the Time [has] visibly taken body, and crystallised itself" (*Past* 61). "Crystallised," a favorite metaphor in *Past and Present*, denotes both hardness and fragility, the possibility of breakage into fragments, into chaos.

Carlyle's sense that such chaos in males may be prevented only by the most rigid control is suggested by his later vigorous defense of Governor Eyre in the controversy of the mid-1860s surrounding Eyre's brutal suppression of what seemed to Carlyle a dangerous insurrection.[16] Carlyle's defense of Eyre's ironhanded rule is couched in the language of Victorian masculine discourse. Carlyle wrote Kingsley that Eyre's "conduct had been that of a faithful, valiant, wise and manful representative of the English Government" (Workman "Carlyle" 93). For Carlyle "manful" encompasses several models of manliness. To Kingsley he speaks of the need to restore the authoritarian warrior model of manliness exemplified in Abbot Samson and in Cromwell, "From all I had learned of Eyre then or before, my notion would have been, had *my* post been that of English King, to appoint Eyre *Dictator* over Jamaica for the next 25 years, as pretty much the one chance there was for saving the West Indies or it" (Workman 93). He wrote to Eyre praising him in terms of the Victorian definition of manliness as a form of sanity characterized by restraint of the potentially destructive energy in one's self and in others, "The insane uproar rising round such a man, as recompense for such service done, was a summons to all sane citizens to stand forth as your vindicators" (Workman 96–97).

Unable to find such real-life exemplars of the "wise and manful" in the earlier Victorian decades, Carlyle turned instead to history, and to history envisioned within a typological mode. In *Past and Present*, Abbot Samson, the celibate male as hero, is the anti-type of his biblical precursor, since his psychic armor is matched to the powerful internal flow of desire and rage. Abbot Samson's virtue is that he can forge a psychic control sufficiently powerful to contain the potent interior force, can construct himself as "iron energy" (95). This monk is a far cry from Browning's impotent Unknown Painter.

Abbot Samson's "copious ruddy beard" (74, 77) signifies the fire of male sexuality burning within. Indeed, it is the very power of Samson's male desire that makes his celibacy heroic, that makes the achievement of control a noble struggle. In the "man himself there exists a model of governing, something to govern by! There exists in him a heart-abhorrence of whatever is incoherent, pusillanimous, unveracious, – that is to say, chaotic, *un*governed; of the Devil, not of God" (92). Furthermore, unlike the biblical Samson, he can keep in check not only his sexuality, but also the equally diseased chaotic power of convulsive rage, the "Berserkir-rage" (165) that in Carlyle's racial mythology powers Anglo-Saxon superiority. He can "suffer faults, damage from his servants, and know what he suffered, and not speak of it" (100).

Carlyle rather adroitly confirms the suppression of sexuality as the index of manliness by transforming the celibate Abbot Samson into the very sign of virility, the hardened phallus. Abbot Samson is introduced as "stout-made, stands erect as a pillar" (74), a "firm-standing man" (75) who has reached his forty-seventh year "still in an erect clear-standing manner" (77). Samson recounts how on his dangerous passage through Italy to Rome, "I ... pretended to be Scotch, and putting on the garb of a Scotchman, and taking the gesture of one, walked along; and when anybody mocked at me, I would brandish my staff in the manner of that weapon they call *gaveloc*, uttering comminatory words after the way of the Scotch" (75). That one of the very few first-person passages given to Abbot Samson should link his actions to Scotland exemplifies what is clear throughout the text, the need of the author from Ecclefechan to equate asexuality with manliness, to transform the celibate male into the phallic hero.

Samson's mental powers are equally phallic. Traditionally, the female has been associated with the unformed, the masculine with the forming principle.[17] Like Ruskin in his masculinist definition of the Imagination Penetrative as "the penetrating possession-taking faculty ... the highest intellectual power of man" (*Works* IV: 251), the equally asexual Carlyle also identifies creative power with male sexual potency, more specifically with the act of penetrating the female. Teufelsdröckh "sheers down, were it furlongs deep, into the true centre of the matter; and there not only hits the nail on the head, but with crushing force smites it home, and buries it" (*Past* 22). Samson's mental force is equally innate, penetrative, male, able to bring order to the fluid formlessness of the psyche as well as the social disorder of the monastery: "The clear-beaming eyesight of Abbot Samson, steadfast, severe, all-penetrating, – it is like *Fiat lux* in that inorganic waste whirlpool; penetrates gradually to all nooks, and of the chaos makes a *kosmos* or ordered world!" (95).

Carlyle's fantasy of masculinity, then, associates the fluid interior or inner chaos of the male with disease; projects this uncleanness onto the female or the racial Other; looks to the control of this unclean yet vitalizing energy by the construction and maintenance of a rigid psychic carapace; sees the practice of celibacy as an heroicized model for the practice of manliness as the control of sexuality; paradoxically valorizes celibacy as phallic hardness; and in the reform of St. Edmundsbury equates manhood with the dissolution of the self through submission to the male leader within an all-male community. It is striking that this constellation of male fantasies projected onto the monks of St. Edmundsbury resembles that of the proto-fascists described by Theweleit, the soldier males of the Freikorps established in Germany between the world wars. Yet, given the long-standing association of Carlyle with fascism, it is also important to note crucial differences between the male fantasies of these soldier males and those presented by Carlyle, differences that suggest the attractiveness of Carlyle's redefinition of manliness for the male readers of the early Victorian age.

In the mental life of the Freikorps and of Carlyle we see the interconnected fantasies of bodily dissolution, of the danger of women to male corporeal integrity, of the pleasure in violence as eruption or flood. For the fascist soldier males, the highest value attaches to those moments when control is lost, those instants of violence in which the desire within overflows in the orgasmic pleasure of killing, particularly of killing women. But for all his attraction to the dissolution of boundaries, to similar moments of eruption and of ferocity, as in the Menadic women of the French Revolution, Carlyle is also repelled by, deeply fearful of, such loss of control. For all his metaphors of battle, for all his later attraction to the imperial violence of Governor Eyre, Carlyle in the 1830s and 1840s is not concerned with creating a warrior society. Instead, his project is to metamorphose the traditional gentry warrior model of manliness to the service of industrial capitalism, to turn male energy from warfare to material production. For the new chivalric man, the sword has become a "Tool," his mace a blacksmith's hammer, his steed a locomotive:

Man is a Tool-using Animal... He can use Tools, can devise Tools: with these the granite mountain melts into light dust before him; he kneads glowing iron, as if it were soft paste; seas are his smooth highway, winds and fire his unwearying steeds. Nowhere do you find him without Tools; without Tools he is nothing, with Tools he is all. (*Sartor* 30)

And for the new Hero as Man of Letters, for the Victorian bard of a manly industrialism "the proper Epic of this world is not now 'Arms and the Man'... no, it is now 'Tools and the Man'": that, henceforth to all time is now our Epic" (*Past* 208).

Although for Carlyle as for the men of the Freikorps, the trope of an internal seminal energy underlies the fantasy of the male psyche, rather than looking to orgasmic eruption in violence or in sex, Carlyle valorizes a tempered repression, a consistent dynamic equilibrium, a controlled uninterrupted flow of interior fluidity into productive work. For Carlyle, the technology of the new male psyche reproduces the primary technology of the new industrial age. Just as industrial England has transformed the fluid energy of water into water power through canals and water-wheels and the chaos of fire into the controlled productive power of steam, so the new industrial man must channel his "untutored energy" (*Sartor* 21), the formless internal lava, his "central heat" (*Past* 96) into regulated, constructive forms of power. To adopt the quite appropriate language of machines, the problem in the technology of the self, as in the technology of the steam engine, becomes the creation of a psychic "governor" to regulate the natural energy of maleness as the steam governor regulates the volatile energy of fire and water. In Abbot Samson, indeed, "there exists a model of governing, something to govern by" (92). For Carlyle in *Past and Present*, his Bible of industrial manhood, the image of the ideal male psyche, of the psychic equilibrium or reserve that marks bourgeois manhood, is the steam engine, fire and water moderated in a consistent flow of energy harnessed to productive purpose: "'To repress and hold-in such sudden anger he was continually careful,' and succeeded well: – right, Samson; that it may become in thee as noble central heat, fruitful, strong, beneficent; not blaze out, or the seldomest possible blaze out, as wasteful volcanism to scorch and consume!" (96). In the "noble central heat, fruitful, strong, beneficent" of Abbot

Samson we see prefigured the furnaces of Manchester and the paradoxically energetic reserve of industrial manhood.

THE MASCULINE PLOT

In constructing a new form of manhood for the new industrial era, Carlyle saw as central to that project the masculinizing or, more accurately, the re-masculinizing of literature itself, of its production, its function, its form. Threatened by what he saw as the increasing feminization of literature, Carlyle sought to reshape "The Hero as Man of Letters" for the industrial era by reaffirming the manliness of literary "Labour," returning literature to its proper form as the script for the achievement of true manhood, and establishing a literature that would transmit such masculine wisdom to an audience of men within a wholly male community of letters. As Browning and the Pre-Raphaelites were to do, in many ways in emulation of Carlyle, in his early writing Carlyle self-consciously shaped a masculine poetic for his age. As latter-day Virgil or Milton, Carlyle set out to sing the new English epic, the epic of industrial manhood: "The proper Epic of this world ... is now 'Tools and the Man'" (*Past* 208).

As manliness is defined by difference from what is marked as female, masculine writing for Carlyle is defined by difference from the female literature of his own time, more specifically, from domestic fiction. To Carlyle, this female fiction poses a particular danger to the precarious stability of manhood, as clear a danger as the Menadic women of the French Revolution or the female Chartists of the middle ages presented to patriarchal society. In its stimulation of eroticism, its scripting of male life within the marriage plot, and its devaluing of manly work, such fiction opens the floodgates of sexual desire and thus threatens to dissolve the fragile boundaries of the male psyche and turn male energy from productive labor within the industrial sphere.

In opposition to the psychic danger of such sexualized literature, here characteristically displaced onto the female, Carlyle develops an opposing masculine poetic whose primary psychic action is the regulation rather than the arousal of desire. Set in a world without women, its erotics focus upon the sexually chaste bonds of man to man. Its masterplot is not the movement through courtship to marriage, but rather rejection of the domestic sphere as the way toward the achievement of manhood. Closure comes with the sublimation of dangerous male desire into productive work and initiation into a male community rather than with joining in marriage.[18] This poetic is exemplified in *Past and Present*, its manifesto is "The Hero as Man of Letters," and its psychological sources laid bare in Carlyle's curious, self-suppressed essay of 1848, "Phallus-Worship."[19]

In "Phallus-Worship" we can see the Carlylean fantasies of the male body and of the body politic giving shape to his masculine poetic. As in the imagined worlds of the past, so in the present, the primary danger to manhood lies in male desire slipping from control and in the potential of such sexualized desire for shattering the fragile crystalline structure of male identity. In "Phallus-Worship" Carlyle characteristically displaces desire onto the female Other, represents the unrestrained female as the agent of disorder and, conflating the social and the psychological, sees the overflow of sexualized desire as the chief danger to the social order. In this manuscript, he attributes the Revolution of 1848 to the increased sexual openness of contemporary novels written by female novelists, particularly the French Other, George Sand, and even the English Geraldine Jewsbury: "These universal suffrages, national workshops, reigns of fraternity, and generally red or white republics with their fraternities and phenomena are to me very mainly a George-Sand Novel come forth from the land of dreams, intending to enact itself as a fact under this sun" (22). The blame for social unrest is projected onto the sexual female, but, as the title suggests, the object and source of this desire remains the phallus. The latent structure of the essay remains Carlyle's ambivalence toward male sexuality. Within his male fantasy these outbreaks of revolutionary energy are, characteristically, eruptions or emissions of the sexualized fluid within, a fluid that may be overtly associated with the mysterious female, but carries connotations of the male fluid interior, the seminal: "The New Sand religion is not yet developed ... an Egg of Eros swimming on the dark immensities; still albuminous, requiring to be *hatched*" (22).

Indeed, the curious history of "Phallus-Worship" shows Carlyle acting out his own fantasies. His contact with the eroticized writing of George Sand must have been so arousing, the sexual arousal so seemingly polluting, the sexuality so contaminating that he could not complete the essay, could not show the unfinished work to his wife

Jane (20). In this exemplary case of male hysteria as sexual panic Carlyle could only control desire by confining or enclosing it. He ultimately tied the uncompleted manuscript in a "string-tied brown paper-bag" (20) and hid it in a drawer.

If Sand is the "melodious Anti-Virgin" (22), then Carlyle is the singer of male virginity, of sexual and psychic control. If Sand and other women produce the "Phallus Bible; – its new testaments and its old" (23), then Carlyle and other men will write a new Bible, exemplified by *Sartor Resartus* and *Past and Present*, of productive repression of the phallus, of male desire. In the past, that is before the feminization of literature, "when Literature was the speech of men" (22), manhood or the shape of a "Man's life" was not "represented as made all or mainly out of Love. Love satisfying or not plays but a small part in it, business, ambition, accumulation, loss, victory, defeat in thousands of other provinces fill up the life of man and woman there" (22–23). Like the manly writing of the past, the male poetic of the present must not intensify the erotic but rather desexualize an eroticized desire, what Carlyle here calls "Love," into the constructive activity of bourgeois man, "business, ambition, accumulation."

Carlyle set out the program for such a masculine poetic in the crucial and influential lecture "The Hero as Man of Letters."[20] As with the later "Phallus-Worship," the motivation of this lecture is overdetermined, arising from myriad masculine anxieties. It is in part a response to the rise of the Hero as Woman of Letters, the challenge of writers like Sand and Jewsbury who had begun to occupy the formerly all-male territory of the sage. And, like the work of other early Victorian male writers, the lecture also responds to the increasing instability in the construction of the category "Man of Letters" itself, the emerging opposition between the category of "man" and the category "writer," the difficulty of affirming the manliness of letters in a utilitarian and commercial age. As Carlyle in his typological rhetoric sees a transhistorical ideal of manhood manifested in differing forms through history, so he sees the essence of man as writer-hero as simultaneously transhistorical, divinely ordained and yet as manifested in new forms over time. Energizing this manifesto is the pressing need to construct a new formation of the male writer for the industrial present, a newly heroic Man of Letters who "is altogether a product of these new ages" (*Heroes* 383).

Underlying Carlyle's vision of the modern "Hero as Man of

Letters" and of the new masculine poetic is the same fantasy governing his monastic utopia of the past and his vision of the industrial future, the bonded community of celibate males: "Men of Letters are a perpetual Priesthood, from age to age" (385). As monasticism provides an attractive figure for Carlyle's ideal psychological and social order, so a celibate "Priesthood" provides a rich if self-contradictory figure for the Carlylean vision of a new masculinized literature. For one, the term signifies not only the exclusion of women, but also, like monasticism, endows this exclusion with a sacred aura, naturalizes the reoccupation of the high position of priest or sage by men, situates male lineage as a return to the biblical order. And by making literary work, like the work of the male sphere, a sacred calling, the equation of writer with priest validates the rejection of domestic life for the sacred fellowship of letters.

In *Past and Present* the monk represents the heroic or virtuoso case of the regulation of desire that defines manhood. The Man of Letters as priest again equates celibacy with virility by focusing on the control of male desire as central to the formation of the male writer. In sharp contrast to the poetic ideal of Browning and the Pre-Raphaelites, and to that of his romantic predecessors, Carlyle's figure of the ideal writer as celibate priest insists on the primary function of literature as the disciplining rather than the arousal of desire. Like the ordered life of the monks, the ordered life of the male writer as priest represents control of the female as the chaos of desire within the self.

Seeing literary continuity as a "perpetual Priesthood, from age to age" also evokes, as does the monastic ideal, the dream of a wholly male community. As in the social dream of the monastery, the exclusion of women from the literary community generates the compensatory fantasy of male self-creation, male self-engenderment. To Carlyle, all history moves by male self-generation from father to son without the contagion of sexuality: "The Centuries too are all lineal children of one another; and often, in the portrait of early grandfathers, this and the other enigmatic feature of the newest grandson shall disclose itself" (*Past* 45). Like Carlyle's monks, the celibate "Priesthood" of letters reproduces both literature and writers "from age to age" without the assistance of women.

This Priesthood of Letters preaches to a congregation that, like the monastery and the cotton mill, is envisioned by Carlyle as entirely male. Men of Letters are "teaching all men that a God is still present in their life" (385). "Our pious Fathers" knew well "what importance lay in the speaking of man to men" (387). This imagining of literature as "the speaking of man to men," a continuation of Wordsworth's ideal of the poet as "a man speaking to men" ("Preface" 737), remains a crucial strategy within early Victorian masculine poetics. With women now seeming to dominate the reading public, the exclusion of women not only from authorship, but also from the audience marks the formation not only of gendered literary forms, but also of a specifically gendered wisdom that can only be circulated among men because it can only be understood by men. This masculinist idea of a separate male knowledge that must be hidden from the female and communicated in secret, often in darkness, among men is inscribed in *Past and Present* as in male texts throughout the century. Abbot Samson preaches to the monks over the coffin of St. Edmund "on that old midnight hour in St. Edmundsbury Church" (122). Lippo shares his life story and his artistic views with the men of the night watch. At the end of the century, Marlow at nightfall on the deck of the *Nellie* reveals to a circle of professional men the secret of Kurtz's life and of his death, a secret that, famously, must be kept from the Intended.[21]

Within a truly masculine literature, then, not only must the audience be "men," but the speaker must be a "man," manly. In the early Victorian decades as throughout the century, the formation of such a manly speaker or writer generated several contradictions. The first, crucial to all male writers and artists of the period, lies in the opposition of the bourgeois model of manhood as active engagement in the commercial and technological world to the romantic ideal of the male writer as detached observer. This issue is quite nicely registered in Ford Madox Brown's pictorial celebration of the Carlylean ideal of work. As the poem he composed for *Work* (plate 1) demonstrates, Brown envisioned work in the Carlylean mode as the primary technology for desexualizing male desire:

> Work! which beads the brow and tans the flesh
> Of lusty manhood, casting out its devils!
> By whose weird art transmuting poor men's evils,
> Their bed seems down, their one dish ever fresh.
>
> (for the picture called "Work")

In *Work* Carlyle is rather notoriously represented watching from the sidelines as muscular, idealized navvies do the heavy digging. Brown's

Plate 1 Ford Madox Brown, *Work*.

accompanying text itself labors mightily to close the gap between manly muscular engagement in the building of England and passive, feminized contemplation: "At the further corner of the picture, are two men who appear as having nothing to do. These are the brain-workers [Carlyle and F. D. Maurice], who, seeming to be idle, work, and are the cause of well-ordained work and happiness in others – sages" (Ford *Brown* 190).

Carlyle shared Brown's middle-class jealousy of what seemed the untroubled masculinity, the "happiness" of the working class so clearly manifested in their evident delight in muscular work, a form of class-bound muscle envy that runs throughout the century, as in Ruskin's road-building experiment at Oxford. Yet, although Carlyle tried to reconcile his detached intellectuality with muscular labor, in *Past and Present* as in Brown's *Work* the gap between physical and mental labor, between working-class industrial manliness and middle-class industrial manliness remains unbridged. Carlyle's subject position in his history of monasticism and in his comments on the industrial present and future is that of a middle-class observer of labor, much like his figure in Brown's painting, rather than of a participant in the act of muscular labor. Carlyle longs for, but never represents from the inside his idealized manliness as physicality.[22]

To escape the self-contradiction of the term "brain-workers," Carlyle, as the Pre-Raphaelite Brotherhood were to do in their art practice, inscribes in his writing the equation of his literary practice with non-literary, indisputably masculine forms of labor in order to bring the new Hero as Man of Letters within the male sphere. *Past and Present* represents the author's "brain-work" not as emotive and morbid, but as rational and progressive. Carlyle's is not the inward spiritual journey of the romantics. Rather, in *Past and Present* Carlyle fashions himself as intrepid explorer of the past, the quester for fact, the seeker of the palpable and material. As nineteenth-century Hero as Man of Letters, Carlyle becomes objective historian, participant in the manly work of expanding scientific knowledge. He quite specifically presents himself as contemporary scientist, interpreting the material remains of the past in the manner of a pre-Darwinian naturalist. The medieval monk is

an extinct species, we say; for the live specimens which still go about under that character are too evidently to be classed as spurious in Natural History ...But fancy a deep-buried Mastodon, some fossil Megatherion, Ichthyosaurus, were to begin to *speak* from amid its rock-swathings, never so indistinctly! The most extinct fossil species of Men or Monks can do, and does, this miracle. (*Past* 49).

Within a figural aesthetic, this formation of writer as scientist can coexist with another formation of manliness inscribed in *Past and Present*, the Man of Letters as prophet or sage, for the detailed observation of both the Book of Nature and the Book of History reveal the presence of the divine. In the 1830s and 1840s, the literary terrain of sage had been recaptured from female occupation, restored to an all-male territory, so that adopting the stance of sage becomes a mode of asserting the manliness of the text. In large measure due to the examples of "The Hero as Man of Letters" and *Past and Present* the model of sage became particularly attractive to Victorian writers and artists in establishing the manliness of their work. Tennyson's late fashioning of himself as sage stands in sharp contrast to the aura of the feminine that marked his early poetic career. Holman Hunt looked specifically to Carlyle and the Carlylean model of artist as prophet in fashioning his post-Brotherhood construction of himself as artist-sage (plates 18 and 19).

Furthermore, Carlyle's definition of his masculine poetic clearly identifies his literary project with that of the Captain of Industry. Both seek the transformation of men into factory workers. As the Manchester mill-owner adapts agricultural laborers to the clock-bound discipline of factory work, so the manly author lures his readers from the rhythms of Eros and the mental wanderings of dream to the regulation and desexualization of desire that defines manliness in the industrial worker. The work of literature is, in Brown's words, to be "the cause of well-ordained work and happiness in others" (Ford *Brown* 190). Carlyle defines the heroic writer for the industrial present as continuing the undertaking of earlier pragmatic, pre-romantic Protestant writers occupied with enforcing the work ethic. He quotes his exemplar of the heroic male author, Samuel Johnson, "'In a world where much is to be done, and little is to be known,' see how you will *do* it" (*Heroes* 409).

The notion implicit in the ideal of "the speaking of man to men," the very idea of man "speaking," presents yet another formal paradox for Carlyle and for nineteenth-century masculine poetics in general, a paradox encapsulated in the old saw about Carlyle writing forty volumes on the virtues of silence. In Carlylean terms, after all, the ideal of the "speaking" man becomes self-contradictory, a truly manly literary voice an impossibility since a truly manly man would be silent, his inner chaos held under tight control. This double-bind implicit in the idea of manly writing appears as early as Wordsworth's "Preface" where the poet as critic reconciles the romantic ideal of poetic creation as expression with the nineteenth-century ideal of manliness as reserve by transforming the "spontaneous overflow of powerful feelings" into "emotion recollected in tranquility" (740) in order to achieve a "language really used by men" (734).[23] For Carlyle, writing as self-expression was particularly dangerous as allowing the feared "overflow" or flood of the chaotic, diseased interior with the consequent liquefaction of ego boundaries. Indeed, the dissolution of a controlled prose, moments or eruption mark Carlylean style.

With romantic or expressive form, particularly first-person narration, marked as dangerous or unmanly, Carlyle found in the *Chronicle* of Jocelin of Brakelond a prefigurative example of a truly masculine narrative form that could resolve the formal paradox of a literature of silence. In the *Chronicle* and in *Past and Present* the exemplary manly man occupies the center, unselfconscious, generally silent. There are some public speeches by Abbot Samson, but no movement into the consciousness of this manly hero. We have the comments of Jocelin, the gossip of the other monks, and the comments of the Carlylean authorial persona. But manliness is represented neither by the voice of Jocelin nor the voices of the other monks, and certainly not by the editorial persona. Instead, male voices describe, admire, puzzle over Samson, the unspeaking exemplar of manliness at the center. The very act of speaking signifies their own unmanliness, their distance from the silence as reserve that marks true manhood. In marked distinction to a romantic literature of self-expression in the lyric and the ode, this form – multiple voices speaking about a silent, emotionally opaque masculine hero – valorizes severe control of the psyche, manly reserve, the virtues of silence. Carlyle's use of dramatized speakers, then, provides a way of regulating and checking his own emotions, of preventing the "overflow of powerful feelings" that marks his excursions into the first person. More generally, the oft-noted turn from lyric to dramatic forms in the male poetry of the early Victorian decades, particularly in Tennyson and in Browning, manifests this same male fear of expressive literary forms as potentially releasing the rush of desire that might overwhelm the fragile boundaries of the male self.

This masculine narrative form, although projected into the past, registers the pervasive change in the construction of nineteenth-century masculinity described by Richard Sennett in *The Fall of Public Man*. As in the monastery, bourgeois men on the streets of nineteenth-century London and Paris fell silent. Reserve became the mark of public order. As in Carlyle's imaginative world, reserve was seen as necessary to prevent the involuntary eruption of inner life, to ward off the revelation of personality to others. Public life became focused not on individual expression or theatrical presentation of the self, but, as in the elevation of Samson to Abbot and in the politics of spectacle in contemporary America, on the heroic leader who acts out the emotions of less manly men, of spectators absorbed and fascinated by the ruler, as eager as Jocelin and as Carlyle to penetrate his secret.

This same masculine narrative form – this circle of male voices seeking the secret of the silent male hero – appears again with the reemergence of the masculine poetic in the later nineteenth and early twentieth century. In *Heart of Darkness*, another masculine fiction, Kurtz remains the silent center whose secret other, more limited men such as Marlow and the Russian seek. In Ford Madox Ford's trilogy *Parade's End* (1924–28), Tietjens stands as the silent embodiment of a Tory ideal of manhood within the gentry formation of man as warrior. Early in her novelistic career, Virginia Woolf satirizes this masculine narrative method, as well as the formation of masculinity as reserve in *Jacob's Room* (1922). Here, Jacob is never given a voice. Instead, the silent, wholly reserved male hero exists only as the object of feeling expressed by others, primarily women, the epitome of what Woolf saw as an emotionally limited masculinity that finds its goal and its own self-destruction in war.

This early Victorian masculine poetic, then, situates its silent heroes and less than manly speakers within a fictional world imagined as wholly male. In a strategy that resembles the moves in nineteenth-century American writing to locate all-male societies in marginal spaces such as the whaling ship, the great river, the territories, British writers often set the masculine wild zone in remote geographic space, the ships of the British Navy, the colonies, or the imperial war to which flees the unmanned speaker of "Locksley Hall." For the English Victorians, such wholly male imaginative space is most often displaced in time, alternative masculinities situated in the past or in the future. Lippo exemplifies a manly artistic identity that is carefully identified with a specific historical moment that has now disappeared. Although the young Pre-Raphaelites did not don the hoods of the Nazarenes, they still imagined themselves as re-creating the male artistic world of the early Renaissance. Achieved manhood can be displaced far forward, as far as life after death, as in Tennyson's vision of union with an androgynous Hallam[24] or in Andrea del Sarto's deeply ironized dream of artistic fulfillment in Heaven. *Past and Present* projects ideal manhood back to the middle ages and far forward to a yet unrealized organic industrial age.

But whether projected into Heaven or into the twelfth century, into the colonies or the Crimea, such all-male space is central to the re-imagining of masculinity in this period. Although such spaces may represent markedly different values, early Victorian masculine poetics move to establish an imagined zone beyond bourgeois society in which the formations of entrepreneurial manliness do not apply and alternative masculinities may flourish.[25] As the example of Carlyle shows, this displacement of manliness into another space and time indicates the inability of early Victorian male writers to imagine a manly life in their own time and their assumption that an integrated manhood can be achieved only with great difficulty, if at all, within industrial England.

This imagined world of men outside contemporary England, exemplified by the monastery of *Past and Present*, becomes necessary as the only space in which can be realized the masterplot of the masculine poetic, the achievement of manhood. In "Phallus-Worship" Carlyle preaches that the primary plot in female domestic fiction, the marriage plot, offers a destructive script for the lives of men. A manly literature, as manliness itself, is defined by a different script, the quest for manhood. Carlyle's gendering of plot depends upon the early Victorian construction of gender. The female was imagined in essentialist terms. Such qualities as passivity, emotional instability, mothering, and subordination to men were seen as innate, as fixed within the flow of time. For women, the initiation into adult life does not involve psychic development. Instead, physical change in menarche and social change in marriage enables the essential nature of the woman to emerge and to be fulfilled in the bearing of children and in service to husband and family. But if femininity is defined as the manifestation of an essential female nature, there remains a crucial distinction between maleness and manhood. Male desire may be essential, but manhood is an ongoing process, a plot, a narrative over time that charts achieving and maintaining the tense regulation of male desire.

In the early Victorian period, this masculine plot, this passage to manhood had become increasingly problematic.[26] The need for males raised by women to differentiate themselves from the female was intensified and made more difficult by changing social conditions. With industrialization, work was removed from the home so that middle-class males no longer grew up in the company of men, no longer worked with their fathers in the field or at the forge. Instead, boys and young men increasingly spent early years in the care and company of women. Extended education and later marriage increased this time in the female sphere, delaying entry of young men into the male sphere. With the Victorians' increasingly sharp gender distinctions, the need to reject the female values of youth, to leave the feminized home, became more acute. Furthermore, there was no longer a single homogeneous ideal of male identity, no longer one, but a number of competing constructions of manliness to choose among. In a society of increasing class mobility, one no longer simply adopted the masculine style of one's father. And there was no single public ritual marking the passage to manhood.

In Victorian America, one manifestation of the social and psychological need in young men to mark the movement from boy to man, from female sphere to male sphere, from feminized home to male workplace was the efflorescence of male secret societies such as the Masons and Oddfellows, whose sole purpose appears to have been the creation and the acting out of secret rituals to initiate new members of the society into manhood. As Carnes shows in fascinating detail, nineteenth-century American men invented and acted out what now seem bizarre rites of male initiation. In darkness, businessmen dressed as American Indians or Egyptian priests administered mock torments and embraces of reconciliation to young men who felt their need for the passage to manliness unsatisfied by the churches and the commercial world of their daylight hours. Such rituals have an uncanny resemblance to the invented rituals, so popular at the time of writing this book, that appear to satisfy this same need in contemporary American men. Once again businessmen and professionals dress as native Americans, and in the primal setting of the forest recover their lost manhood under the guidance of such father figures as Robert Bly.

In early Victorian England the demand for rites of passage to manhood was as acute as in America. If this need was satisfied for some in all-male institutions such as the public schools or colonial service, for many others of the middle class this psychological and social need, like so much else in the nineteenth century, was displaced from public ceremony to the individual psyche and achieved not in the company of others but through the private rituals of reading, a crucial practice in achieving bourgeois identity.[27] Thus, reading literature structured by the masculine plot becomes a replacement for absent public rites of passage, a vicarious experience that satisfies the newly intensified and newly problematized emotional need for masculine identity as differentiation from the female, a newly necessary private rite that assists the male reader in attaining the arduous equilibrium of bourgeois manhood.

Whether in invented ritual or literary fictions, in the darkness of secret initiation rites, or in stories of the British Navy, of the public school, and of the monastic community, this early Victorian masculine plot takes a specific form. The young man must leave his mother, reject domestic life to enter a male community. In this new male world, he is granted masculine wisdom by the males of the community and tested. Often the testing involves rejecting the sexual temptations of women, who are always presented as a danger to the male community and to the individual quest for manhood. The final achievement of manhood involves the rejection of the female or mother, often figured by the casting off of female clothing, and bonding with the father or more often a surrogate father. This process of bonding involves, first, ritualized rejection by the father, then acceptance by the surrogate father sealed by chaste bodily contact within carefully controlled rituals of male–male physicality. Because this masculine plot opposes the marriage plot, the hegemonic script of bourgeois manhood, closure is often ambiguous. The members of the secret Order of Redmen must leave the lodge for the company of their wives, and the resolution in nineteenth-century masculine literature is equally unstable.

This pattern is exemplified in an early Victorian novel, Marryat's very popular *Peter Simple* (1834).[28] Peter leaves his family, including a weak father, for the community of men in a life at sea. His first days on shipboard are threatened by a female, by the sexual advances of a Mrs. Trotter. When she is finally sent ashore, removed from the all-male society, Peter learns his first bit of masculine knowledge: "Women [are] at the bottom of all mischief" (15). The windy tales told Jim by his fellow sailors may seem tedious to the modern reader, but register the need to absorb masculine wisdom in the company of men. Peter's manliness is also signified by his chastity, his ability to withstand even the allure of the women of the tropics. Removed from his own bourgeois family, Peter finds a surrogate father, O'Brien, who, in the chaste ways of this male community, was, in Peter's words, "very fond of me" (59). Captured by the French along with O'Brien, Peter is tested. To escape with O'Brien, Peter must dress like a girl (much like Huck Finn), but on reaching England, having proven his manliness by his courage, he sheds this female clothing. The closure remains ambiguous, the opposition between the marriage plot and the masculine plot typically unresolved. We see Peter at the end wealthy and married, but the book never tells of his leaving again for the navy. Any conflict between his warrior manliness as the commander of men at sea and his bourgeois manliness as breadwinner husband on land remains unwritten, perhaps unnarratable.

This same masculine plot governs several of Tennyson's poems of the early Victorian period, particularly "Locksley Hall," a tale of masculinization that scripts a movement toward manhood that runs counter to the marriage plot. As in *Maud*, the perilous psychic balance of manliness has become unstable as the male self dissolves in a feminized overflow of the inner life. For the Victorians, the opposite of manliness is madness. Only by controlling this dangerous heterosexual eroticism, only by rejecting "Phallus-Worship" can manhood be achieved:

I am shamed through all my nature to have loved so slight a thing.
Weakness to be wroth with weakness! woman's pleasure, woman's pain –
Nature made them blinder motions bounded in a shallower brain.
(lines 148–50)

Like Carlyle, Marryat, and Conrad later in the century, Tennyson in "Locksley Hall" projects dangerous male desire onto the female Other, quite specifically the racially dark female Other, the "dusky" (line 168) woman of the tropics, the primitive world. The speaker here, like Conrad's Marlow, moves toward manliness by repudiating the uninhibited heterosexual desire displaced onto the dark female and by shifting his primary affective ties to other men. The attainment of manhood as joining "in this march of mind" (line 165) suggests not only bonding with other men and the sublimation of desire into manly work, even if that work is war, but also, as in

Carlyle's monks, escaping the terrors of the individual male ego by dissolving the self within the mass, by moving in step with other men. Since such male–male ties are dangerously situated on the boundary between the homosocial and homoerotic, the speaker must leave contemporary England for a space abroad, for imperial warfare, where close masculine bonding into adult life is permitted within a warrior model of masculinity that opposes the bourgeois system that compels marriage: "Hark, my merry comrades call me, sounding on the bugle-horn,/They to whom my foolish passion were a target for their scorn" (lines 145-46).

This same masculine plot also shapes the central chapters of *Sartor Resartus*. The movement from "The Everlasting No" through the "Centre of Indifference" to "The Everlasting Yea" traces "in a psychological point of view" (128) the achievement of manhood. Like the workers of St. Ives, in "The Everlasting No" Teufelsdröckh is unmanned. In "a state of crisis, of transition" (121), he is isolated, removed from family. His mental state is represented as bodily disease to be cured, as "a hot fever of anarchy and misery raging within" (121). Within a metaphorics of abjection, this unmanly state appears as the dissolving of the boundaries of the male self into its primal liquid form. Teufelsdröckh's "mad Pilgrimings" become a "general solution into aimless Discontinuity" (121).

Most importantly, the masculine plot involves the search for the true father, for adult masculine wisdom. The "Everlasting No" sets forth a false vision of manhood both in the assertion that the unformed male is "fatherless" (128) and in the substitution of a false father figure: "The Universe is mine (the Devil's)" (128). Only by rejecting the "Everlasting No" which asserts that an authentic father can no longer be found and that masculine wisdom is impossible to attain can the male initiate his own initiation, engender himself: "It is from this hour that I incline to date my Spiritual New-birth... perhaps I directly thereupon began to be a Man" (128).

Within the masculine plot, the male passes through another stage that Carlyle calls the "Centre of Indifference." Like the monks before the coming of Samson, Childe Roland before he turns on to the path toward the Dark Tower, the speaker of "Locksley Hall" before setting off to war, Teufelsdröckh displays a listlessness, a feminized passivity, what "the Psychologist [can] surmise... [as] no longer a quite hopeless Unrest" (128). Without a productive channeling of their desire, men remain unmanned, a condition limned in the pervasive Carlylean fear of castration: "Thou art wholly as a dissevered limb" (138). In this nadir of unmanliness, the still to be masculinized male remains outside the community of men: "For thee the Family of Man has no use; it rejects thee" (138). If in its use as cliché in our own time the term "Family of Man" includes women and children, Carlyle's use of the phrase exemplifies his pervasive fantasy of male self-engenderment, of a "Family of Men."

"The Everlasting Yea" marks Carlyle's closure of the masculine plot as the achievement of a newly configured industrial manhood. Within the now psychologized plot of manhood, this is a purely psychic metamorphosis figured in the Carlylean trope of the innate sickness of maleness transformed into health: "By benignant fever-paroxysms is Life rooting out the deep-seated chronic Disease" (145). Dissolution of the boundaries of self, the death by drowning that during this period represents the male anxiety of reversion to the fluidity of self is stayed: "On the roaring billows of Time, thou art not engulfed, but borne aloft into the azure of Eternity" (145). And this psychological equilibrium, this control over the flux of the psyche, is reached only by rejecting earlier formations of masculinity. The famous exhortation, "Close thy *Byron*; open thy *Goethe*" (145) is a demand to repudiate the construction of manliness represented by Byron – a hero as man of letters *manqué* offering the public only the overflow of personal emotion, an epitome of eroticized aristocratic idleness. In contrast, Carlyle sees in Goethe the new exemplar of industrial manliness as the desexualization of desire, the channeling of male desire into production: "Be no longer a Chaos, but a World, or even Worldkin. Produce! Produce! Were it but the pitifullest infinitesimal fraction of a Product, produce it, in God's name!" (148).

And yet the manliness attained in *Sartor Resartus*, as in *Past and Present* in the next decade, is not linked with the bourgeois ideal of marriage. Indeed, within this masculine plotting, as in "Locksley Hall," manhood is made possible only by rejecting marriage and even heterosexual desire itself. Teufelsdröckh can move to manhood only by severing his emotional bonds with Blumine: "'Farewell, then Madam!' said he, not without sternness, for his stung pride helped him" (112). Rather than entering marriage, Teufelsdröckh enters the transhistorical community of men by adopting the masculine wisdom transmitted by men to men "in all times." Central to this community of masculine wisdom is the celibate male or "Priest" equated here as throughout Carlyle's writing of these decades with the "Poet":

There is in man a HIGHER than Love of Happiness: he can do without Happiness, and instead thereof find Blessedness! Was it not to preach-forth this same HIGHER that sages and martyrs, the Poet and the Priest, in all times, have spoken and suffered; bearing testimony, through life and through death, of the Godlike that is in Man. (145)

To enter the timeless male community, like the monks of St. Edmundsbury, Teufelsdröckh must paradoxically lose his self in order to save it: "The Self in thee needed to be annihilated" (145). He can release himself from the anxieties of seeking manliness only by abandoning his individuality through immersion in the bonded male community. And only in this abandonment of individuality within an all-male continuity can the male move from the situation of socially mobile industrial man in being "fatherless" (128) and find the true father. But for Carlyle in *Sartor Resartus* no single male appears as the father, as the strong authoritarian masculine figure. Abbot Samson and the Captain of Industry lie ahead. Rather, in his psychologized writing of the 1830s, Carlyle looks to the true father as a God within, still seeks the center of male authority in "the Godlike that is in Man, and how in the Godlike only has he Strength and Freedom" (145).

When in the 1840s Carlyle turned to the Condition of England question, he saw this social issue, as he had seen the shaping of the psyche in *Sartor Resartus*, as a Condition of Manliness question. In *Past and Present* he presents the reformation of industrial society, whose analogue is the monastery, as the individual and the communal achievement of manliness.

In *Peter Simple*, a priest says of O'Brien, Peter's surrogate father, "His commission as a captain...was all the same as going into a monastery as a monk, for he could never marry" (297). The equation of maritime manliness with that of the monk points to the shared configuration of masculinity in the life narrative of Peter Simple, the speaker of "Locksley Hall," Teufelsdröckh, and Abbot Samson. The biography of Abbot Samson embedded in *Past and Present*, like that of other masculine heroes, emphasizes the process of clear differentiation from the female, particularly from the mother. Indeed, the youthful sign of Samson's heroism is the preternatural revelation that he move toward manliness by early separation from his mother. At the age of nine he dreams of being rescued from the Devil by St. Edmund. When his mother takes him to St. Edmund's shrine to pray, the little boy says, "See, mother, this is the building I dreamed of!" In a figural repetition of the biblical story of Samuel, "His poor mother dedicated him to St. Edmund, – left him there with prayers and tears: what better could she do?" (74). In "Fra Lippo Lippi," youthful entrance into the cloister resonates with the male terror of emasculation. In *Past and Present*, as Samson's dream suggests, entry into the monastery is charged with feelings of liberating separation from the mother and from heterosexual desire, as well with the urge for bonding with the father and for a chaste homoeroticism within a male community. In later years, Abbot Samson would read the dream as prophesying that he would have been snatched by "the pleasures of this world... had not St. Edmund flung his arms round me, that is to say, made me a monk of his" (75).

As in Samson's life, so in the reformation of the monastic community, the narrative follows the masculine plot. Before the reign of Abbot Samson the monks are feminized men. Like Pictor Ignotus or Teufelsdröckh in the Centre of Indifference, with no outlet for their energy they are smitten with a psychic paralysis, a female passivity. They engage not in manly work, but in traditional female pursuits, "idle gossip... listless gossip" (73). As if taking on the psychic life associated with middle-class Victorian women, they are "dull, insipid men" (73). Abbot Samson makes them true monks, that is, true men.

If there is a dominant note in Carlyle's technology of the self, it is his attraction toward the total control of the dangerous, polluting seminal energy within, a psychic ideal signified by the limit case of monastic celibacy. In one of the very rare accounts of happiness in *Past and Present*, the authorial voice states, "In general the more completely cased with Formulas a man may be, the safer, happier is it for him" (129). For the ordinary man, as distinct from such virtuosos of manliness as Abbot Samson, for Carlyle's monks and Theweleit's soldier males, such safety and happiness may best be achieved by ceasing the personal struggle to contain the diseased chaos within through bonding with other men in submission to the stronger male. Only by drawing on the psychic heroism of the superior man can the ordinary man achieve the ideal of reserve as full control over inward energy. As with Teufelsdröckh, one has to lose one's self in order to gain one's self; one has to lose one's virility in order to find it.

The rhythms of the movement toward manhood in *Past and Present*, like those of nineteenth-century initiation rites, show such bonding found, rejected, then restored. The path to manhood begins with the ceremony of bonding with the father. Such fellowship is symbolized in a ritualized physical contact among men, a chaste embrace. Before the reform of the monastery begins, Abbot Samson gives "his new subjects seriatim the kiss of fatherhood in the St. Edmundsbury chapterhouse" (94).

But if the course of heterosexual love does not run smooth in the marriage plot, neither does the path toward masculine bonding. The monks mutiny; they reject the father. Abbot Samson has them bound, chained. Their consequent submission to the stronger male, to the father (the etymological root of "abbot" is, of course, "father"), indicates their progress toward manliness: "On the morrow morning we decide on humbling ourselves before the Abbot, by word and gesture, in order to mitigate his mind" (104). This gesture of submission stills the anger of the Abbot and within this male fantasy transforms the rage of the father into love, an emotional pattern central to nineteenth-century initiation rituals. The monks cast off the feminized self by submission to the strong male or father. The achievement of manhood, then, is marked by repetition of the chaste physical embrace with the heroic male and with other men, communal acceptance of the social and psychic control of the male leader cemented by allowing a momentary emotional overflow linked to male–male physical contact: "[Abbot Samson] arose weeping, and embraced each and all of us with the kiss of peace. He wept; we all wept" (104). Ritually reunited with the father, the community achieves communal manhood.

Abbot Samson has achieved his own heroic manliness because he too has moved through the same ritual of submission to an even stronger male. In the ceremony of being named Abbot, Samson faces the anger of the King: "If you manage badly, I will be upon you!" Samson then abases himself, "steps forward, kisses the King's feet." Such submission becomes the path to manhood for the anger of the father is transformed into acceptance: "'By God's eyes,' said the King, 'that one, I think, will govern the Abbey well'" (86). Submission, self-regulation, the signs of manliness are, paradoxically, limned in what, to give the term a different valence, we might call

Phallus-Worship. Samson falls at the King's feet, but "swiftly rises erect again" and sings "in clear tenor-note ... with firm voice, firm step and head, no change in his countenance whatever" (86). Again, Carlyle transmutes male celibacy into phallic virility.

The achieved manliness of the community is marked by a final ceremony which centers on the ritualized, therefore safely controlled, touching of the male body. Abbot Samson disinters the body of the father of them all, St. Edmund. Samson in the company of only a select group of monks unwraps the "Sacred Body" (124) and abases himself "saying he durst not proceed farther, or look at the sacred flesh naked. Taking the head between his hands, he thus spake groaning: 'Glorious Martyr, holy Edmund ... turn it not to my perdition that I have so dared to touch thee, I miserable and sinful; thou knowest my devout love, and the intention of my mind'" (124). In a striking passage suffused with barely controlled male–male bodily, even phallic, desire, Samson then

> touched the eyes; and the nose which was very massive and prominent ... and then he touched the breast and arms; and raising the left arm he touched the fingers, and placed his own fingers between the sacred fingers. And proceeding he found the feet standing stiff up, like the feet of a man dead yesterday; and he touched the toes, and counted them. (124)

Such fearfulness surrounds exposing and touching the flesh of another male, particularly of the father, that the act can only be carried out for the community by the high priest, the strongest and most controlled male. Samson tells the monks "that it had not been in his power, nor was it permissible or fit, to invite us all to the sight of such things" (126). But on hearing of the act of male physical contact carried out by their surrogate, the community is bonded still more strongly: "At hearing of which, we all wept, and with tears sang *Te Deum laudamus*; and hastened to toll the bells in the choir" (126).

To Carlyle, this is the "culminating point of [Abbot Samson's] existence" (127). And it may be the "culminating point" of Carlyle's work as the Hero as Man of Letters in marking out the new masculine poetic whose closure is achieved not with marriage, but with the achievement of a very particular form of manhood. As models for the lives of industrial workers, having rejected the mother and the feminine, ritually reconciled with the father, submissive to a single leader, their arduous personal struggle to maintain their psychic balance transferred to a stronger male, their inchoate energy channeled into productive work, their male–male desire transformed through ritual into chaste affective ties with other males, these monks have indeed become men.

MONASTICISM MANLY AND UNMANLY

The emotional trajectory of Carlyle's masculine plotting, then, moves from connection with the female toward intense male–male ties. The achievement of such chaste bonds between men becomes the very index of manhood. As DeLaura notes, for Carlyle "Love is indeed the unexplored basis of the 'Hero' doctrine, of the passionate attachment of men to a leader" ("Hopkins and Carlyle" 76). In Carlyle's ideal world without women the "love" of man for man is the most valued of emotions. Jocelin says of Samson, "I loved him much" (74), that he was "much loved by some, not loved by all" (75). And even King Richard "forgave him, and even loved him… Thou brave Richard, thou brave Samson! Richard too, I suppose, 'loved a man,' and knew one when he saw him" (117).

This utopian vision of chaste male love within an all-male society was attractive to Carlyle's male readers for several compelling yet contradictory reasons, since the early Victorian decades contain several contradictory views of male–male relationships. Untouched by any construction of the "homosexual," men found in deep same-sex affection powerful emotional, even spiritual value, value sanctioned by institutional practice within the university, by a long literary tradition, and by the Bible itself. In the early 1840s Charles Kingsley, the apostle of muscular manliness, formed a deep attachment to a fellow Cambridge student, Charles Mansfield, an attachment strikingly similar to that of his Cambridge contemporaries, Hallam and Tennyson. This relationship, which continued even after his marriage, Kingsley later described with a quite Carlylean unselfconsciousness and in a vocabulary similar to that of *Past and Present*, "He was my first love" (Chitty *The Beast and the Monk* 52). In 1843 he wrote his wife-to-be, "There is something awful, spiritual, in man's love for another." And he even paid his wife what must have seemed to him an erotic compliment, "Had you been a man we should have been like David and Jonathan" (Chitty 52).

Early Victorian male readers, then, found deeply attractive in *Past and Present* the imaginative creation of a society as well as a male self grounded in the intense affective ties of man to man, in the chaste male–male "embrace" and "kiss," and in the sacralized communal rituals of touching the male body. The reviewer for *Blackwood's* sees the primary emotive and even moral value of Carlyle's book to be its positive treatment of male–male relations: "We are accustomed to view his [Carlyle's] works, even when they especially regarded communities of men, and take the name of histories, as, in effect, appeals to the individual heart, and to the moral will of the reader" (Seigel *Carlyle* 212). Ralph Waldo Emerson, another nineteenth-century sage troubled by issues of manhood,[29] sees the attraction of the book to "all men" in the soft, affectionate, almost erotic feeling toward other men that he calls "manly tenderness": "[*Past and Present*] grapples honestly with the facts lying before all men, groups and disposes them with a master's mind, – and with a heart full of manly tenderness, offers his best counsel to his brothers" (Seigel 219). To such readers, the book's "tenderness" toward other men carried no hint of transgressive eroticism, no taint of effeminacy, but rather bore the aura of that which is truly "manly."

Furthermore, this utopian world of male love in the past becomes compelling as figuring and prefiguring the management of male desire in the industrial present. *Past and Present* represents the movement to manhood as the forging of masculine bonds, of "manly tenderness" within "communities of men," and thus provides in the monastery an historical analogue that heroicizes the affective ties of the work-centered male sphere within the industrial present. But for Carlyle male–male desire, the essential energy source for industrial labor, must always be desexualized, channeled into productive purposes.

If *Past and Present* represents the valorization of chaste male love, it simultaneously manifests the beginnings of that edginess about such love that was to increase through the nineteenth century. By the 1840s and 1850s the boundary between the homosocial and the homosexual had become an increasingly contested territory, the site of preliminary border skirmishes. Carlyle's rather paradoxical project of representing a manly monasticism exemplifies that urgency, so characteristic of male writing in these decades, to defend normative homosocial male bonds, the center of the hegemonic bourgeois formation of manliness, from the new threat of the unmanly masculine bonds within what was seen as an emerging and dangerous, if undefined, construction of masculinity. Like all early Victorian masculine writing, *Past and Present* defines its masculinity relationally, not only through differentiation from the female or feminized, but also from the new formation of the unmanly informed by the homoerotic.

Strikingly, this new gay construction of masculinity was for the early Victorians also represented in a discourse of monasticism. One historical context of *Past and Present* is the Tractarian revival of celibate religious communities for both males and females. There was Newman's male community at Littlemore as well as several female religious communities founded by Pusey. Before marriage, Fanny Kingsley was deeply attracted to such a Puseyite convent and even Kingsley himself was attracted to a monastic life. And there was the advocacy of a celibate clergy. Richard Hurrell Froude wrote in 1833, "Colleges of unmarried priests would be the cheapest way of providing effectively for the spiritual wants of a large population" (Hill *Religious Order* 304).

In the periodicals, debate about the Tractarians was occupied, if not preoccupied, with monasticism as the limit case of regulating male sexuality. An *Edinburgh Review* essay of 1843 on "Puseyism, or the Oxford Tractarian School" attacks "the celibacy of the clergy" and "the monkish institute" along with such other anti-progressive follies as "superstitious reverence for relics" and "the worship of the saints" (533). An essay in the same journal of 1844, "Recent Developments of Puseyism" notes that in the Puseyite *Lives of the Saints* "the penances, pilgrimages, the monasticism, and the grotesque and degrading superstitions of the Middle Ages, are commended to our ardent veneration" (364). Unlike Carlyle, and more like Browning and the Pre-Raphaelites, this *Edinburgh Review* author sees as one of the chief abuses of the cloistered life advocated by the Tractarians the suppression of sexuality:

Such is the revived admiration of monasticism, that one of these authors commends the hateful practice of consigning children to a monastic life on the sole authority of their parents – one of the most odious abuses of the whole system, – (*Life of St. Stephen*, 2, 5.) He is almost as bad as the holy Ambrose, who recommends young girls to retire to nunneries *against* the will of their parents! (364).

Within the 1840s, then, the resurgence of celibate monasticism as well as of female religious communities in England became a site for expressing deep anxiety about the manliness of male–male relationships. If the homosocial ties of the industrial male sphere are valorized by Carlyle's monastery, a deeply threatening re-valuation of such ties appeared to critics to be manifested in Anglo-Catholic monasticism and in the Tractarian advocacy of a celibate clergy. For the early Victorians, Tractarian and High Anglican religious practices were associated not only with ritualism, but what in the gender vocabulary of the 1840s was termed the "effeminate."[30] When applied to the Tractarians, discussion of what the *Blackwood's* reviewer of *Past and Present* called "communities of men" (212) or what Emerson terms "manly tenderness" takes on a distinctly anxious, threatened, sharply homophobic taint. In the early 1850s, even before his celebrated controversy with Newman, Kingsley expressed his own deep attraction/repulsion toward Newman in such terms: "In him and all that school, there is an element of foppery – even in dress and manner; a fastidious, maundering die-away effeminacy, which is mistaken for purity and refinement; and I find myself unable to cope with it" (Chitty *The Beast and the Monk* 236). Such linking of effeminacy with the Tractarians was not idiosyncratic, but pervasive. "Puseyite" became a code word for the unmanly as homoerotic. Within the historicist discourse of monasticism, the *Edinburgh Review* essayist of 1843 attacks "The Oxford Tractarian School," those who "plead for the restoration of Monasticism" (554), by setting them against the true English reformers of an earlier age. His comparison of the feminized or effeminate Tractarian male community to the manly community of the sailing ship is charged with a sadistic homophobia: "There is as great a difference between *their* tone and that of the Reformers, as between the playful tap of a coquette's fan and the vigorous stroke of a boatswain's lash" (553).

The *Edinburgh* article of 1844 on "Recent Developments of Puseyism" that reviews, along with the "odious" works of the Tractarians, *Chronica Jocelini de Brakelonda* also describes Puseyite medievalism as feminized, as a Keatsian aestheticism removed from the manly world of material fact: "They are ignorant that their sensitive fancy, which now luxuriates amidst the images of self-created beauty, would recoil with corresponding loathing from the actual deformities of the reality" (366). Anticipating Pater, the article speaks of the "effete system of the Middle Ages" (368). Against this effeminacy of monasticism past and present, the reviewer sees the Chronicle of Jocelin as well as *Past and Present* as a bracing antidote, for these works show monk Samson not as aesthete, but as aggressive commercial man devoted to the accumulation of assets: "[Abbot Samson] was a man deeply in earnest in increasing the wealth and power of his monastery, and in asserting its secular privileges" (568).

Within this public debate about homoeroticism registered within monastic discourse, it is this association of male celibacy and male communities with this new unmanliness as effeminacy that fuels Carlyle's intense, unfocused, often hysterical outbursts against "Puseyism" in *Past and Present*: "O Heavens, what shall we say of Puseyism, in comparison to Twelfth-Century Catholicism?" (119–20). In the chapter "Practical-Devotional," the contemporary opposite of manliness, the exemplary "Dilletantism" of the age, is "Puseyism" (119). Here, Carlyle gratuitously includes a curious poem that refers to the controversy surrounding Tract *XC* of Newman: "The Plan He shap'd His Worlds and Æons by/ Was – – Heavens! – Was thy small Nine-and-thirty Articles?" (120).[31]

Characteristically, in his attack on Puseyism Carlyle does not consider doctrinal issues, but rather employs a psycho-social analysis that sees theological disputes as emerging from different formations of manliness. Since this new gay formation of manliness was also figured within monastic discourse by the Puseyite monasticism of his own time, in *Past and Present* Carlyle is compelled to distinguish between a true and a false, a manly and an unmanly monasticism as a way of differentiating productive homosocial from prohibited homosexual bonds in contemporary relationships among men. The authorial voice attacks the "noisy theoretic demonstrations and laudations of *the* Church, instead of some unnoisy, unconscious, but *practical*, total, heart-and-soul demonstration of *a* Church" (120). Given the clear association throughout of social disorder and even of speaking itself with the unmanly, the "noisy" followers of Pusey become feminized or effeminate men, the spiritual equivalents of the female Chartists of the twelfth century in opposition to the authentic, strong and "unnoisy" manliness of "Twelfth-Century Catholicism" (120) exemplified in the life of Abbot Samson. But we can also see taking shape in Carlyle's use of the term "theoretic" the constellation of qualities that will throughout the century and into our own time serve to distinguish the gay male from the hearty Englishman. The Tractarians occupy the position of interiority, of intellectual speculation, which is implicitly associated with a kind of delicacy, as in

Carlyle's opposition of the "light adroit Man of Theory" to the "burly figure of this thick-skinned ... almost stupid Man of Practice" (160).

Carlyle's epic of "manly tenderness" within a community of men, then, evades the homophobia directed at the Tractarians by himself as well as by other early Victorian men, successfully negotiates this problematic of the masculine poetic – valorizing male–male bonds within an all-male world while not overstepping the boundary into the proscribed homosexual – by deploying one of the more powerful devices of that poetic, displacing the intensities of male–male desire to an imaginative space beyond the homophobic constrictions of contemporary bourgeois society. The Tractarians, as well as the Pre-Raphaelite Brothers ran into homophobic opposition not because they idealized monastic brotherhood in an imagined past, but because they established such male communities in the present. Carlyle evades the homosocial/homoerotic bind by placing his male community in the twelfth century. Transposed to the middle ages, the joining of men into communities is transformed into the highest expression of Christian worship. When historicized, the affective ties of man to man are moralized rather than sexualized. Like monkish celibacy, male love, even male–male physical contact, exemplifies sacred duty:

On the whole, who knows how to reverence the Body of a Man? It is the most reverend phenomenon under this Sun. For the Highest God dwells visible in that mystic unfathomable Visibility, which calls itself "I" on the Earth. "Bending before men," says Novalis, "is a reverence done to this Revelation in the Flesh. We touch Heaven when we lay our hand on a human Body." (126)

By presenting this homoerotic physicality as sacralized manly worship within a typological structure, Carlyle can prefigure the homosocial bonds to be fulfilled within the ideal factory system of the future while avoiding directly representing such bonding in the present time.

As model for the ideal cotton mill, Carlyle's monastery bound by masculine love imaginatively resolves a major problematic in the construction of manliness within industrial society. Patriarchal power depends upon close homosocial relations within the male sphere, and yet, given the imperative of bourgeois society to define manhood through marriage as well as through work, men must avoid what society forbids as the homosexual. *Past and Present* provides an attractive fantasy, a liminal response to this tension within the hegemonic script of bourgeois manhood. Displaced into the twelfth century, associated with the sacred, linked to the moral virtue of work, pervaded by sexual control, Carlyle's fantasy of chaste male love within an all-male community provides a safe imaginative space in which the strain of the homosocial/homosexual bind for bourgeois man is relieved, a place in which is acted out the forbidden desire of industrial man to live wholly in the male sphere, develop intense male–male bonds that do not cross the line to homoeroticism, and, crucially, escape having his virile energy attenuated by the defining act of bourgeois manhood, marriage.

INDUSTRIAL MANHOOD

The masculine poetic and the historicist discourse of monasticism enable Carlyle to displace into the twelfth century an imaginative resolution for the problematics of male identity in the early nineteenth century – controlling male energy, establishing a boundary between manly male–male ties and homoeroticism, separating virility from sexuality, channeling potentially dangerous male desire into productive work. But if the ideological contradictions and psychic strains of his masculine vision are barely contained in the account of achieved manhood in the microcosm of the monastery, they are unresolved in his account of the present industrial world, and of the industrial world to be. The same sense of the male body and of the psychic processes of the male self that govern his fiction of the past shape his account of the present and of the future, but to speak in the Carlylean mode, his male fantasy falters in confrontation with "Fact" (*Heroes* 329), the gritty reality of industrial England. Whereas his account of the monastery shows a compelling facticity, his representation of contemporary industrialism demonstrates an unconvincing fictiveness. This withdrawal to fiction, to allegory and to prophecy in the last sections of *Past and Present* registers the difficulty for Carlyle, as for other early Victorian male writers, in situating an integrated male identity within his own time and place.

As much as, if not more than the medieval past, the industrial present is transformed by Carlyle into the stuff of male fantasy. Although thousands of women were knotting threads and breathing fluff in Manchester cotton mills, Carlyle imagines the modern factory to be, like the ancient monastery, a wholly male world. The female does not enter the world of work, except as the wandering Irish Widow, the carrier of disease and agent of disruption. This fantasized erasure of women from the analysis of modern factory labor, like the choice of the all-male monastery as the exemplar of communal labor, emphasizes that for Carlyle the Condition of England question is primarily the Condition of Manliness question, a gendered matter of reaffirming and recreating manhood in the face of its dissolution. At the workhouse at St. Ives, Carlyle sees imprisoned "within their ringwall and its railings, some half-hundred or more of these men" (8). His concern here, as with the monastery before the reforms of Abbot Samson, is not so much with the economic as with the psychosocial – the loss of male potency, the blockage of male energy: "O, what a waste is there; of noble and thrice-noble national virtues; peasant Stoicisms, Heroisms; valiant *manful* habits, soul of a Nation's worth ... Workers, Master Workers, Unworkers, *all men*, come to a pause; stand fixed, and cannot farther. Fatal paralysis spreading inwards, from the extremities" (9–11, emphasis added). Without the channeling of desire into work, the workers of England are for Carlyle emasculated men, "their cunning right-hand lamed, lying idle in their sorrowful bosom" (7).

For Carlyle, industrial England is but St. Edmundsbury writ large, an extended community of feminized men who have not yet achieved manhood. The social remedy for this dis-ease lies, as in his utopian male community of the past, in working out the masculine plot of manhood achieved, in creating or, within his typological vision, recreating the affective, desexualized bonds among men that Carlyle calls "the union-bond of man to man" (189). For Carlyle the "union-bond," the bond of male community and of submission to the strongest male, is as crucial to the psychic life of the male factory worker as to the monk, as imperative for the orderliness of the factory as for the monastery, central to the transformation of industrial society into the ordered, productive all-male community prefigured by the microcosm of St. Edmundsbury.

The sacralized, distanced monastery provides a safe zone for representing such bonds, but, crucially, *Past and Present* does not concretize such male bonding in the lives of men in the industrial present. The contemporary equivalent of the bonds of monk to monk or monks to Abbot is noticeably absent from the accounts of Manchester. Carlyle's models of the "union-bond" among men in industrial relations do not inhabit the social reality of the present, but are rather displaced into the past, into the future, or into the realm of literary fiction, rhetorical moves that inscribe his inability to imagine and reluctance to represent chaste male–male ties in contemporary life.

Carlyle's most celebrated exemplar of an industrial order based upon male bonding as submission is drawn not from his own time, but doubly distanced as a fictional version of the feudal past. Gurth the swineherd is a figure taken from *Ivanhoe*:

> Gurth ... in him at least the certainty of supper and social lodging when he came home; Gurth to me seems happy, in comparison with many a Lancashire and Buckinghamshire man, of these days, not born thrall of anybody! Gurth's brass collar did not gall him: Cedric *deserved* to be his Master ... Gurth had the inexpressible satisfaction of feeling himself related indissolubly, though in a rude brass-collar way, to his fellow-mortals in this Earth. (211)

In the typical Carlylean pattern, the "satisfaction" of the psycho-sexual and the economic is conflated. But that such "satisfaction" is "inexpressible" suggests several foci of early Victorian male anxiety.

For one, the term "inexpressible" suggests the absence of a language in the 1840s for naming the intense male–male relationship between Gurth and Cedric, a relationship of "rude brass-collar" bonds that involves a good deal of abasement or, to use rather anachronistic terms, a good measure of sado-masochism. The absence of psychoanalytic language does not, of course, point to a limitation in the Victorians and a larger wisdom in us, but rather to the fact that the early Victorians represented male same-sex relations in an historicist vocabulary. It is not that male–male relations dare not speak their name in these decades, but that such relations are nameable only through historicist coding. Yet this use of an historicist code rather than a contemporary vocabulary and images of contemporary life to represent such male–male ties does suggest an unresolved anxiety about such bonds. An affective tie based on psycho-sexual dominance/submission between, say, a worker and a "Master" in a cotton mill of the 1840s would be "inexpressible," difficult to represent within the conventions of nineteenth-century realism.

For Carlyle, the achievement of industrial order is one with the achievement of manhood. The reform of society follows the masculine plot. But when applied to the nineteenth century, the masculine plot runs counter to the marriage plot, the approved script for bourgeois manhood. Carlyle's rejection of heterosexuality, his valorization of the affective ties of men, and call for the loss of ego in the group through submission to a stronger male clearly contradicts the hegemonic bourgeois imperatives of compulsory heterosexuality, marriage, and privileging of the autonomous male subject. In the sections of *Past and Present* dealing with contemporary industrial life, Carlyle attempts to resolve these contradictions by applying the same fantasies that shape his dream of the past, a dream whose imaginative attractiveness, however, resides in its oppositional position in regard to the bourgeois manhood supposedly governing the hearts of Victorian middle-class men. Having erased women entirely from industrial England, Carlyle represents the new heroic industrial manhood by adopting traditional constructions of a masculinity lived within all-male institutions. The Captains of Industry are, notably, warriors, soldier males: "The Leaders of Industry, if Industry is ever to be led, are virtually the Captains of the World ... Captains of Industry are the true Fighters, henceforth recognisable as the only true ones" (268). As "Fighters," the Captains of Industry have neither wife nor domestic establishment. Captains of Industry are indeed Captains, "Leaders" of men within the warrior model of masculinity, rather than breadwinners for a family. Their male energy channeled into leading men, their lives spent in the company of other men, the Captains of Industry are, implicitly, as celibate as Abbot Samson.

In *Past and Present* this opposition between competing scripts for manhood is handled by the refusal of the realist mode, the continuation of the fantastic and the ungrounded. In the realist industrial novels of the period deeply influenced by Carlylean social theory, this same conflict between masculinities is equally destabilizing. Like *Past and Present* these novels attempt to resolve the opposition set out in "Phallus-Worship" between domestic fiction and masculine writing, between the marriage plot that valorizes heterosexual life within the family as the marker of manhood and the Carlylean plot that sees homosocial bonding within a productive male community as the sign of manhood achieved.

In many ways, Elizabeth Gaskell's *North and South* (1854–55) follows the Carlylean plot. Lead by a masculinized heroine, Margaret Hale, the family leaves the domestic space in which the weakened, feminized father presides for the male sphere of Manchester. Here, Margaret confronts a surrogate father, the potential Captain of

Industry, Mr. Thornton. Like Abbot Samson, Thornton faces rebellion in the disorder of the strike by his children or workers represented as a form of working-class unmanliness through Carlylean images of social disruption as the unregulated flow of male energy. Margaret "looked round and heard the first long far-off roll of the tempest; saw the first slow-surging wave of the dark crowd come, with its threatening crest tumble over, and retreat" (226–27). Even more dangerous within the Carlylean context is that the fluid energy of the workers has not only escaped its bounds, but has become sexualized, a reversion manifested in the barely coded public penetration or rape of Margaret by the mob: "A sharp pebble flew by her, grazing forehead and cheek, and drawing a blinding sheet of light before her eyes... They [the workers] were watching, open-eyed, and open-mouthed, the thread of dark-red blood which wakened them from their trance of passion" (235).

The mob dispersed by the military, Thornton, who provides a justification of middle-class hegemony in his manifestation of manhood as reserve, finally contains this overflow of desire in the working class by creating in Carlylean fashion a male community, an industrial St. Edmundsbury, within the walls of the mill. He constructs at the factory a "dining-room – for the men" (444) as a masculinized substitute for feminized domestic space. He even appropriates the female role of homemaker by transforming this function into the traditional masculine terms of the all-male club: "So I coolly took the part assigned to me, which is something liker that of steward to a club. I buy the provisions wholesale, and provide a fitting matron or cook" (445). The reform of the factory, like the reformation of the monastery, culminates in the achievement of male community, again realized in the fantasy of substituting for the bourgeois family the nurturing, self-engendering all-male family:

One day, two or three of the men – my friend Higgins among them – asked me if I would not come in and take a snack... so I went in, and I never made a better dinner in my life... and for some time, whenever that especial dinner recurred in their dietary, I was sure to be met by these men, with a "Master, there's a hot-pot for dinner to-day, win yo' come?"... Nothing like the act of eating for equalising men. (445–46)

A truly Carlylean masculine plot would have ended with this vision of the mill-owner dining and even living within this walled community of men as the contemporary fulfillment of the productive all-male utopia prefigured in St. Edmundsbury. But by the 1850s the realization of such an ideal of manhood had become unthinkable, "inexpressible," tinged with the anxiety that by mid-century surrounded the idea of male communities and was impermissible by its opposition to the bourgeois ideal of manhood. Instead, the masculine plot is short-circuited by the marriage plot. Thornton marries Margaret Hale. The closure comes not from union with other males as it does in Carlyle's monastery, but by entry into heterosexuality in marriage, a movement taking the male from a life lived wholly within the male community into a fully bourgeois rather than a Carlylean form of industrial manhood.

The same contradiction between Carlylean and bourgeois manliness, between the masculine plot and the marriage plot, is also played out in *Hard Times*, a novel dedicated to Carlyle and that works out in scathing comedy the emotional logic of Carlylean industrial manliness. Carlyle's definition of bourgeois manhood as sublimated sexuality rather than heterosexual erotics is worked out with some ambivalence in the most Carlylean figure in Victorian fiction, Josiah Bounderby of Coketown. Bounderby may be the Captain of Industry *manqué* in certain ways, but he does embody the productive industrial celibacy prefigured in Abbot Samson. Although he does not establish a factory community, his mill does seem to flourish. His energy is expended on the construction of a manliness that with his characteristic literalizing of fantasy Dickens represents as necessitating the erasure of the mother as the psychic means of holding to the male dream of self-generation.

His self begins to dissolve when his energy, once devoted to industrial production, becomes sexualized in his desire for Louisa. But there is also the suggestion that as a "bachelor" (83), a construction of masculinity developed in the nineteenth century to code the rejection of heterosexuality, Bounderby is already viewed with suspicion. Social pressure compels him toward a marriage that is necessary to his self-fashioning as bourgeois man, however antithetical such entry into heterosexuality may be to his functioning as a Captain of Industry. Indeed, the imposition on his life of the marriage script is wholly disastrous. The destructive, incompatible marriage fails and Bounderby is disgraced. But he then "resumed a bachelor life" (265) in a celibate relationship with Mrs. Sparsit and in the world of laboring men where his "boundless" male energy can once again be "bound" or sublimated into the productive work of industrialism.

As these industrial novels suggest, the "satisfaction" of masculine bonding figured by Gurth and Cedric is "inexpressible" in that such intense male–male relations both support and disrupt the pattern of manhood set out for bourgeois men in early Victorian England. The rhythm of Carlyle's prose in *Past and Present* suggests that such feelings are also "inexpressible" in that their very voicing disrupts the tense equilibrium of manliness. Within Carlyle's technology of the self, even the verbal expression of desire tends to free the inner chaos from the tight regulation that defines manhood. Since the function of a truly manly literature is not the intensification of desire, but the strengthening of manly reserve, this repressive practice of the self creates a problematic for the male writer who must inevitably evoke or express the very feelings that must be restrained. The emotional pattern of Carlyle's prose enacts this contradiction within the masculine poetic and within this ideal of manliness as reserve in the extreme oscillation of mood, the alternation of frenzy with calm, the shifts from constrained commentary to emotional exhortation that define the Carlylean style.

Carlyle is powerfully drawn to certain emotional states, particularly male–male bonding, submission to another male, and to the eruption of violence in female surrogates which he represents in intense, often frenzied set-pieces that are themselves encased in exhortations to achieve manly reserve, as if the force within could be calmed by repeated mantras of control. These eruptions of the volcanic force within often occur when the authorial voice slides from observer to participant, opening the floodgates that usually hold back the psychic flow of the inner life. In the passage about Gurth and Cedric, the narrator first speaks in a calm generalizing third-person mode about the general need for abasement to a stronger male: "That any and every wiser man, could, by brass collars, or in whatever milder or sharper way, lay hold of him when he was going wrong, and order and compel him to go a little righter" (212). But as the prose shifts to the first person, to the mode of personal confession so rare in Carlyle, manly reserve crumbles. Rather than control itself, the prose represents the desperate need for control:

O if thou really art my *Senior*, Seigneur, my *Elder*, Presbyter or Priest, – if thou art in very deed my *Wiser*, may a beneficent instinct lead and impel thee to "conquer" me, to command me!... I conjure thee in the name of God, force me to do it; were it by never such brass collars, whips and handcuffs, leave me not to walk over precipices! (212).

This disjunction of style, this move between stasis and flood, enacts, then, not manly reserve but male hysteria, the inability to control the fluid chaos within, and demonstrates the crystalline brittleness of male psychic armor. For Carlyle, achieving the "iron energy" (95) of manhood appears so difficult in the present that, as for Tennyson in "Locksley Hall" and *Maud*, the binary of gender becomes not masculinity/femininity, but masculinity/insanity. Carlyle sees the Captain of Industry as confronting in the present not only "unkempt Cotton," a formless nature that is marked as female and to be conquered by manly industry, but also "hallucinating fellow Men" (192). The heroism of the modern Man of Letters, like that of his literary forefathers such as "Poet Dryden," is to confront the essential disorder of the male psyche: "You do walk hand in hand with sheer Madness, all the way, – who is by no means pleasant company!" (*Past* 206). Ideally, then, the heroic, the mythic task of the male writer is to return from that "*Inferno*" (206) of the male self and transform the hellish chaos of the male interior to the psychic regulation that defines manliness: "You look fixedly into Madness, and *her* undiscovered, boundless, bottomless Night-empire, that you may extort new Wisdom out of it, as an Eurydice from Tartarus" (206). The task of the Hero as Man of Letters is thus identical to that of the Hero as Captain of Industry who, depending upon an equally hard-won sanity, must turn the mental rhythms of organic time in agricultural laborers to the mechanical orderliness of the clock, to create what we would now call a disciplined workforce. Carlyle calls on Captains of Industry to "reduce them [workers] to order, begin reducing them. To order, to just subordination; noble loyalty in return for noble guidance. Their souls are driven nigh mad; let yours be sane and ever saner" (272).

For Carlyle, manly work in the industrial age is but a socially useful mode of controlling male insanity: "All Works, each in their degree, are a making of Madness sane" (206). For Carlyle, the most effective work for "making...Madness sane" is not intellectual speculation or literary composition, for eruptions of the inner life unman even the prose of *Past and Present*, but silent physical labor. For Carlyle, the source of manly industrial labor is the fluid seminal energy of the male body. Characteristically this essential maleness in the factory worker as in the writer is also the object of deep ambivalence. The working-class body is primal, monstrous. The "Soul [inhabits] the rudest Caliban of a body" (192), a body inherently diseased, requiring "some Soul... were it only to keep the Body unputrified" (190). In the industrial present as in the past, in England as in the France of 1848, male energy becomes most dangerous when the "god-given Force, the sacred celestial Life-essence breathed into him by Almighty God" (197) slips from regulation to become sexualized as spasmodic, orgasmic, "convulsive energy": "Industrial work, still under bondage to Mammon, the rational soul of it not yet awakened, is a tragic spectacle. Men in the rapidest motion and self-motion; restless, with convulsive energy, as if driven by Galvanism, as if possessed by a Devil" (207).

As in the twelfth century, so in the nineteenth, virile seminal force must be channeled, cleansed, desexualized. For the industrial worker, as for the Captain of Industry and the monk, psychic health, true manliness lies in the sublimation of male desire, its transformation through an industrial-strength celibacy that directs energy from sexuality to regulated industrial labor. Chaotic flood within is transformed from unclean to clean through regulated flow, through the routines of productive work rather than through the "convulsive" unproductive emissions marked as the disease of spermatorrhea: "How, as a free-flowing channel, dug and torn by noble force through the sour mud-swamp of one's existence, like an ever-deepening river there, it runs and flows; – draining off the sour festering water, gradually from the root of the remotest grass-blade; making, instead of pestilential swamp, a green fruitful meadow with its clear-flowing stream" (197). Within Carlyle's tropes of the psyche, "waste waves" (206) must become water power, "weedy gulf-streams" (206) transformed into millraces powering "Undershot" water wheels. A new Plugson must emerge to "plug" the "restless" force within to achieve a tempered rather than a "convulsive energy."

Like the monastic celibacy of Abbot Samson, this new industrial celibacy as the desexualization of male desire is transformed into phallic virility. Carlyle envisions the sacralized "Phallus-Worship" fantasized in the monastery as soon to be fulfilled in time: "We will now quit this of the hard, organic, but limited Feudal Ages; and glance timidly into the immense Industrial Ages, as yet all inorganic, and in a quite pulpy condition, requiring desperately to harden themselves into some organism" (247). The new Captain of Industry will be defined not only by "insight, courage," but, most importantly, by "hard energy" (207).

But, like the "union-bond of man to man" (189), industrial work as desexualized desire is not concretized in the industrial present. Carlyle's abhorrence of the male body as well as his class position as "brain-worker" prevent him from entering the physical reality of working-class toil. In describing both the work of the monastery and the "Labour" of the cotton mill Carlyle's prose fuses the psychosexual and the material. In the conclusion of "The Everlasting Yea," the making of male madness sane and the making of swamp into farm are conflated: "The mad primeval Discord is hushed; the rudely-jumbled conflicting elements bind themselves into separate Firmaments: deep silent rock-foundations are built beneath; and the skyey vault with its everlasting Luminaries above: instead of a dark wasteful Chaos, we have a blooming, fertile, heaven-encompassed World" (148). In *Past and Present* the "fight...with Necessity, Barrenness, Scarcity, with Puddles, Bogs, tangled Forests, unkempt Cotton" (191) figures less the work of land reclamation, colonization and cotton-spinning than what we would call "therapeutic work," the ordering of the puddles and bogs of the male psyche and the tangles of male desire. The merging of mental and material points again to Carlyle's abiding definition of manhood as hard-won mental stability, but the psychological occupation moves the prose from any clear sense of the physical reality of industrial work itself. As in Brown's *Work*, Carlyle stands enviously contemplating the muscular effort of the working class, but it is the factory workers who are doing the heavy lifting.

As much as Carlyle's epic of manliness is powered by personal psychological concerns, the difficulty in creating the stable equilibrium of manhood is compounded by what Carlyle, like his contemporaries, saw as the inadequacy of each of the several competing styles of masculinity available in the 1840s, the absence of any single formation of manliness to which a man might surrender himself, as the monks surrendered to the sacralized community. Rather than wholly rejecting current models of manhood, Carlyle, like Arnold, reconciles these competing formations purely through rhetoric, particularly through the figure of self-contradiction, the oxymoron. He opposes the entrepreneurial formation of manhood, which he dismisses as "Mammonism," yet employs the entrepreneurial work ethic to criticize the gentry construction of manliness as the "Gospel of Dilettantism." His own version of heroic manhood in a "Working Aristocracy" paradoxically links the aristocratic male, whose identity is defined by being beyond the necessity of work, with industrial labor. The equally self-contradictory term "Captain of Industry" binds through language alone the aristocratic ideal of manliness as leadership in war with the bourgeois ideal of manliness as industrious labor. Chivalric battle and industrial work become conflated. The cotton-mill owner becomes a "Chevalier" (191), the workplace a "Field of Honour" (192). The industrialist may become a "Knight" in battle with "unkempt Cotton" as well as with the chaos within "hallucinating fellow men" (192).

The new paragon of manliness, then, is limned in a rhetoric of contradiction, but, unlike Abbot Samson, he is not concretized in the world of fact. Instead, *Past and Present* displaces the new masculinity into the future. Applied to industrialization, the masculine plot shows not manhood achieved, but manhood as potential. Rather than look about him to see industrial manhood realized, the speaker in "Locksley Hall" can only dip "into the future": "Men, my brothers, men the workers, ever reaping something new;/ That which they have done but earnest of the things that they shall do" (lines 117–18). The final Book of *Past and Present* is titled "Horoscope," a vision of things to come.

Carlyle's turn to the future may be read positively within the genre of the utopian or, more contextually, within the mode of the prophetic. In this final section Carlyle is clothing himself in the mantle, to be worn now only by men, of the sage, the reader of future time. Situated within the still formless, yet unhardened industrial age, he employs typology as prophecy. If Abbot Samson is the type of true manliness in the past, Plugson of Undershot is the anti-type in the present, and the Captain of Industry the fulfillment in future time of the manliness figured throughout the Bible of History. But Carlyle's use of typological form also suggests his own uneasiness about the possibility of realizing an heroic industrial manhood. The figural mode is based upon incarnation of the transcendent within historical fact. If the example of Abbot Samson exhibits a compelling historicity, as does the portrait of the unemployed at St. Ives, the representation of the Captain of Industry moves into the visionary style of the biblical prophets.

In the crucial chapter "Captains of Industry" within "Horoscope," the movement from the realist mode is pronounced. The Captain of Industry lacks even a personal name. He, or rather "they" since the title and language uses the plural rather than the individualized singular, is defined only by differentiation from earlier forms of manhood: "Let the Captains of Industry consider: once again, are they born of other clay than the old Captains of Slaughter" (268). The Captain of Industry, then, moves out of history, outside the figural mode of historical incarnation. Fulfillment of true manhood in future time becomes a belief grounded not in the facts of nineteenth-century life but compelled by Carlyle's intense iteration. But even this faith is attenuated by qualifiers: "The Leaders of Industry, if Industry is ever to be led, are virtually the Captains of the World; if there be no nobleness in them, there will never be an Aristocracy more" (268).

The slippage in his account of the present from historical fact through novelistic fiction to allegory and visionary prophecy, like the self-contradictory names of an ideal masculinity, indicate Carlyle's difficulty in resolving the oppositions of early Victorian manhood and of grounding the achievement of true manliness in contemporary social fact. The abrupt shifts in his prose from reserve to "volcanoism," from manly control to male hysteria, dramatize not the regulated desire that defines industrial manhood, but the very madness and hallucination that the new Hero as Man of Letters seeks to control. *Past and Present* in its idealization of the monastery provided for its male readers a compelling and in many ways antihegemonic fantasy of productive celibacy as the discipline of desire within chaste male–male bonds. But Carlyle's translation of this same fantasy into the emerging industrial society demonstrates his inability fully to resolve the psychological and social strains within early Victorian manhood. Instead, his accounts of the present and of the future dramatize the fragility and the instability of his own ideal of manliness, as well as the more general difficulty of forming a new model of manhood in the industrial age.

CHAPTER 2

The problematic of a masculine poetic: Robert Browning

Like Carlyle's prose, Browning's poetry of the early Victorian decades – *Dramatic Lyrics* (1842), *Dramatic Romances and Lyrics* (1845), *Men and Women* (1855) – is grounded in that period's discourse of masculinity, occupied with the points of problematization within that discourse, and expressed within the coding of an historicized monasticism.

For Browning, as for Carlyle and the Pre-Raphaelites, the central issue within masculinity is the management of male energy. More specifically, for Browning the major problematic becomes the productive regulation of a highly sexualized male energy in the practice of the male poet. If for Carlyle the repression coded by monastic celibacy exemplifies a virtuoso technology for controlling male desire, Browning is equally obsessed with monasticism as a limit case of male sexual regulation, but his valuing of the sign of monasticism differs dramatically. For him the monastery becomes not an all-male utopia, but a site of male psychic imprisonment containing a gallery of men who demonstrate varied shapes of psychic deformation, of male madness created by the extreme containment of natural male sexuality. And if Browning is the great early Victorian celebrant of heterosexual desire, he is also drawn to the affectionate bonding between men. Like the fantasies of masculine bonding in Carlyle, Browning's poems of these decades inhabit the troubled boundary between the homosocial and the homosexual.

As much as Browning may differ from Carlyle in valuing practices of managing male desire, the masculine plot as the quest for manhood achieved, however deeply ironized, also structures his writing. Like Carlyle, Browning was occupied with the quest for a viable form of artistic manhood, with constructing for his own time a new Hero as Man of Letters or, more specifically, a new Hero as Man of Poetry. And his poetry of this period, particularly the artist-poems – "Pictor Ignotus," "Fra Lippo Lippi," "Andrea del Sarto" – represent the project and problematics of forging a masculine poetic that would ground the manliness of the poet in the normative values of bourgeois masculinity.

MASCULINITY DEFORMED

Underlying Browning's occupation with forms of madness in men is the concern, shared with his contemporaries, about the intense difficulty of maintaining manliness as a tense self-disciplining of sexuality and about the potential for deformation of the self through this ongoing management of sexual desire.[1] For Browning, as for Tennyson and Carlyle, the primary binary within the discourse of manhood is not manly/feminine, but manliness/madness.[2] Employing a model of sexual pathology implicit within early Victorian masculine discourse, Browning dramatizes a psychological process in which the uneasy equilibrium in the management of desire breaks down as the emotional reserve that defines manliness is carried to an extreme, as the floodgates shut on the flow of male sexuality. In ways that resonate with his criticism of the puritanism of his own time, he codes in the limit case of monastic celibacy the ways that repression of male sexuality leads to voyeurism and to the murder of women, to the distortion of male art through mimetic failure, and to aestheticism as a fetishizing of the art object that substitutes for the natural flow of male sexual energy.

"Soliloquy of the Spanish Cloister" (1842), one of Browning's earliest dramatic monologues, exemplifies his use of monastic celibacy as limit case to represent the deformation of male mental life and of sexualized male energy by the enforced containment of male desire. In contrast to the contemporary work of Carlyle, Browning's poem equates male chastity with male madness. If Brother Lawrence is a virtuoso of male self-control, one of the rare male innocents in Browning's work, the speaker exemplifies the average sensual man turned monstrous when natural energy is distorted by sexual repression, an intimation of what Lippo might have become had he remained within the cloister. Like the unhistoricized lover of Porphyria, who occupies another madhouse cell, the Spanish monk represents an extreme case of the emotive and erotic constrictiveness valorized by the normative construction of manliness as reserve within Browning's own society. Driven inward, the speaker's innate desire takes on the configurations of early Victorian male fantasy. As in Carlyle's male fantasies, the male sexuality so threatening to the self is displaced onto the female. Women become primal, animal. Their fetishized hair, "like horsehairs," is associated with fluidity, "Steeping ... in the tank." As in Tennyson, the sexualized female is cast as the racial Other, the Latin "brown Dolores":

> *Saint*, forsooth! While brown Dolores
>   Squats outside the Convent bank
> With Sanchicha, telling stories,
>   Steeping tresses in the tank,
> Blue-black, lustrous, thick like horsehairs.   (lines 25–29)

For Browning these dark women do not function as dangers to manhood as the sexual female does within the masculine plot. Rather, underlying this poem is its extreme projection of the other side of the Victorian problematic of manliness, not the Carlylean longing for chaste masculine bonding within an all-male community, but the urge to shatter bourgeois constraints on heterosexual virility.

From the unmanly voyeurism of the Dolores section, the monologue shifts to another deformation of male desire in the anachronistic allusion to the growth of Victorian pornography.[3] By introducing the "scrofulous French novel/ On gray paper with blunt type" (lines 57–58) the poem shatters the historicist frame of monastic discourse. Rather than displacing issues of masculinity into the safe imaginative zone of the past, the text here shifts psychic action to the present, to the "French novel" that, as in Carlyle's hysterical fear of George Sand, embodied the danger of "Phallus-Worship" as the destructive freeing of male sexuality. For Browning, pornography exemplifies the driving of male desire into the inner cloister of the mind, the warping of virility by the puritanical constraints of bourgeois England. Indeed, within the world of print culture the commodification of male desire takes an extreme and destructive form. In a world mediated through the imprecision of "blunt type" men no longer need to purchase the body of the woman, as does Lippo in a more hearty age, but are able to buy print descriptions of women to ruminate over, if not within the privacy of one's monastic cell, then within the analogous privacy of one's suburban study.

In this case history of male madness as enforced celibacy, the inability to regulate the energy of male sexuality is registered, as in other Browning poems, by a breakdown of language that signifies the breakdown of mental self-discipline. As in the rhythms of *Past and*

Present, the monologue of this monk oscillates between rigid imposition of control and mental "volcanoism" (*Past* 96). The dissolution of the linguistic order enacts the speaker's dissolution into the flux of primal maleness:

> *Hy, Zy, Hine...*
> 'St, there's Vespers! *Plena gratiâ*
> *Ave, Virgo*! Gr-r-r – you swine!   (lines 70–72)

This deformation of male mental life as grounded in what Browning sees as the unnatural restraint of heterosexual desire, again coded in the limit case of clerical celibacy, structures Browning's more complex dramatic monologue, "The Bishop Orders His Tomb at Saint Praxed's Church" (1845), a poem that connects distortions in the management of sexuality to distortions in the practice of art that resonate with Browning's own time. For this cleric, male desire or, more specifically male heterosexual desire, is the primary ground of male identity. Within this stream of consciousness, erotic recollection of the mother of the gathered sons surfaces at the beginning and concludes the monologue, "so fair she was!" (line 125). Of course, male celibacy is not observed by the Bishop as it is by Abbot Samson. Yet, with clear nineteenth-century resonance, the flow of male sexuality is forced underground, thereby blocking the positive transformation of male sexual energy into artistic creation. For Browning any inhibition on virility causes a destructive reification of male energy, and his critique of the Bishop's artistic practice as consumer rather than producer of art exemplifies the basic assumption of a masculine poetic, the dependence of artistic potency on sexual potency.

Within the gendered poetics of its time, "The Bishop Orders His Tomb" dramatizes a conventional form of unmanning, the emergence of a male hysteria in which, as in Tennyson's "Locksley Hall" and *Maud*, manly reserve dissolves to loose the flux of inward feeling. But, in distinction to Tennyson and to Carlyle, this feminization as dissolution is attributed to conditions of sexual constraint that resonate with the bourgeois respectability of Browning's own society. Regression to a feminized overflow of feeling as the sign of failure to achieve manly balance between sexual control and sexual expression is registered here, as in "Soliloquy of the Spanish Cloister," by linguistic dislocation, the unmediated juxtaposition of extremes of Christian asceticism and an unrestrained sexuality. Such unmanly mental chaos is concretized by the frieze the Bishop imagines for his tomb, an ironic emblem of his unmanning and, more generally, of the internal tensions of early Victorian manhood:

> The Saviour at his sermon on the mount,
> Saint Praxed in a glory, and one Pan
> Ready to twitch the Nymph's last garment off,
> And Moses with the tables. (lines 59–62)

Within this model of male pathology in which sexuality forced inward destroys the equilibrium of mental life, desire is transformed to eroticized fantasy, as in "Soliloquy of the Spanish Cloister" and "Pictor Ignotus." For the Bishop, this male fantasy takes a particularly degraded form. He transforms Christianity into a dream of violence, "Big as a Jew's head cut off at the nape" (line 43), and an erotic reverie, "Blue as a vein o'er the Madonna's breast" (line 44). His most extreme fantasy, emerging as he perceives the reality of death, is that of horror as abjection. He envisions *in extremis* the liquefaction of the boundaries of the male body. In an hallucinatory vision the grave opens up to reveal in the dissolution of the body in death the fluid interior that defines primal, essential maleness: "Gritstone, a-crumble! Clammy squares which sweat/ As if the corpse they keep were oozing through" (lines 116–17).

Of crucial concern to Browning within this psycho-sexual analysis of the Bishop is how male desire forbidden open expression in life becomes invested in the acquisition and delectation of the art object, in what came in the nineteenth century to be termed "aestheticism." As Pater was to do in the 1860s, Browning defines the aesthetic as exemplified in the Bishop not in moral or religious terms, but as another deformation of manliness under conditions of social inhibition, as a discipline of sexual energy that transfers desire from the forbidden sexual object to internalized eroticized sensation stimulated by an art object. Within the historically coded debates about reconciling masculinity and poetry, aestheticism as this eroticizing of the observing and savoring of the art object represents a particularly unmanly mode of managing male sexuality since male desire is channeled into the consumption of art rather than, as in the happier example of Lippo, being acted out in the body and also sublimated into the production of art. Since the channeling of desire into productivity defines bourgeois manliness and the transformation of sexual energy into creative work marks early Victorian masculine poetics, the aesthetic remains in opposition to normative masculinity throughout the century.

"My Last Duchess" provides another case history of male pathology, another imbalance in the management of male sexuality, another example in historicist form of the psychic perils of early Victorian masculinity. In the Duke, Browning presents the limit case of the practice of reserve as sexual inhibition that defines normative Victorian bourgeois manliness. The palace of Ferrara, like the palace of the Medici in Florence, is another madhouse cell, and for Browning cell resonates with the cloister and with the prison. The Duke's palace is another of Browning's palaces of art as prison in which men live cut off from the expression of normal heterosexuality. But here the constraints on a natural sexual life are not those generated by puritanical prohibition, as in Browning's cloisters. If monasticism becomes the historicized limit case of the evangelical ideal of sexual asceticism, the Duke becomes the historicized limit case of the aristocratic reserve adopted by the Victorian bourgeoisie as a class marker.[4] This practice of manly self-control defined the bourgeois male and justified his dominance over the men of the working class whose uncontrolled emotive and erotic expressiveness is registered here, ironically, through the eyes of the Duke, who looks condescendingly at the incident of the "bough of cherries some officious fool/ Broke in the orchard for her" (ll. 27–28). It is this class-bound psychic practice of reserve, transposed into the Renaissance, that prevents the Duke from reaching out to the Duchess, from attaining a manly sexual life: "And I choose/ Never to stoop" (lines 42–43).

That this psychic armor is fragile, that the equilibrium of manliness as reserve can be achieved only through continuous, intense psychological strain is registered in the very form of the Duke's speech. In the monologues of the Spanish monk and of the Bishop, as well as in the rhythms of Carlyle's prose, lapses in manly mental control are marked by a disjunctive rhetoric that juxtaposes extremes of desire and of constraint without any mediation. In the Duke, the fragility of his self-regulation is figured in the stammer, the momentary inability to speak that interrupts his otherwise assured aristocratic rhetoric in bargaining with the envoy. These lapses indicate his cognitive failure to engage the emotional energy contained within himself by the practice of reserve and evidence the characteristically early Victorian practice of displacing a threatening male sexuality onto the female Other.[5] The first instance appears as the Duke attempts to confront the spontaneous overflow of emotion represented in the now dead female:

> She had
> A heart – how shall I say? – too soon made glad,
> Too easily impressed. (lines 21–23)

The next confrontation with such threatening emotive openness comes as the Duke fails to understand an exchange that lies outside the class-bound constraints of his aristocratic, or in Victorian terms, gentlemanly performance. In his confrontation with the Duchess, the Duke confronts a crisis of manhood in that the Duchess challenges both the formation of manliness as reserve as well as the Duke's use of such manliness to justify his social position. The female here refuses to recognize the class position that, with clear reference to the Victorian bourgeoisie, is ostensibly validated by sexual and emotional constraint:

> she liked what e'er
> She looked on, and her looks went everywhere.
> ...
> She thanked men, – good! but thanked
> Somehow – I know not how – as if she ranked
> My gift of a nine-hundred-years-old name
> With anybody's gift. (lines 23–24, 31–34)

Within Browning's early Victorian model of male pathology, the female Other as the longed for yet threatening possibility of erotic and emotive release must be contained by being destroyed. For the sexually restrained male, of whom the earliest example is Porphyria's lover, male fantasy turns to intense control of and finally to killing the female who functions as a projection of repressed male desire. Famously, "My Last Duchess" does not provide an account of the fate of the Duchess, but Browning's later comments that the Duchess may have been shut up in a convent, the sign within monastic discourse of confined sexuality, suggests Browning's analysis of the male urge to contain the flood of desire which endangers the integrity of the psyche should a man "stoop" or succumb. The Duke's desire for the figure of "Neptune...Taming a sea-horse" (lines 54–55) draws upon this same early Victorian imaginary in associating the female as projection of male sexuality with the animal, the primal, the fluidity of the sea. Ironically, the Duke as deformed male identifies himself with the god of the sea, the controller of fluid energy, the man who can set Eros within a "bronze" (line 56) stasis.

Like "The Bishop Orders His Tomb," "My Last Duchess" represents aestheticism as a degraded and unmanly practice of sexual regulation in its transfer of male erotic energy from the sexual act to contemplation of the flesh cast in bronze or captured in paint. Like the Bishop, the Duke displaces Eros into art. In its difference from the Browningesque ideal of manly art as produced in necessary conjunction with a rich fleshly life exemplified in Lippo, the Duke's eroticized aestheticism exhibits a particular male pathology within art practice. His response to the portrait registers a deformed male sexuality, complete with overtones of fetishism and of necrophilia – "Looking as if she were alive" (line 2), "There she stands/ As if alive" (46–47) – comparable to that of the equally reserved murderer of Porphyria who sits in erotic bliss contemplating the woman he has just killed. Within the psycho-social theorizing that informs Browning's writing of art practices as forms of managing male sexuality, setting the portrait within a chamber hidden by a curtain, an image that anticipates Pater's later image of the "narrow chamber of the individual mind" ("Morris" 148), suggests this interiorization of Eros. Erotic desire reified, the art object has become the private property of the Duke: "none puts by/ The curtain I have drawn for you, but I" (lines 9–10). And this gesture of ownership also signifies the commodification of the artistic product that in the artist-poems becomes a central feature of Browning's representation of the degradation of male creative potency in the nineteenth century.

"My Last Duchess," "Soliloquy of the Spanish Cloister," "Porphyria's Lover," and "The Bishop Orders His Tomb," then, present extreme projections of the normative practice of middle-class sexual self-discipline, instances of masculinity deformed within the limit case of male celibacy. In thus interrogating the formation of masculinity to which he had committed himself on undertaking the vocation of poet, Browning registers his own ambivalence toward bourgeois manhood, an ambivalence that is also inscribed in his artist-poems, the works that most directly register his project of reconciling the hegemonic formation of the masculine with the practice of the male poet.

A MASCULINE POETIC

"Soliloquy of the Spanish Cloister" was originally titled "Cloister (Spanish)" and paired with "Camp (French)," the poem we now know as "Incident of the French Camp." The pairing is illuminating as representing a crucial conflict about masculinity in Browning's youth, a pull between the attractions of the "cloister," the isolated space of the poet, and the "camp," the male sphere. In his youth Browning had moved in the worldly circles of his father, who held a position in the Bank of England. In his early twenties Browning even travelled in the company of international men of affairs as far as Russia. He had as a young man seriously considered a career in diplomacy, and with his family connections the path to a position in banking at the highest level was open to a young man of his intelligence and cosmopolitan manner. But it is significant that given the opportunity for indisputably manly work within the male sphere, Browning chose to be a poet, a career that he selected not to repudiate the normative manliness exemplified in diplomacy and finance, but to affirm the manliness of the poetic vocation. As Maynard perceptively notes, "But, however great or small Browning's untapped abilities as a financier or worldly administrator may have been, what matters is that he felt himself competent as a man among the men of his age and that, in choosing to devote himself to literature, he considered not that he was unsuited to the more usual pursuits of his time but that he could serve a more significant role as a writer and poet" (*Browning's Youth* 120).[6]

In choosing the career of poet, Browning sought not to live in a palace of art, not to isolate himself from but continue to live within the male sphere. His poems of the 1840s and 1850s inscribe the contradictions emerging from this choice by representing within monastic discourse the difficulty of creating a poetic grounded in the normative masculinity of the early Victorian age.

For the early Victorian bourgeois man, concern about manliness was set not only on the restive border between the homosocial and the homosexual, but also in the competitive arena of the marketplace where manhood marked as aggressive energy and commercial success was tested against other men. Primarily, middle-class man was judged by the criteria of entrepreneurial manhood.[7] As Davidoff and Hall note in their study of the Victorian middle class, the bourgeois masculine persona... was organized around a man's determination and skill in manipulating the economic environment... His puny strength was also pitted against the stern course of a more novel destiny, the market. The contrast between such intense self-generated activity and the awfulness of these necessities [supporting his family] could undermine even the bravest confidence. Far from carrying the blustering certainty of the late Victorian paterfamilias, early nineteenth-century masculine identity was fragile... The mood in which middle-class men faced their world was best expressed by a seed merchant... [who] bitterly remarked: "I may be a man one day and a mouse the next." (*Family Fortunes* 229)

Entrepreneurial manhood with its emphasis on engagement in the male sphere of work, its valuing of strength and energy, and its criterion of commercial success measured by support of a domestic establishment generated particularly acute anxiety for the early Victorian male poet, for this definition of male identity conflicted with the ideal of the poet based on a romantic model in many ways constructed to oppose the new formation of bourgeois man. This romantic model valorized isolation from the commercial or male sphere, emotive openness and imaginative inwardness, passivity, and even the drive toward dissolution and death. These discontinuities in gender roles for the male poet are well summarized by Mermin: "For the Victorians, writing poetry seemed like woman's work, even though only men were supposed to do it... Male Victorian poets worried that they might in effect be feminizing themselves by withdrawing into a private world" ("Damsel" 67).[8] The deep ambivalence about the value of this feminized romantic poetic identity in relation to the entrepreneurial model of manhood is exemplified in Tennyson's poetry of the 1830s and 1840s, the classic instance for the Victorians as for ourselves being the evocatively ambiguous death of the Lady of Shalott.[9]

For early Victorian male poets one historically crucial strategy for resolving this basic disjunction was the project of situating the source of poetry not in the qualities of isolation and emotional intensity associated then as now with the feminine, but rather in the attributes of energetic activity, commercial endeavor, and phallic sexuality identified with entrepreneurial manhood. This enterprise, continued into the twentieth century, undertakes to construct a distinctively masculine poetic not in opposition to, but from the elements that comprise, the bourgeois formation of manliness.

This early Victorian project of creating such masculine poetry is exemplified in Browning's artist-poems – "Pictor Ignotus," "Fra Lippo Lippi," "Andrea del Sarto." The importance of these poems lies in their proclamation of a poetic whose sources are the elements of hegemonic Victorian masculinity.[10] Their connection with the work of other early Victorian writers and artists, such as Ruskin and the Pre-Raphaelites, lies not so much in formalist terms as in the shared effort to create a manly style and a manly construction of Christianity.[11] These artist-poems mark the formation at mid-century of a masculine poetic that, identifying creative power with sexual potency, has continued into our own century, particularly in America.

Within this poetic sequence, Lippo stands, then, for Browning and for his age as the exemplar of the manly artist. In this figure of the robustly heterosexual monk painting religiously powerful work while in the employ of the exemplary mercantile patron, Browning dramatizes a valorized constellation of male sexual energy, artistic potency, commercial success, and moralized art that seems to reconcile artistic achievement with bourgeois manhood. But as much as the male(?) critical tradition has continued to read Lippo as the "successful" artist, Browning's representation of the exemplary manly painter also reveals inherent contradictions within a masculine poetic. In particular, the portrait of Lippo shows how the entry or, in Ruskinian terms, the unfortunate "fall" of the artist into the sphere of commerce generates a debilitating commodification of male energy, both artistic and sexual. Just as Foucault's rewriting of the history of sexuality has shown that the supposed liberation of sexuality in our own time has generated new internalized forms of constraint, so Browning turns the whiggish Victorian narrative of male sexual/commercial/artistic liberation upon itself to show that the emergence of the male poet into the supposedly free individualistic activity of capitalism generates new forms for imprisoning male desire.[12]

As the manifesto of a masculine poetic, these poems are set within a liberationist historical narrative that conflates the emergence of capitalism, the formal development of visual art, and the liberation of male sexuality, all subsumed within the Victorian master narrative of progress. Lippo exemplifies the successful artist not merely because he has moved from medieval formalism to a more modern sacred realism, but because this formal "progress" is inseparable from his move from the patronage of the Church to that of a merchant prince and his escape from the imprisoning celibacy of the monastery to energetic heterosexual activity. Within the gendered, historicist categories of early Victorian aesthetics, this highly sexed artist-monk represents the possibility of creating a popular realist religious art while maintaining a truly manly gender identity. Indeed, Browning is writing not only art history and economic history, but also, as a kind of Victorian Foucault, the history of male art as the history of male sexuality. The similarity to Foucault even extends to Browning's ironizing the narrative of sexual liberation and subverting the Repressive Hypothesis that appears to structure these artist-poems.

Underlying the conflation of sexuality/art/commerce in "Fra Lippo Lippi" lies the Victorian model of male identity – the assumption that manliness lies in the proper regulation of an innate, distinctly male form of energy. It would be tempting, but anachronistic, to apply to Browning's psycho-sexual representation of the male artist a Freudian model that sees this energy as essentially sexual, as libido sublimated into other activities such as painting or entrepreneurship. Rather, Browning's model, like that of other early Victorian theorists of masculinity, posits a powerful unitary male desire that can find expression in artistic creation, entrepreneurial activity, phallic sexuality, or any combination of these. Within this construction of manhood, then, art-making, love-making and money-making are valued as signs of true manliness, productive expressions of natural, God-given male energy.

For Browning's male contemporaries, the dominant figure for the instability of male poetic identity is the opposition between male and female qualities. Tennyson and Arnold often show the artist as an isolated, enclosed female or as a feminized male figure observing, but not participating in, the activity of the commercial, often sexualized male sphere. These artist surrogates usually carry positive qualities to which the poet is attracted if not wholly committed. The "high-born maidens" such as the Lady of Shalott in poems of the early Tennyson represent the poet's attraction to a passive imaginative openness. For Arnold the celibate monks of the Grande Chartreuse embody those traditional values of communal Christianity dissolved by the modern individualist quest for gain. The Arnoldian voice empathizes with the impotence of the desexualized monks unable and unwilling to join the progress of the "Sons of the world" (line 161).

For Browning in "Fra Lippo Lippi," "Pictor Ignotus," and

"Andrea del Sarto," however, the central trope for the problematic of male poetic identity is the conflict between the imprisonment and the freeing of male energy. Browning's artist-poems, like Tennyson's early poetry, also associate the romantic model of poet with the feminine; the unknown painter is figured as a "nun" (line 48). But for Browning the feminized male poet/artist is not valued. Rather, for Browning the Unknown Painter and Andrea are male artists *manqué*, emasculated, lacking or repressing the male energy exemplified in Lippo. Nor does the unwillingness of Pictor Ignotus to engage in commerce convey positive value as it would, for example, in Ruskin. Instead, in Browning's Renaissance artist-poems the escape of the male figure from enclosure to join the commercial and sexualized world of men becomes the crucial act of man-making.[13] Within the liberationist narrative of this sequence, "Fra Lippo Lippi" represents the male becoming manly by rejecting institutional constraints upon male desire in order to join the inevitable historical movement toward the expression of such desire in commerce, art, and phallic sexuality.

For Browning, the Unknown Painter watching furtively from his cloister signifies unnatural sexual repression. His "sanctuary's gloom" (line 63) exemplifies those destructive effects on the male psyche of imprisoning male desire that are dramatized within the coding of clerical celibacy in "Soliloquy of the Spanish Cloister" and "The Bishop Orders His Tomb," as well as in the more secular "Porphyria's Lover" and "My Last Duchess." In "Pictor Ignotus," male desire wells up only to be stifled by external and internalized discipline. The longing to move from the patronage of the cloister to that of the nation-state, the "Kaiser" (line 28), or of the art market itself, the "burgh" (line 30), takes its special value in the text from its identification with repressed desire, with dream. The feeling so "wildly dear" (line 40) in this context is more authentic than the less emotive, more conscious "voice [that] changed it" (line 41), that calls for constraint within the celibate cloister:

> Nor will I say I have not dreamed (how well!)
>   Of going – I, in each new picture, – forth,
> As, making new hearts beat and bosoms swell,
>   To Pope or Kaiser, East, West, South, or North,
> Bound for the calmly-satisfied great State,
>   Or glad aspiring little burgh.   (lines 25–30)

The impulse to emerge from Church patronage into the art market finds expression in sexualized terms, in the *double entendre* of tumescence. The "I," imagined by the Unknown Painter as embodied in an easel painting rather than in an *in situ* fresco, is fantasized as "making new hearts beat and bosoms swell" (line 27). The art market itself appears to him as the site of orgiastic sexual activity:

> Glimpses of such sights
> Have scared me, like the revels through a door
> Of some strange house of idols at its rites! (lines 41–43)

The crucial moment for Lippo and the Unknown Painter is escape or failure to escape from imprisonment in the cloister, the sign in early Victorian artistic discourse of formal backwardness, anti-capitalist economics, and unnatural male chastity. In the positive reading of Lippo's career, the flight from the monastery signifies the achievement of a masculine poetic in representing the artist as entering the male sphere, engaging in heterosexual activity, and consequently developing a manly style. For Browning, the rise of realism is identified not only with the rise of the market, but also of the phallus.

In "Pictor Ignotus," as throughout the artist-poems, Browning draws upon the early Victorian psycho-sexual theory of mimesis, a theory that also underlies the practice of the Pre-Raphaelite Brotherhood as well as the responses of its early critics. For Browning repression of male sexuality, coded as monastic celibacy, generates a pathology within the male psyche, a deformation not only of the body but of the mind. When applied to art practice, particularly to the question of representational accuracy, and here the limit case for the early Victorians becomes the work of early Italian monastic painters, this deformation of masculinity is manifested in a distortion of the ability to see and accurately to represent the external world, particularly the male body. An unmanly celibate life generates an unmanly art. In his review of Anna Jameson's *Sacred and Legendary Art*, Kingsley says of the early Italian painter-monks, "They were prone to despise all by which *man* is brought in contact with this earth – the beauties of sex, of strength, of activity, of grandeur of form; all, that is, in which Greek art excels: their ideal of beauty was altogether *effeminate*... [having] that ascetic and *emasculate* tone, which was peculiar to themselves" ("Sacred and Legendary Art" 217, emphasis added).

For Browning, as for Kingsley, the foundation of a manly art, like the foundation of manliness itself, is the proper management of male desire. Since for these early Victorians, the art work manifests the maker's mode of regulating sexuality, the history of art, which is the history of art by men, becomes the history of specific technologies of male sexual self-discipline. Lippo's repudiation of a symbolic for a realist art is conflated with his movement from monastic celibacy to sexual liberation represented as a movement from the unnatural to the natural: "You should not take a fellow eight years old/ And make him swear to never kiss the girls" (lines 224–25). Mimetically accurate art is thus marked as a manly style, the inevitable effect of removing unnatural restrictions on male sexual potency. The painting of the still virile Lippo appeals to the innate male energy still present if repressed and awaiting liberation within the monks. When Lippo shows his realist art to the audience of men, even these celibates respond according to the innate manly impulse that survives beneath the puritanical rules of the monastery. Seeing the

> covered bit of cloister-wall.
> The monks closed in a circle and praised loud
> Till checked, taught what to see and not to see,
> Being simple bodies. (lines 165–68)

By associating the exemplary artist not with the monastery, but with the new house of Medici, Browning connects artistic manhood with what most Victorians saw as the inevitable movement of history toward a mercantile economy. Lippo approaches the condition of economic man as artist, artist as economic man. Unlike the Unknown Painter, he has a name, has become an individual unit working for his own economic well-being, whether joining a religious community for material rather than spiritual sustenance or accepting the Medici patronage for its food and shelter.[14]

In representing the exemplary male artist as moving from precapitalist anonymity to individual art production, Browning is attempting to show that manly engagement in commerce as well as a liberated sexual life are the preconditions for a manly style, a style that he associates here with a sacred or figural realism. The Prior tells Lippo to represent only the transcendental world:

> Make them forget there's such a thing as flesh.
> Your business is to paint the souls of men –
> ...
> Give us no more of body than shows soul! (lines 182–83, 188)

Instead, Lippo sees that his "business" is not only with "the souls of men," but with connecting spirit to the occupations of commercial life, the palpable and material world of individual subjects and tangible objects:

> folk at church,
> From good old gossips waiting to confess
> Their cribs of barrel-droppings, candle-ends, –
> To the breathless fellow at the altar-foot,
> Fresh from his murder, safe and sitting there
> With the little children round him in a row
> Of admiration, half for his beard and half
> For that white anger of his victim's son
> Shaking a fist at him with one fierce arm,
> Signing himself with the other because of Christ
> (Whose sad face on the cross sees only this
> After the passion of a thousand years). (lines 146–57)

Like other early Victorian writers and artists, such as Carlyle and the Pre-Raphaelites, Browning found in the typological mode a method of reconciling this occupation with the materiality of the secular world with transcendental purpose: "This world's no blot for us,/ Nor blank; it means intensely and means good" (lines 313–14).[15]

Within Browning's masculine poetic, the enabling figure for this transcendental realism is not a female muse, a figuration that would have resulted had Browning chosen, for example, to use Vasari's description of Lippo later in life married to a nun. Rather, Lippo is supported by Cosimo di Medici, the world historical figure embodying the predestined movement toward capitalism. The patronage of Cosimo indirectly suggests the Victorian hope, shared by Dickens and other Victorian men, that art, flourishing under the patronage of latter-day Medici, would remain within the male sphere. At a banquet in Birmingham at which Dickens praised the mercantile, that is male, leaders of that city for encouraging the fine arts, John Forster "proposed 'The Birmingham Society of Artists' and praised the 'merchant princes' of Birmingham, Manchester, and Liverpool as the Medici of a new era" (*Speeches* 158).

Like Dickens and Forster in Birmingham, Lippo exemplifies the Carlylean ideal of the Hero as Man of Letters in being a man speaking to men. He relates his sexual history (which is, of course, one with his artistic and economic life) to the watch, a group who, as males, are permitted to be out in the night streets. And he shows little

The problematic of a masculine poetic

impatience in pausing on his way from the brothel in order to sketch for a painting and describe his artistic principles, but then artistic production and art discourse are as much a release of male energy as sex itself. This monologue indicates Lippo's rhetorical power, and by implication that of the manly poet, to draw upon homosocial ties, upon beliefs shared with other men. Lippo persuades the men of the watch not only to sympathize with his sexual exploits, but to share his artistic principles. Yet the bemused sense of brotherhood attributed to the watch is ironized, open to opposing readings of the masculine poetic. The silent agreement of the watch with Lippo's art doctrine implies that a religious or moralized realism is a truly manly art in that it can be understood and valued by men of all classes, including the males reading the text. But this scene also presents for ironic contemplation the complicity of men, again including the male reader, in the masculinist double standard implicit in a masculine poetic, the assumption that men, unlike women, quite naturally need a sexual release for the powerful energy also manifested in their art.[16]

Truly at ease with other males, Lippo's psyche turns to the transformation of women into works of art. The objectification of the female is, of course, a prominent theme for Browning. In "Porphyria's Lover" and "My Last Duchess" Browning presents male sexuality distorted by being denied outlet in the flesh as transformed into murderous rage against women. But here the male gaze emerging from an artist who is in touch with his own and with the female body is presented as transforming sexualized vision not only into mimetically accurate representation of the body, but also into the ability to see the female "face" as sign of subjectivity, of spirit, of "soul":

> Take the prettiest face
> The Prior's niece ... patron-saint – is it so pretty
> You can't discover if it means hope, fear,
> Sorrow or joy? won't beauty go with these?
> Suppose I've made her eyes all right and blue,
> Can't I take breath and try to add life's flash,
> And then add soul and heighten them threefold?
>
> (lines 208–14)

But if the text values Lippo's ability to transform heterosexual desire into moralized and empathetic representation of the female, it also shows the Victorian male imagination as haunted by another vision of the female Other. As Carlyle fastened upon the Menadic women, Lippo's male fantasies turn also to the castrating woman, embodied in the Salome myth. In almost an hallucinatory mode, Lippo sees one man of the watch holding "John Baptist's head a-dangle by the hair" (line 34). The Prior sees his niece as "Herodias, I would say – / Who went and danced and got men's heads cut off!" (lines 196–97). The Prior's slippage from the singular to the plural (not "a man" but "men's") suggests the deep anxiety about manliness registered within the poem. Read from another perspective, the text reveals, as much as Carlyle's early writing, the fear that within the new mercantile world, virility and entrepreneurial manhood are fragile, endangered, vulnerable to the destruction of the phallus as signifier of the essential male energy that generates male social power and male artistic potency.

For all the Browningesque optimism and success that readers from Browning's time to ours have found or projected onto Lippo, Browning's brief history of male desire in these artist-poems, like Foucault's history of sexuality, subverts the Repressive Hypothesis, the liberationist narrative of manhood. While seeming to show the freeing of male energy with the coming of capitalism, the poems also imply the opposite, that bourgeois manhood and particularly the conditions of art production within a mercantile society generate new constraints upon male desire – the attenuation of artistic energy in marriage, the alienation of this energy by the demands of the mercantile patron, and the commodification of phallic sexuality itself. In these artist-poems, entrepreneurial manhood is but pre-capitalist imprisonment writ large.

In early Victorian male poetry, escape from enclosed space – the tower on the island, the palace of art, the monastery – signifies, however differently valued, the moment of man-making. Within that trope, Lippo's flight from the monastery exemplifies the male artist rejecting the emasculating repression of artistic, commercial and sexual energy represented in "Pictor Ignotus." But "Fra Lippo Lippi" shows another escape, equally crucial to the achievement of manhood, the flight from the house of Cosimo of the Medici. In setting the monologue in an all-male zone comparable to Carlyle's community of men, Browning suggests that the palace of commerce has become not a palace of art, but rather a new prison. Having rejected the cloister in his quest to become a man, the exemplary male artist must now flee the "banking-house" (line 99), an act that resonates with Browning's own path toward manhood, for the bawdy house in order to preserve his manhood. And the silence of Lippo's male auditors implies an agreement, or at least an understanding presumably shared by bourgeois male readers that male desire may be constricted as well as liberated by the structure of entrepreneurial manhood.

For the imprisoned male artist, the demand of the Church for repetitive, unimaginative work has continued under the patronage of the merchant prince. The Unknown Painter immured in the cloister must paint "the same series, Virgin, Babe and Saint" (line 60). Lippo, free for the moment, tells the men of the watch:

> And I've been three weeks shut within my mew,
> A-painting for the great man, saints and saints
> And saints again. (lines 47–49)

The enervation of these Renaissance artists resonates with Victorian fears about creativity in their own age. The continued production of "saints and saints" by both the Unknown Painter and Lippo suggests the concern about mechanical reproduction that, most notably in Ruskin, is the central sign in early Victorian aesthetic discourse of uncreative artistic labor.[17]

As individual producer, Lippo may no longer have to satisfy the institutional patron, the Church, but must now satisfy the individual patron, the merchant prince, who sets equally debilitating controls upon the expression of male energy. After returning from the brothel, Lippo must:

> rise up to-morrow and go work
> On Jerome knocking at his poor old breast
> With his great round stone to subdue the flesh. (lines 72–74)

Lippo's celebrated complaint reveals an inherent contradiction in this masculine poetic. Lippo has entered the employ of a mercantile patron, a new "Master" (lines 17, 78, 226), a repeated term that resonates with the Victorian term for mill-owner. Yet under the terms of employment he is compelled to create a product at odds with his manhood, with the sexualized energy that is the very source of artistic potency, of artistic success.

In showing Lippo as an artist forced to paint what he does not practice as a man, that is, to repress his sexual being, Browning criticizes the limitation upon male desire set by Victorian public morality, a topic of his poems with contemporary settings such as "Respectability." This disjunction in Lippo's life resonates, then, with the feelings of mid-Victorian male writers, such as Dickens and Thackeray, who also felt the constraint that the respectability demanded by bourgeois manhood placed upon their sexual and thus their creative energy.

This failure to achieve an integrated management of desire is registered in this poem in eruptions of desire similar to those that disrupt the psychic flow of the Spanish monk and the dying Bishop. Here male desire satisfied neither by alienated artistic labor nor by commercialized sex bursts out with a Carlylean "volcanoism" in snatches of song, expressions in lyric mode of an unfettered sexuality that abruptly and with the logic of repressed desire shatter the rhetorically controlled narrative of his life and of his masculine artistic principles.[18] The first emerges through association with the imprisoning workplace:

> I could not paint all night –
> Ouf! I leaned out of window for fresh air.
> There came a hurry of feet and little feet,
> A sweep of lute-strings, laughs, and whifts of song –
> *Flower o' the broom,*
> *Take away love, and our earth is a tomb!*
> *Flower o' the quince,*
> *I let Lisa go, and what good in life since?* (lines 49–56)

Another eruption of song counters his memory of language imposed upon desire:

> They tried me with their books:
> Lord, they'd have taught me Latin in pure waste!
> *Flower o' the clove,*
> *All the Latin I construe is "amo," I love!* (lines 108–11)

For Lippo, as for Victorian male artists and poets, one strategy for coping with the opposition between sexual desire and the demands of bourgeois patrons and of the art market is to create an art that is duplicitous, covertly sexual. In Lippo's masterpiece, the female is represented as virginal, saintly, but is still the object of the sexualized male gaze:

> the little lily thing
> That spoke the good word for me in the nick,
> Like the Prior's niece ... Saint Lucy, I would say.
> (lines 385–87)

Within this history of male sexuality, the covert sexuality of the art is one with the covert practices of sexuality in the artist's life. That a poem about the male artist centers on an excursion to the whorehouse is crucial to the poem's critique of the masculine poetic. The visit to the brothel is a sign not of success as a male, but rather of the difficulty in reconciling male creativity with entrepreneurial society. Within the proto-Freudian hydraulic metaphor underlying Browning's, as well as Carlyle's, model of male desire, the need for sex with a prostitute suggests that the male artist's labor under mercantile patronage, in "the munificent House that harbours [him]" (line 29), does not provide a full release of male desire. The escape from the art workshop would not have been so pressing had his energy been expressed through an artistic practice less occupied with self-flagellating male saints. Within this model, fluid male energy must emerge elsewhere, here in degraded, commodified form.

In Lippo's trip to the brothel, as in the marriage and the artistic practice of Andrea, Browning suggests that a mercantile system may generate the commodification and reification of male desire in both sexuality and in art. The coin, the "quarter-florin" (line 28) that Lippo flaunts, signifies pride in his artistic achievement, but it also connects cash payment for uncreative art with cash payment for loveless sex. That the artist uses prostitution in order to maintain his artistic potency signifies degradation in both areas of male life. Indeed, male sexual activity is here reduced to purely utilitarian value within entrepreneurial artistic activity. These trips to the red-light district, then, are as functional for Lippo as for any Victorian businessman. After a night of R & R, Lippo can return to the workplace, refreshed for a new day of re-producing pictures of saints for his "Master."

Typically the unrepresented response of the male auditors is indeterminate, the indeterminacy here signifying the characteristic Victorian ambivalence about male sexuality. The decision not to arrest Lippo suggests general male complicity in the belief that illicit sex, a "secret life," is necessary for the male artist and for males in general. And yet the sexual double standard articulated by Lippo is simultaneously ironized as a sign of the potential degradation of the emotional life within bourgeois manhood.

In "Andrea del Sarto," Browning brilliantly concludes the subversion of the masculine liberation narrative by showing how a fully formed entrepreneurial masculinity generates its own "mind-forg'd manacles" through the self-policing of male desire. Here Browning dramatizes the artist as economic man internalizing bourgeois structures of manhood that attenuate and deform male energy itself.[19] Even Andrea's awareness of his own desire is set into the ledger of profit and loss: "I know both what I want and what might *gain*,/ And yet how *profitless* to know, to sigh" (lines 100–1, emphasis added). Indeed, Andrea sees his artistic enterprise within a dream of God as the head of a rather large firm and himself as a clerk worried about his pension:

> All is as God over-rules.
> Beside, *incentives* come from the soul's self;
> ...
> God, I conclude, *compensates*, punishes.
> 'Tis safer for me, if the *award* be strict,
> That I am something *underrated* here,
> *Poor* this long while, despised, to speak the truth.
> (lines 134–35, 141–44, emphasis added)

Rather than linear progress, then, as an historical sequence these three artist-poems show a pattern of circular return if not decay. The male artist as self-employed producer exhibits the same emotional lassitude, the same unmanliness as the pre-capitalist cloistered monk.

For this bourgeois male artist, as for Lippo, both artistic and sexual activity have become reified. For both, art production has become a means for purchasing sex. Verbal slippage in Andrea's monologue indicates that the artist's work has become only a way of making money, rather than an expression of a powerful, sexualized energy:

> If you would sit thus by me every night
> I should *work* better, do you comprehend?
> I mean that I should *earn* more, give you more.
> (lines 205–7, emphasis added)

As Andrea uses his entrepreneurial ability to purchase the simulacrum of affection, the language characteristically conflates consumer demand and desire:

> I'll *work* then for your friend's friend, never fear,
> Treat his own subject after his own way,
> Fix his own time, accept too his own *price*,
> And shut the *money* into this small hand
> When next it takes mine. Will it? tenderly?
> (lines 5–9, emphasis added)

The identification of sexuality and money pervades the poem, as in "Let my hands frame your face in your hair's gold" (line 175), where "gold" refers both to Andrea's artistic sense of color and to his transformation of his wife into a commodified sexual object, a prostitute.

In both poems, then, the representation of the entrepreneurial male artist problematizes the same issue, the commodification of male energy in the artist as figured through the purchase of sex. This similar reification of desire in the two painters has been occluded in the (male?) critical tradition that has marked Lippo as the "successful" and Andrea as the "failed" artist. My Norton Critical Edition typically introduces "Andrea del Sarto" in the following terms: "Contrasting markedly with the exuberant 'Fra Lippo Lippi,' this is Browning's classic study of moral and aesthetic failure" (184). This inability to see the "failure," the transformation of desire into money in each, may be attributed to the unconscious acceptance by (male?) critics and readers of the very masculine double standard that Browning problematizes in these poems. Critical tradition reads Lippo as exemplifying "normal" male heterosexuality – hearty, aggressive, dominating, predatory – and seems to assume, as willingly as the night watch, that the buying of sex is a functional necessity for the entrepreneurial male, an "exuberant" overflow of male energy. Andrea is read as having failed because the wife rather than the husband is purchasing sex outside marriage. One could imagine a dramatic monologue in the voice of Andrea's wife, similar to Angela Carter's fine prose fiction "Black Venus" narrated in the voice of Jeanne Duval, the object of Baudelaire's "Black Venus" cycle.

This displacement of male energy from art to sex, and to sex distorted by commodification, pervades the writing of early as well as late Victorian male poets. Indeed, the oft-noted concern of Victorian male writers with the prostitute, with the purchase of sex, functions as a displacement of their own concern with the commodification, the purchase and sale of their own sexualized desire under mercantile patronage and within the art market. As D. G. Rossetti wrote in a letter to Ford Madox Brown in 1873, "I have often said that to be an artist is just the same thing as to be a whore, as far as dependence on the whims and fancies of individuals is concerned" (*Letters* II: 1175).

Rossetti's "Jenny" (begun 1848, publ. 1870), a dramatic monologue of a man of letters in contemporary life, exemplifies the identification of male artistic and sexual pathology in a form quite similar to that of Browning. Here, too, the male speaker has escaped the world of art, the room "so full of books" (line 23) limned in the trope of imprisonment – "Whose serried ranks hold fast, forsooth,/ So many captive hours of youth" (lines 25–26) – to turn to the prostitute as a source of refreshment from his unsatisfying artistic labors.[20] But, as in Browning's poems of collectors, "The Bishop Orders His Tomb" and "My Last Duchess," the degradation of Eros in men is indicated by the transference of desire from the flesh to the eye – "Why, Jenny, as I watch you there" (line 46) – and internalized into the erotic fantasy of a penetrative imagination that reads the female as object – "You know not what a book you seem,/ Half-read by lightning in a dream!" (lines 51–52). In this poem of deformed, commodified male sexuality, the ironic form of the dramatic monologue, and this is one of Rossetti's few poems in that genre, suggests that the speaker does not recognize the source of this inhibition as lying within himself, that his failure to manage his own sexuality is one with the failure of potency in his literary work.

In part, this inhibition is presented as the internalization of the puritanical standards of nineteenth-century society, particularly of the split between virgin and whore, here seen in the speaker's highly ironized distinction between the prostitute and "cousin Nell... fond of fun" (line 186). This same deformation of male sexuality also appears in Lippo's inability to reconcile his trips to the whorehouse and his erotic feelings toward the Prior's niece whom he represents as Saint Lucy. Furthermore, the sexual impotence of the speaker in "Jenny," identified in the standard Victorian equation with his impotence as writer, is connected to the characteristic abhorrence of male sexuality itself, which the speaker fantasizes as primal and animalistic in day-dreams of streets where "flagrant man-swine whets his tusk" (line 346). Here, too, closure comes not with sexual climax, but with the giving of money to the female. As in "Andrea del Sarto," the failure of the male artist is limned by the commodification of male sexual energy, the substitution of money for desire.

This same commodification in Lippo, the irony of a sexy male artist painting for pay the lives of saints in the desert after his own visit to the whorehouse, points to the fault lines in Browning's project of reconciling a masculine poetic with bourgeois masculinity. Browning shows the entrepreneurial male artist facing a basic contradiction. As "Respectability" suggests, the Victorian code of public morality would "supply a glove" (line 20), constrain the expression in life and in art of the very desire that is for the artist/poet the source of male artistic power. The result for Lippo, and by extension for male Victorian artists and poets, is an accepted yet secret life as a man and a covert representation of this secret life in art, as in Lippo's private association of the angel wings in his painting with

> a spread of kirtles when you're gay
> And play hot cockles, all the doors being shut,
> Till, wholly unexpected, in there pops
> The hothead husband! (lines 380–83)

Like Arnold's male poet at the Grande Chartreuse, as an historical figure Lippo stands "between two worlds" (line 85), at the cusp between past and present. More specifically, Lippo stands between and embodies two formations of manhood. He has escaped the pre-industrial feminized monastic life for the manly world of commerce, but, unlike Andrea, he is not wholly fallen into bourgeois manhood. He is not married, not the breadwinner for a family. No longer under the patronage of the Church, he is supported by a merchant prince but not yet fully dependent upon market-driven demand. The focus on Lippo's sexual adventure incorporates into his manliness the construction of manhood against which middle-class manliness defined itself – the earlier gentry association of the true man with the rake, the sexual freebooter, with the ideal of "wenching" (Davidoff and Hall *Family Fortunes* 110). In good part, the identification of success with Lippo derives from the poem's fusion of these two competing forms of manhood, the combination of the sexual freedom of the gentry with the entrepreneurial energy of the bourgeois, a fusion displaced into the past that could be desired but never achieved by the proper bourgeois in the nineteenth century.

Browning's sense of inherent contradiction between the masculine poetic and entrepreneurial manhood is also suggested by his separation in these artist-poems of artistic success from marriage, one of the defining elements of bourgeois manliness. Like Carlyle's dream of an all-male community, Browning's artist-poems provide a covert historicized expression of bourgeois male uneasiness about compulsory matrimony. Just as Browning does not show Lippo as successful and married, he does not show Andrea, the failed artist at the moment in Vasari's account when he fell in love with a young woman, when male passion was strong. Rather, Browning chooses to represent the "Faultless Painter" at that point when marriage and domesticity have diminished male energy.[21] In Andrea, a moderately successful artist as businessman, who, much like a Victorian R.A., manages with diligent effort to market art commodities in order to support a respectable domestic establishment, Browning links the attenuation of erotic life in marriage to the loss of power in art.

However much this dissociation of masculine art from marriage contradicts the possibility of a fully bourgeois artistic manhood, the strategy is consistent with the need of a masculine poetic to remove the feminine from the creative process. And yet, even in exemplifying a masculine art in "Fra Lippo Lippi," Browning suggests that certain qualities that neither he nor his age could associate with the masculine – a rich, even "soft" (line 371) emotive life, a self-effacing relation to others – are necessary to the creation of art and poetry. Since the possession of these qualities by the male artist would contradict the very definition of the masculine self, they are projected onto an Other, onto the female. To perform this ideological work in "Fra Lippo Lippi," Browning returns to a traditional strategy of poetry written by men, the creation of a female muse separate from the male self, yet a necessary supplement to the work of the male artist. The Prior's niece as Saint Lucy becomes the male artist's "light," his Beatrice, his savior. She "steps" into Lippo's painting "sweet angelic... soft," bearing the very qualities against which masculinity defines itself. The painting, then, becomes a masterpiece not as the exemplary manifestation of masculine artistic sensibility, but rather as the fusion of the masculine and feminine into an androgynous vision:

> Then steps a sweet angelic slip of a thing
> Forward, puts out a soft palm – "Not so fast!"
> – Addresses the celestial presence, "nay –
> He made you and devised you, after all,
> ...
> Like the Prior's niece... Saint Lucy, I would say.
> And so all's saved for me, and for the church
> A pretty picture gained. (lines 370–73, 387–89)

The instability and uncertainty in Browning's representation of a masculine poetic appears most clearly in the (ir)resolution of Andrea's vision of the "New Jerusalem." Given the representation in this poem and in "Fra Lippo Lippi" of the psychic costs to the male artist of commercial pressures and bourgeois marriage, this vision of artistic practice within a sacred space and in the company of men "without a wife" suggests the difficulty of achieving a satisfactory life as a male and particularly as a male artist within the current bourgeois social arrangements. The complete satisfaction of male desire is displaced from this world to the next:

> What would one have?
> In heaven, perhaps, new chances, one more chance –
> Four great walls in the New Jerusalem,
> Meted on each side by the angel's reed,
> For Leonard, Rafael, Agnolo and me
> To cover – the three first without a wife,
> While I have mine! (lines 259–65)

The most celebrated lines of "Andrea del Sarto" – "Ah, but a *man's* reach should exceed his grasp,/ Or what's a heaven for?" (lines 97–98, emphasis added) – pose the same rhetorical question, one answer to which is that only in an imagined moment in the Renaissance or in the "new chances" of "heaven," rather than in the Victorian present, can "a *man's* reach," an integrated masculinity, true manhood be achieved. After all, the resolution of gender anxieties in the afterlife rather than in the life of Victorian society is common in the work of other early Victorian poets, both male and female. In *In Memoriam* Tennyson describes a new, heterodox ideal of masculinity as possible only in a heaven presided over by an androgynous Hallam.[22] In "To George Sand," Elizabeth Barrett Browning calls upon "my sister" to endure "in agony" the constraints of gender in this world "Till God unsex thee on the heavenly shore."

And yet this subversion of the masculine poetic by seeing its attainment as possible only outside history is contradicted by Browning's characteristic method of presenting the sensibility of a dramatized speaker. Within this ironic mode, Andrea's inability to realize a manly art is attributed neither to the bourgeois construction of gender nor to contradictions within a masculine poetic itself, but rather to the attenuation of virile energy through individual weakness: "So – still they overcome/ Because there's still Lucrezia, – as I choose" (lines 265–66). The male artist's turn toward heaven is ironized as yet another passive daydream, another sign of Andrea's unmanly desire to withdraw from the energetic activity of his age.

If "Andrea del Sarto" indicates a failure to realize a masculine poetic, the poem leaves open the possibility of its achievement to the man of energy, to the truly manly artist. "Fra Lippo Lippi" has been seen as representing this manly artist, but in being set just prior to the emergence of a fully bourgeois society and in suggesting the psychic degradation and commodification of creative energy within such a society, the poem undercuts the possibility of realizing this poetic. And even if we see Lippo within the Victorian typological structure employed by Carlyle as prefiguring the manly artist of the nineteenth century, Browning's poems about contemporary male life such as "Respectability" and "Popularity" do not show the historical type realized in present time. As a manifesto for a masculine poetic, then, these artist-poems suggest the shape of a manly art, but set within Browning's characteristic structures of irony, historicism, and typology the poems represent equally well Browning's uncertainty that the reconciliation of entrepreneurial manhood and poetic practice could be achieved in his own life and in his own age.

QUESTIONING THE MASCULINE PLOT

Browning's uneasiness about the bourgeois formation of masculinity within his own time emerges in his persistent turn in the poetry of these decades to the masculine plot, the narrative of initiation into manhood that counters the marriage plot and thus provides early Victorian men an imaginative expression of their restlessness with the normative manliness of middle-class English life.

Like the biography of Abbot Samson, the life of Brother Lippo is set within the early Victorian narrative of male initiation. Yet the initiation of Lippo plays against, even parodies the masculine plot exemplified in the monastic career of Samson. Through the agency of the female, both Lippo and Samson leave feminized domestic space for the male space of the cloister, Samson through a naturalized maternal self-sacrifice, Lippo as prisoner in shackles:

> Old Aunt Lapaccia trussed me with one hand,
> (Its fellow was a stinger as I knew)
> And so along the wall, over the bridge,
> By the straight cut to the convent. (lines 88–91)

Once within the male community, following the ritual of Victorian male initiation, each encounters a surrogate father. But for Lippo the male mentor is degraded, corrupt, a "good fat father" who conveys only a caricature of masculine wisdom to the initiate:

> "So, boy, you're minded," quoth the good fat father
> Wiping his own mouth – 'twas refection-time, –

"To quit this very miserable world?
Will you renounce"... "the mouthful of bread?" thought I.
(lines 93–96)

Unlike Carlyle's Samson and his worker-monks, Lippo flees the celibate all-male community of the monastery. In Browning's poem, the path to manliness does not lie in the virtuoso performance of bourgeois sexual reserve, but in the liberation of male artistic and sexual potency. And yet, it must be emphasized, Lippo escapes to the secular version of the all-male community, the palace of the Medici, the historical analogue, like Carlyle's monastery, of the nineteenth-century all-male world of work. For Browning, who escaped from his own father's banking house, the locus of artistic manhood remains a determinedly male world, a place from which women have been erased. Browning's own Oedipal issue of rejecting the work of his father in banking is here negotiated as Lippo finds a new father, a wiser older male in Cosimo the exemplary banker who, for all the ambivalence of the poem about commodification, embodies the masculine wisdom of the emergent capitalist age.

But for all his attraction to the world of men, in "Fra Lippo Lippi" Browning resists the conventional closure of the masculine plot with artistic manhood achieved within the chaste affective bonds of an all-male community. Nor does he adopt the closure of the marriage plot with manhood realized in the escape from male community into marriage. Again it is noteworthy that Browning might have chosen to see Lippo's path to artistic manhood as culminating in the marriage described in Vasari. Instead, as if representing the tensions of early Victorian masculinity as well as Browning's own unease in scripting the personal life of the male artist, the life of Lippo shows desire satisfied neither in the male sphere nor within the domestic sphere. In "Fra Lippo Lippi" as in "Andrea del Sarto," the exemplary case of male desire vitiated in marriage, the tension between the masculine plot and the marriage plot in the lives of bourgeois Victorian men remains unresolved. Lippo exists vividly in a male wild zone set beyond both the ordered male community of the banking house and the domestic interior of "Andrea del Sarto."

Browning's attraction to the plot of masculinization as well as his difficulty of representing manhood achieved appears most complexly in "Childe Roland to the Dark Tower Came" (1852), the poem that is most overtly cast within the masculine plot and that most clearly ironizes and subverts this plot. Like so much male literature of the early Victorian decades, this historically displaced narrative of male initiation becomes a safe imaginative site for engaging the specific problems of constructing manhood in the new industrial age. "Childe Roland" provides a literary equivalent for the ritual of initiation into a manhood that had become increasingly problematic in the early industrial age. The young men of America in the nineteenth century found a manhood available neither in their work nor in their personal lives by participating in ritual inductions into invented male communities of Redmen or ancient Egyptians. Carlyle displaces his rituals of male community to a dream of the medieval monastery as proto-factory. "Childe Roland" presents another imagined ritual of male initiation, another invented tradition in which the chivalric quest is inflected to engage the specific issues of achieving manliness in his own time. That the Browning poem most directly occupied with initiation into manhood should also be the Browning poem that most clearly diverges from the manly style of realism suggests how, like his male contemporaries who set the quest for manhood far removed in space and time from contemporary England, Browning also felt the difficulty, not to say impossibility, of representing an integrated manhood within the bourgeois world.

Here again, the masculine plot begins with the young man, the "Childe," separated from family, living within a world from which women have been erased and seeking to be accepted within the male community, "The Band." Here again, the initiate encounters a father surrogate, a male mentor in the "hoary cripple" (line 2) who provides "counsel" (line 13). This father figure *manqué*, like the "fat father" of "Fra Lippo Lippi," provides a comment on the failure of such paternal wisdom within the nineteenth century. And yet, although this father surrogate provides a wisdom that is ultimately fatal, he does set Childe Roland on the pathway toward a particular form of manhood. This quest for manliness takes the youth over a landscape that is connected to the wasteland of the mechanized present through the logic of dreams, and Browning confessed that the poem had come to him in a dream:

> What bad use was that engine for, that wheel,
> Or brake, not wheel – that harrow fit to reel
> Men's bodies out like silk? with all the air
> Of Tophet's tool, on earth left unaware,
> Or brought to sharpen its rusty teeth of steel.
>
> (lines 140–44)

The problematic of a masculine poetic

The end of this journey through the surreal industrial world, so perplexing to readers from Browning's day to ours, emerges from the tensions about Victorian manhood out of which the poem grows. The specific quality of the manhood achieved by Childe Roland is marked not by his success in actions, but by his adopting a particular state of mind. The quest for manhood is here radically psychologized. Adopting the form of dream, rather than resurrecting the deeds of heroic men set in the real world as in Marryat's maritime stories and in Carlyle's monastic history, suggests the nineteenth-century internalization of middle-class manliness as self-discipline. No longer is manliness defined as physical prowess, but as control of the interior life, the ability to continue even with the possibility if not the certainty of failure, the self-policing that controls fears arising from within. In Childe Roland's quest there are no battles with dragons or with evil knights. The monsters he encounters on his quest are not actual, but oversized creations of an imagination that threatens to slip from manly control. Parodically enlarged rats replace the dragons of St. George: "It may have been a water-rat I speared,/ But, ugh! it sounded like a baby's shriek" (lines 125–26). This quester engages the ghastly Oedipal projections of his own inner fears:

> good saints, how I feared
> To set my foot upon a dead man's cheek,
> Each step, or feel the spear I thrust to seek
> For hollows, tangled in his hair or beard! (lines 121–24)

Within the anxieties about masculinity in the early Victorian decades, Browning's psychologizing of the traditional chivalric quest points to the fact that for bourgeois men within the new industrial world, unlike working-class men whose muscular labor is so envied from afar by Brown, Carlyle and Ruskin, manliness no longer depends upon muscular strength. Within the banking house, the diplomatic corps, the new professions, as well as the practice of poetry, manhood is no longer defined by physical abilities. Rather, as this poetic internalizing of masculinization suggests, within the early Victorian discourse of masculinity middle-class manhood depends not upon bodily, but upon psychological strength, upon the ability to maintain the psychic balance that, although often registered in tropes of the physical, as in the Andromeda myth so beloved of male Victorian writers,[23] depends upon the kind of psychological fortitude exemplified by Childe Roland.

Bourgeois manliness, then, is no longer marked by bodily strength and physical courage, but by the internalization of certain practices of psychic regulation, and the achievement of manhood so defined is recognized by induction into an all-male community. Here, the success of Roland in the quest is registered not in a physical victory, but, as in nineteenth-century initiation rituals and in *Past and Present*, by acceptance into the "The Band" of men. The nature and indeed the outcome of the mysterious battle to be is not relevant. Manliness lies in the display of mental fortitude within an induction ritual observed by his "peers" (line 195). Within the psychologized terms of the poem it is appropriate that closure as the achievement of manhood comes not with a represented act of battle nor even with an initiation into this Brotherhood of "peers," but rather with his internalized *feeling* of belonging to and being accepted by this male community: "I saw them and I knew them all." Within Browning's dream vision, the very purpose of the quest becomes manhood achieved as masculine bonding, a goal to be gained at the price of life itself and that, as in the vision of the New Jerusalem in "Andrea del Sarto," may be satisfied fully only in the afterlife:

> There they stood, ranged along the hill-sides, met
> To view the last of me, a living frame
> For one more picture! in a sheet of flame
> I saw them and I knew them all.   (lines 199–202)

THE ATTRACTION OF MASCULINE BONDS

Browning's turn to the masculine plot rather than the marriage plot, to narratives that close not with heterosexual union but with membership in an all-male "Band," as well as the sense within the artist-poems of marriage as attenuating virile energy, suggests his representative difficulty in negotiating the passage between homosocial and domestic life. Browning's poems of the 1840s and into the 1850s show an oscillation between the attraction of male–male ties and the pull of heterosexual union, display the same covert opposition to compulsory matrimony that made Carlyle's *Past and Present* so attractive to male readers.

This irreconcilable contradiction within a Victorian manliness defined paradoxically by resistance to heterosexual desire and by heterosexual potency, so characteristic of male literature in these decades, is exemplified in the paired poems written during his

The problematic of a masculine poetic 105

courtship of Elizabeth Barrett, "Meeting at Night" and "Parting at Morning" (1845). The first, "Meeting at Night," represents a frenzied journey to heterosexual satisfaction described in resolutely, if not embarrassingly, phallic terms:

> And the startled little waves that leap
> In fiery ringlets from their sleep,
> As I gain the cove with pushing prow,
> And quench its speed i' the slushy sand.   (lines 3–6)

The release of male desire is here orgasmic, "the quick sharp scratch/ And blue spurt of a lighted match" (lines 9–10), as seminal energy is rapidly dissipated or, in Victorian slang, "spent." To look ahead, Browning's use of the metaphor of flame to valorize the orgasmic potential of male sexuality differs markedly from Pater's "hard gem-like flame" that locates male erotic intensity in the practice of tumescence.

In "Parting at Morning," as in Tennyson's contemporaneous poems of masculinization, in the clear light of day the speaker recognizes that to linger within the night-time world of heterosexual desire is to lose one's manliness, to exhaust one's male energy unproductively in the "spurt" of orgasm. As if following Carlyle's critique of eroticized literature as unmanly, Browning appropriates and transforms an erotic literary form into a manly repudiation of a vitiating heterosexuality. Within a masculine poetic, the second poem achieves a masculine form by desexualizing the traditional aubade in which as dawn breaks the male lover laments leaving his beloved. As a puritan avatar of the work ethic, the male god of the sun rises and "looked over the mountain's rim" (line 2) as if peeking into the homes of the slothful, those truant from the workplace. The divinity of bourgeois masculinity, the sun outlines the road to manliness as the rejection of non-productive desire. "And straight was a path of gold for him," with "gold" as color conflated, as in "Andrea del Sarto," with "gold" as money. The "path of gold" is not a yellow-brick road, but rather the natural "path," the undeviating manly career track to commercial success. Laid out by sun and sea, the "straight...path of gold" is naturalized as much as is the historical movement to capitalism in the artist-poems. Furthermore, much as the speaker of "Locksley Hall" finds his manhood in riding the divinely constructed railroad, the "ringing grooves of change," so this male speaker must also join the movement of men through history along this "path of gold." Closure within these matched poems comes not with heterosexual erotic fulfillment, but with entering a community of men, joining the commercial society in a move that resonates with the authentic nature of the male self, "the need of a world of men."

This "need of a world of men" suggests Browning's desire to be a masculine poet by inhabiting the male sphere, the arena of manly action. "Need" also suggests his longing for the company of men that at times moves toward the homoerotic. In later years, Browning was deeply troubled by what he saw as the homoeroticism of the poetry of the new generation. In 1870, he wrote to Isabella Blagden,

"Yes, – I have read Rossetti's poems... you know I hate the effeminacy of his school, – the men that dress up like women, – that use obsolete forms, too, and archaic accentuations to seem soft... how I hate "Love," as a lubberly naked young man putting his arms here & his wings there, about a pair of lovers, – a fellow they would kick away, in the reality. (*Dearest Isa* 336–37)

And yet, in the 1840s and 1850s his own masculine poetry, so insistently occupied with all-male groups, registers the intensity of male–male desire. One does not have to apply the biblical sense of the term "knew" to Childe Roland's "I knew them all" to see that Browning shares with his male contemporaries the fascination as well as the strain of that boundary area between the homosocial and the homosexual.

"Fra Lippo Lippi" exemplifies one element of a masculine poetic, that artistic power depends upon heterosexual potency. But the poem also represents the opposing element of that poetic, that manly artistic achievement depends upon bonding within an all-male community. Setting the discussion of art within the red-light district exemplifies this opposition. The visit to the brothel represents the necessary heterosexual potency of the artist. The conversation with the watch in a zone from which respectable women are excluded suggests masculine bonding as equally critical for the artist. The focus of the poem on the relationship with the men of the watch, rather than, for example, with the prostitute as in "Jenny," foregrounds not heterosexual, but rather homosocial ties as central to artistic manhood. As in "Childe Roland," the strongest emotion is that of male–male union. The emotional trajectory of the poem is that of the masculine plot, the move from discord between men, "a gullet's gripe" (line 20), to the achievement of a chaste affective, even physical bond between men, "Your hand, sir, and good-by" (line 390). As an erotic triangle,[24] the scene typifies the expression of a forbidden homoerotic desire through the female body. Here, Lippo is speaking of a sexual experience within the brothel to a group of men who, by their appearance within the night and their acceptance of the double standard, are assumed to be frequenters of these same brothels. The male–male bond is created, supported and validated by channeling homoerotic desire through the bodies of the "sportive ladies" (line 6) shared by these men.

Within a poetic that situates manly art practice within a community of bonded men, negotiating the homosocial/homosexual boundary becomes a crucial issue and depicting the management of homoerotic desire a central concern. In "Fra Lippo Lippi" Browning represents an ideal artistic life situated within a male community and supplemented by heterosexual activity that, rejecting marriage, binds the artist more closely to other men. If a controlled homoeroticism informs Browning's representation of the exemplary manly artist, a failure to regulate homoerotic desire characterizes his exemplary unmanly artist. The psychic paralysis manifested in Andrea del Sarto's lifeless art arises, in the familiar Victorian pathology, from the mismanagement of his sexuality, but his is a sexuality whose primary force, the poem suggests, is not heterosexual but homoerotic.[25] His desire turned inward and transformed into unproductive fantasy dwells on the earthly paradise lived with Francis I: "That Francis, that first time,/ And that long festal year at Fontainebleau!" (lines 149–50). These male fantasies take on a distinctly bodily, erotic tone, a remembrance of male flesh touching male flesh, of breath touching skin, a sexual intensity absent from Andrea's feelings about his wife:

> In that humane great monarch's golden look, –
> One finger in his beard or twisted curl
> Over his mouth's good mark that made the smile,
> One arm about my shoulder, round my neck,
> The jingle of his gold chain in my ear,
> I painting proudly with his breath on me,
> All his Court round him, seeing with his eyes. (lines 153–59)

Andrea's final vision of an afterlife turns to "one more chance" (line 260) to recreate these male–male bonds. His longing to work "in the New Jerusalem" with "Leonard, Rafael, Agnolo" (line 263) suggests the masculine ideal of sustained artistic energy as possible only within the company of men. The reference to marriage as impediment – "the three first without a wife,/ While I have mine!" (lines 264–65) – resonates strongly with the opposition between bourgeois marriage and artistic potency felt so strongly by early Victorian men, Browning among them. This dream vision of an ideal masculine bond in heaven, closely analogous to Tennyson's dream in *In Memoriam* of union with Hallam, presents within the defenses of historical displacement and irony a longing for a new form of marriage, for a male marriage beyond the confines of bourgeois masculinity.

In Browning's poetry of these decades, "Saul" most clearly brings to the surface the homoeroticism implicit in the centrality of male–male bonds within a masculine poetic. In this poem, David exemplifies the Carlylean Hero as Man of Letters, a man whose poetic power emerges in speaking to other men, a poet on the divinely sanctioned mission of curing male madness so that the Hero as King may resume authoritarian rule. Within the masculine plot of initiation into manhood that structures the poem, David's achieved manliness is marked as acceptance by the surrogate father into the community of adult men, an acceptance sealed, as in *Past and Present*, by physical contact between the initiate and the sacralized body of another man.

But here the masculine ideal of poetry as communication among men drifts beyond the limits of the homosocial. Although the retelling of a biblical story, the poem has a distinctly Greek quality, for it presents a boy bonding with a powerful and aristocratic older man. David is brought to Saul by another adult male and ushered into the tent with a kiss that, albeit the same mark of chaste male–male affect so important in *Past and Present*, resonates here with man-boy desire and with pandering: "Said Abner, 'At last thou art come! Ere I tell, ere thou speak,/ Kiss my cheek, wish me well!' Then I wished it, and did kiss his cheek" (lines 1–2). Once in the tent, alone with Saul, the young boy praises the older man in terms resonant with an admiration of phallic virility:

> And the tent shook, for mighty Saul shuddered: and sparkles 'gan dart
> From the jewels that woke in his turban, at once with a start,
> All its lordly male-sapphires, and rubies courageous at heart.
> So the head: but the body still moved not, still hung there erect.
>
> (lines 63–66)[26]

In the first nine stanzas, published before Browning's marriage, David sings a highly secular song of virility and muscularity, a paean to male physicality: "Oh, our manhood's prime vigour! No spirit feels waste,/ Not a muscle is stopped in its playing nor sinew unbraced" (lines 68–69). In terms more Hellenic than Hebraic the song continues as praise of the physical and sensual life: "All the heart and the soul and the senses for ever in joy!" (line 79). The heterosexual is here erased as the song turns to masculine bonding. David sings of "the friends of thy boyhood" (line 89). Closure comes with admiration not of spiritual "gifts," but of body's beauty in Saul:

> And all gifts, which the world offers singly, on one head combine!
> On one head, all the beauty and strength, love and rage
> ...
> High ambition and deed which surpass it, fame crowning them – all
> Brought to blaze on the head of one creature – King Saul!
>
> (lines 92–93, 95–96)

The original version of the poem (1845) ended with this culminating vision of male beauty. The stanzas added in 1853–54, after Browning's marriage, turn more toward religious speculation, but the physicality resonant with admiration for the male body so marked in the original stanzas continues. The poem reaches closure within the masculine plot as David attains artistic manhood in enabling Saul to regain manly control of his psyche. As in *Past and Present*, this entry into manhood is marked by male–male physical contact, here of man and boy. But in spite of the attempt to control this male–male desire by transforming such "love" into Christian "love" within a typological scheme, here, as in Andrea's memories of King Francis, the homoerotic energy emerges in an erotically resonant language of the male gaze focused on the beautiful boy and in a physical gesture of bending back the head that stops just short of a kiss:

> thro' my hair
> The large fingers were pushed, and he bent back my head, with kind power –
> All my face back, intent to peruse it, as men do a flower.
> Thus held he me there with his great eyes that scrutinized mine –
> And, oh, all my heart how it loved him! (lines 228–32)

Within the typological theology of the poem, David's desire to "help" what he terms his "father" (line 233) prefigures the Christian love to be incarnated in Christ, whose Crucifixion is foreshadowed in

Saul outstretched on "the great cross-support" (line 29) of the tent. But in "Saul" we can also see figured the conflation of erotic and sacred feeling in contemplating the adult body of Jesus that remains unsettled and unsettling not only in this poem, but throughout the visual and verbal art of the period. The next chapter will consider the efforts of the Pre-Raphaelite Brotherhood to reconcile the erotic attraction of the body of Christ both to men and to women with a manly religious art and a manly visual style.

CHAPTER 3

Artistic manhood: the Pre-Raphaelite Brotherhood

In January of 1853, William Michael Rossetti wrote, "The P.R.B. is not, and cannot be, so much a matter of social intercourse as it used to be. The P.R.B. meeting is no longer a sacred institution, – indeed is, as such, well-nigh disused" (Fredeman *P.R.B. Journal* 99). Like so many Victorian discussions of artistic issues, William Michael's comments are situated within the monastic discourse that registers the problematics of artistic manhood. The dissolution of the Brotherhood evokes the dissolution of the monasteries, those abandoned "sacred institution[s]" that, like St. Edmundsbury, are now "well-nigh disused." Like Carlyle's monastery, the PRB had hovered on the boundary of the sacred and the secular, a band of unmarried, if not wholly celibate, males, joined together under obedience to a strict rule in manly, religiously charged labor devoted to the high calling of art. The ties of the male community had been that of "social intercourse," a rather nice Victorian phrase for what we would now call the homosocial, chaste affective bonds between men.

During the 1840s and into the early 1850s the Brotherhood shared the project of Carlyle and Browning, forging within the gendered field of early Victorian aesthetics a specifically masculine aesthetic, creating or, in their historicist terms, re-creating a manly visual art that differentiated manly practice from the feminine by associating art production with the work of the male sphere, that took as its subject and as its goal the regulation of male desire, and that was energized in its practice by male–male bonding. Like Browning and Carlyle, the Brothers expressed this aesthetic through the figure of monasticism. In employing the cloistered religious life as the trope for the psychic and physical deformations generated by sexual repression and in their occupation with narratives of rescue and of escape from imprisonment, the Brothers focus on the main problematic of early Victorian manliness and of a masculine aesthetic, the regulation of male desire and the relation between sexual and artistic potency. And yet, quite ironically, because their early critics perceived Brotherhood art within another formation of early Victorian monastic discourse, these early efforts toward a manly religious painting were at first received as unmanly, as the unhealthy subversion of normative heterosexual masculinity.

By mid-century the increasing hegemony of bourgeois manliness and the Tractarians' establishment of celibate male as well as female religious communities had heightened uneasiness about male communal life and intensified the difficulty of reconciling the attractions of masculine bonding with the bourgeois imperative of compulsory matrimony for men. The dissolution of the Brotherhood, the transformation of a male artistic community into individual men pursuing diverse styles of artistic manhood illustrates the problem of constructing a form of masculinity that would reconcile the opposition between bourgeois manliness and the practice of art. But, as dissimilar as the post-Brotherhood lives of John Everett Millais, Holman Hunt, and Dante Gabriel Rossetti may appear, each took its shape from the continuing need to resolve this opposition in order to achieve a viable form of artistic manhood. The diversity of these post-Brotherhood careers and styles demonstrates, then, not the monolithic character of Victorian manliness and manly artistic practice, but rather the varied possibilities for artistic manhood as well as for a masculine aesthetic and a manly visual style in the nineteenth century. And if the post-Brotherhood work inscribes these new constructions of artistic manliness, it also registers the contradictions and psychic strains within these formations, the inability fully to reconcile art practice with the available Victorian masculinities so as to achieve an integrated artistic manhood.

A MASCULINE VISUAL STYLE

In 1850, in language that has since become notorious, Dickens described the Jesus in Millais' *The Carpenter's Shop* (plate 2), the first Pre-Raphaelite work to draw public attention, as a "hideous, wrynecked, blubbering, red-headed boy, in a bed-gown." He also saw "such men as the carpenters [as] might be undressed in any hospital where dirty drunkards, in a high state of varicose veins, are received" ("Old Lamps" 265). This severity, particularly in the focus on a perceived distortion in representing the male body, was shared by

Plate 2 J. E. Millais, *Christ in the House of His Parents* (*The Carpenter's Shop*).

other critics. To *The Art-Journal*, *The Carpenter's Shop* exhibited "the vulgar errors of men whose ignorance never raised them beyond the coarsest representation of humanity – who would wring the soul by distorting the body" ("Review" 175). For *The Athenæum*, this same revulsion at the Brotherhood's depiction of men was informed by the same early Victorian mood of abjection, the same fear of the potential decay of the male body that pervades the writing of Carlyle and Browning:

It is difficult in the present day of improved taste and information to apprehend any large worship of an Art-idol set up with visible deformity as its attribute... In all these [early Italian] painters the absence of structural knowledge never resulted in positive deformity. The disgusting incidents of unwashed bodies were not presented in loathsome reality; and flesh with its accidents of putridity was not made the affected medium of religious sentiment in tasteless revelation. ("Review" 590)

The celebrated reception of *The Carpenter's Shop* and other Brotherhood paintings at the Royal Academy exhibition of 1850 illuminates the male anxieties pervading the gendered field of early Victorian artistic practice. Although, as Carlyle complained, the early Victorian Man of Letters was directly threatened by the commercial success of the Woman of Letters, the Man of Art suffered little direct financial and status competition from women. In the 1840s women were still largely excluded from painting as a professional career. Although women could exhibit at the Royal Academy, they were relegated to amateur status by their exclusion from membership. Whereas early Victorian writers such as Carlyle self-consciously developed literary forms that signified their manliness by their difference from feminized forms such as domestic fiction, male artists did not confront a form of painting marked as female. Instead, the primary problematic for the early Victorian male artist became valorizing his practice or, in the applicable Victorian term, his "work" as art producer with the criteria that defined bourgeois manhood – wealth, prestige and, most importantly, respectability.[1] For the male English artist of the early and mid-Victorian period the chief drive, albeit with some conflict about serving the cause of beauty and art, was toward middle-class status as manifested in the amassing of wealth, in marriage as elegant domesticity, and particularly in the manly status to be achieved by inclusion in that new nineteenth-century formation of masculinity, the professional man.[2]

Artistic manhood

Albeit nominally imitating the artists of the early Renaissance, the Brothers are continuing another pre-bourgeois formation of artistic manhood, the model of the romantic artist. To the Brothers, the romantic poet and painter lives in isolation from and opposition to the male sphere of getting and spending. As the example of Percy Shelley, a one-star Immortal to the Brothers, seemed to show, the romantic artist also lives outside the bourgeois norm of regulated heterosexuality within marriage. Furthermore, the romantic poet lived a life centered on masculine bonding, as the friendships of Shelley and Byron, Wordsworth and Coleridge exemplify. The Brotherhood, then, extends this romantic model of artistic manhood into what was to become one of the dominant formations of artistic manhood for the nineteenth century, even if more dominant in France than in England, the avant-garde model. Indeed, the Brotherhood appears as the first avant-garde group of artists in England.[3]

Nineteenth-century avant-gardes, of course, defined themselves by opposition to the bourgeoisie and certainly the monastic model adopted by the Brotherhood signifies a rejection of certain crucial qualities of bourgeois masculinity. By taking a secular vow of poverty, by a purposeful downward mobility exemplified by their residing in *déclassé* lodgings in working-class districts, the Brothers spurned the Victorian ideal of rising in class status. Ostensibly, though certainly not in practice, the Brothers saw their project as the revival of a religious, moralized art freed from commercial considerations.

But for all their oppositional stance, avant-gardes exist in a dialectical relation to bourgeois society. Indeed, their well-advertised lives as Brothers within a Brotherhood appropriates the construction as well as the contradictions of bourgeois masculinity. In one sense, the valorization of homosocial life as monastic Brothers provides an oppositional model to the bourgeois idea of compulsory marriage. And yet, as in the Carlylean monastery, their self-fashioning as worker-monks within an all-male community idealizes and sacralizes the affective ties of the male sphere and presents an analogue to the bonded activity of men within factories. Furthermore, in its homosocial formation, this avant-garde group also mirrors the structure of artistic manhood that appears on a larger scale in the dominant art institution of the time, the Royal Academy, whose members persistently fought to exclude women from full membership. Here men worked together to hang each other's works, watched each other paint on Varnishing Day, and found the highlight of their year in the banquet before the Annual Exhibition, a festival of masculine bonding from which wives were excluded.[4]

Furthermore, in their project of shaping a masculine aesthetic the Brothers, like Carlyle and Browning, sought to develop a manly visual style by appropriating several significant elements of entrepreneurial manliness. Several formal features that mark the practice of Hunt, Millais, and to a lesser extent Rossetti during the Brotherhood period signify their desire to ennoble their art by incorporating their work into the male sphere, into the area of masculine knowledge, and into what was seen as the progressive historical movement of Victorian England.

To see the practice and the style of the Brothers as participating in bourgeois manliness we can turn to the crucial text of Victorian aesthetics, *Self-Help; with Illustrations of Character, Conduct, and Perseverance* by Samuel Smiles, the author, as the title page notes, of *The Life of George Stephenson*. Along with chapters devoted to financiers, industrialists, inventors, and scientists, the true inhabitants of the male sphere and exemplars of manly work, Smiles includes a chapter significantly titled, given the industrial ethos of the book, "Workers in Art." This chapter represents a conduct book for the practice of a particular construction of artistic manhood as the reconciliation of art and entrepreneurship. A Victorian Vasari, Smiles provides "illustrations" from the history of art, what Codell rightly calls an "entrepreneurial hagiography" ("Spielmann" 12), that set, or squeeze, the lives of artists into the model of the self-made man. For Smiles, the male artist (women, of course, appear only as helpmates to their husbands) begins in humble surroundings unpropitious to artistic achievement, perseveres through "painstaking labour" (182) and "indefatigable industry" (189) to attain the artistic skill that marks the mature artist. Like Michelangelo and Leonardo, Turner manifests "a career of...labourious industry" (189). For Smiles, artistic maturity is defined primarily by achieved skill in mimetic accuracy, by mastery of the technology of reproducing nature so as to transform nature into commodities for sale on the art market. This "industry" is represented as the regulated, disciplined expression of powerful male energy. Like Carlyle, Smiles employs the vocabulary of fluid energy, of inward male potency channeled to productive purposes: "Energy enables a man to force his way through irksome drudgery and dry details, and carries him onward and upward in every station in life" (254). In opposition to the spontaneous overflow of emotion or the orgasmic river of Xanadu, the Smilesean artistic metaphor suggests slow orderly progress: "[Wilkie] became an artist; working his way manfully up the steep of difficulty" (211). Through this technological control of the external world the artist achieves financial success and a higher social station.

If we set the Brotherhood program into this Smilesean, bourgeois model of artistic manliness, the labile figure of monasticism assumes Carlylean shape as the desexualization of male energy, devotion to disciplined labor, and the production of masculine knowledge within a male community. The Brothers' communal artistic enterprise takes shape as an attempt to found a specifically English art on a valorization of scientific knowledge and of the entrepreneurial work ethic that underlies Smiles' aesthetic and that in the 1840s and into the early 1850s seemed to distinguish the English from less favored, less manly nations. Like Smiles, the Brothers sought to situate the artist among the industrialists and technologists.

The art produced by the Brothers, particularly by Hunt and Millais, is conceived as a distinctly masculine form of knowledge. Hunt and Millais deal with objects, individuals, events by deploying the practices of the male sphere. Those qualities that seem most bizarre in the twentieth century, such as lengthy on-site observation or the precise hard-edge detailing of grass, flower, brick wall, and wood shaving, valorizes this art within its nineteenth-century context as the application of controlled scientific observation to art production, the transformation of nature into art commodity. Much as Carlyle's comparison of unearthing the life of a monk to unearthing a fossil equates his work as Man of Letters with that of the paleontologist, transmitting detailed knowledge of nature in painting identifies the practice of the artist with that of the scientific naturalist, a similarity remarked with some condescension by the comments of *The Art-Journal* of 1850 on Millais' *Ferdinand Lured by Ariel*: "The emphasis of the picture is in its botany, which is made out with a microscopic elaboration, insomuch as to seem to have been painted from a collection of grasses, since we recognise upwards of twenty varieties; there may be more; and such is the minute description of even one leaf, that the ravages of an insect are observable upon it" ("Review" 175). The celebrated Pre-Raphaelite occupation with historical accuracy, however inaccurate in practice, also sought through detailed observation of tangible objects and extensive research to equate the labor of the artist with that of the new scientific historian.

Notably absent from Brotherhood practice is the romantic quest for inspiration, the sense of self as Aeolian harp. Masculine knowledge is not conferred in moments of revelation, but acquired through hours of hard work, not absorbed through wise passiveness but achieved through strenuous activity. For the early Hunt and Millais there are no dream visions. Although Smiles is sometimes torn between the romantic cult of genius and the Victorian ethic of work, he typically subordinates inspiration to industry. His is not a study of geniuses, but of "Workers in Art." As religiously charged as their early art may be, like the work of Carlyle's monks, the Brothers' practice is informed by this secular cult of labor. The strenuous physical hardship of their practice – the laborious search for the right wall or flowered bank, the long hours in darkness and cold waiting for the right shade of moonlight – suggest bourgeois guilt energizing their desire to resolve the contradiction pictured in Brown's *Work* (plate 1) by showing that they are not mere "brain-workers," but manly men engaged in physical activity and encountering bodily challenge. Such practice acts out the Smilesean and the Carlylean sense that artistic worth is validated by long and unremitting labor, not by moments of heightened perception. "Going To Nature," the celebrated motto of the group, means moving away from the self. Such valuing of art production by the hours of physical work spent, by what Smiles called "labourious industry" (189), informs Ruskin's charge against Whistler later in the century that the time spent by the artist in production did not justify the price demanded. And Whistler's reply, calling up "the knowledge of a lifetime," reminiscent of a contemporary physician justifying his bill, echoes this same artistic calculus grounded in the work ethic.

Within a binary that equates the emotive with the female, this adherence to close observation and prosaic hard work, this focus on the sharply observed natural detail rather than the intensely experienced nuance of emotion, this occupation with the external rather than the internal world, this retreat from self-consciousness brings the practice and the artistic style of the Brotherhood into the configuration of a masculine aesthetic emerging in the early Victorian decades. And yet, as in the masculine poetics of Carlyle, Tennyson, and Browning, the intense drive toward a thoroughgoing objectivity and a complete suppression of the dangerous inner life, the withdrawal from feeling and the refusal of subjectivity engenders a return of the repressed. The more rigid the manly control, the stronger the swerve toward mental instability, the greater the danger of madness. The intention of erasing the consciousness of the observer through the intense focus on the object paradoxically generates a hallucinatory, surreal aura within Brotherhood work.[5]

This male madness, seen by the age as male hysteria manifested in hyperaesthesia, is exemplified in the hallucinatory detailing of such works as *Ophelia* or *The Scapegoat*. The mood is best verbalized by Rossetti, who often takes as his subject the psychological effect of the Brotherhood aesthetic, that state of subjectivity Pater in his essay "Dante Gabriel Rossetti" brilliantly terms the "insanity of realism" (89). Rossetti's work shows from within how the intense concentration on the object generates a form of instability verging on madness in the male subject. These states bordering on the unmanly loss of emotional control emerge from the powerful focus on the desacralized natural object in such poems as the post-Brotherhood version of "My Sister's Sleep"[6] and particularly in "The Woodspurge." In that poem the poetic vision of the three-part cup repudiates a sacred reading of the flower as figure of the Trinity for a state of concentrated visual apprehension: "One thing then learnt remained to me, – / The woodspurge has a cup of three" (lines 15–16). It is this mental practice of internalizing and thereby intensifying sense impressions that Pater appropriates, terms the "aesthetic," and valorizes as a productive form of male madness in his reworking of the masculine poetic in his essays of the 1860s.

The Carpenter's Shop exemplifies the historically specific problematics of realizing the Brotherhood's masculine visual aesthetic. The first viewers, in what has become a tradition of response, were occupied with Millais' hard-edged rendering of the detail, most notoriously the wood shavings. Dickens noted with no little irony, "It is particularly gratifying to observe that such objects as the shavings which are strewn on the carpenter's floor are admirably painted" (266). *The Athenæum* singles out Millais' "giving to the higher forms, characters and meanings a circumstantial Art-language from which we recoil with loathing and disgust" ("Review" 590–91). The handling of detail always carries historically specific and usually gendered significance.[7] Here, the shavings, unlike many of the equally specified objects such as the dove or the wounded hand, gain such gendered significance by resisting integration into a symbolic or typological scheme. In their non-metaphorical quality, the shavings, like the other non-figural detail, present a Brotherhood version of what Barthes calls the "effect of the real." The emphasis on detail is significant not on the grounds of mimetic accuracy, but for signaling the use of a realist style. Within mid-Victorian gendered aesthetics, evoking this code of realism differentiates this art from the idealizing Grand Style of Raphael and, although couched in the usual Victorian historicist rhetoric of revival, establishes this artistic practice as participating in the forward movement of the age, substituting, to use the title of Dickens' essay, new lamps for old by recreating a scene of the past with the advanced mimetic skills of the present. Such hard-edged objectivity and visual acuteness distinguishes this religious art of the nineteenth century from medieval art and, as in the case of Lippo, this turn to accuracy of detail registers the artist's engagement in the tangible world, his ability to see that world clearly, thereby demonstrating his manliness. Thus the formal use of detail differentiates this art from the medieval style associated with the unmanly Tractarians, signals the manliness of the style, and thereby the value of the artistic work itself.

The creation of this manly style, in opposition to the unmanly painterly styles of past and present associated with monastic celibacy, is crucial to the Brotherhood project, similar to that of Browning, of creating a manly religious art suitable to their own age. But in their effort to revivify devotional art by incorporating it within normative masculinity, the Brothers engaged another problematic of manliness, the issue of the manliness of Christ,[8] the difficulty of reconciling the traditional representation of the life of Jesus with the norms of early Victorian bourgeois manhood.

In *The Carpenter's Shop* Millais seeks to resolve this contradiction by creating a manly Christ through means congruent with the Brotherhood's formation of the manly artist. He constructs Jesus as worker, situating him not in the act of mortifying the flesh, like Lippo's St. Jerome, but as participating in the sphere of artisanal labor. Rather than "brain-workers," the members of the Holy Family are manual workers in wood, much as the Pre-Raphaelite artist is a worker in paint at the easel and in the field. Indeed, the painting becomes the biblical equivalent of Brown's exaltation of manly Carlylean labor in *Work*. As the children in Brown's painting bring food for the adults, so the young John the Baptist brings a bowl of water. Each family member from child to grandmother actively participates in useful physical labor. For all its typological significance, the young Jesus' wound has come from participation in physical work. That Millais carefully modeled the musculature of Joseph's arms from an actual carpenter, much as Brown drew from actual navvies, suggests his concern with representing, albeit from the subject position of middle-class "brain-worker," the muscular actuality of physical labor.

Furthermore, the painting, whose formal title is *Christ in the House of His Parents*, sets Jesus within the center of the bourgeois social formation of manhood, the nuclear family. The novelty of this compositional scheme was noticed by *The Art-Journal*: "He is yet in the home of his parents, that is, of Mary and Joseph, of whom the latter is working as a carpenter" ("Review" 175). That Millais did not choose to depict, say, Christ with his male disciples or with Mary Magdalene, a subject that strongly attracted Rossetti (plate 6), suggests a concern with picturing the family, a center of bourgeois value, as the source of economic support and emotional nurturance, indicating through the typological form the natural, even sacred quality of this element of bourgeois masculinity. Then, too, picturing Jesus in this working family with each person engaged in labor suited to age and gender stresses the humble social beginnings of Jesus. Although Dickens was distressed by Millais' setting Jesus within the working class, the picture does not dwell on the indignities of poverty nor evoke a theology of the poor. Rather, the prefigurative typological imagery invokes the Smilesean, bourgeois life-narrative, the script of entrepreneurial masculinity illustrated in great industrialists and inventors and manifested at its highest, most sacred level in Jesus – the rise from humble origins. The same narrative also applies to artists, and this representation of the young Jesus inscribes one definition of artistic manliness for the Brotherhood, the artist as a humble worker called to a holy mission and achieving manhood in the completion of that mission.

Yet the painting also registers how contemporary anxieties about manliness and particularly about male sexuality complicated and indeed vitiated the Brotherhood efforts to re-create a manly religious art by presenting the historical Jesus, the adult Jesus incarnated in a male body. The historical specificity of this Victorian difficulty is sharpened by contrast to the Renaissance treatment of the sexuality of Jesus in which, for example, artists foreground the genitals of the baby Jesus as a way of indicating the completeness of the Incarnation

Plate 3 D. G. Rossetti, *The Passover in the Holy Family: Gathering Bitter Herbs*.

and the purity of Jesus.[9] But early Victorian writers and artists could deal with the sexuality of Jesus with far less calm. In "Saul" male–male desire associated with the body of a muscular adult Christ is displaced onto King Saul as a prefiguration of Christ. The opposition between Christ's celibate life and the Victorian definition of manhood as encompassing the regulated flow of male desire within marriage further complicated the artistic use of Jesus as the model for contemporary manhood.

Given the difficulty at the mid-nineteenth century of presenting Jesus as a manly man, that is, as a sexual male, the Brothers often avoided depictions of His adult life, presenting Him not in an adult body, but rather in the body of a child. As *The Carpenter's Shop* illustrates, the Pre-Raphaelites preferred to work within the sub-genre of the Childhood of Jesus to show Him before puberty, at the

Artistic manhood

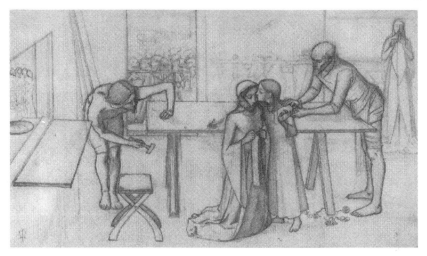

Plate 4 J. E. Millais, Study for *Christ in the House of His Parents*.

moment when, within the Victorian notion of childhood, gender is not yet imposed and dangerous male sexuality not yet present. The drawing that served as the frontispiece in the second number of *The Germ* and the accompanying poem, "The Child Jesus," Hunt's *The Finding of the Saviour in the Temple*, as well as Rossetti's *The Passover in the Holy Family: Gathering Bitter Herbs* (1855–56) (plate 3) all indicate the desire to avoid depicting the adult sexual Jesus. In this regard, typological structure served the Brothers well, as it did Browning in "Saul," by enabling the artist to suggest but not depict that which cannot be pictured, the body of the adult Christ. For *The Passover in the Holy Family*, Rossetti painted "Christ (as a boy)" from "a very nice little fellow whom I picked out from the Saint Martin's School the other day" (Surtees *Paintings and Drawings* 1: 40). In the prepubescent boy, the adult Jesus is present, prefigured but not figured. As Rossetti states in his poem on the drawing:

> What agony's crown attained,
>   What shadow of death the Boy's fair brow subdues
> Who holds the blood wherewith the porch is stained
>   By Zachary the priest? (lines 9–12)

But even picturing the childhood of Jesus presented the problem of representing Him as a manly boy. In a study for *Christ in the House of His Parents* (plate 4), the child Jesus is distinctly unmanly as He kisses His Mother in an emotive feminine gesture. In the painting Millais

Plate 5 Holman Hunt, *The Light of the World*.

has masculinized this feminized boy, whose longish feminine hair is now shortened. In the finished work the boy Jesus exhibits a manly reserve, a stoic endurance of his mother's kiss, detaching himself from the mother as He inwardly contemplates His Mission, the prefigured Crucifixion. As child/man he exemplifies the resistance to the familial and particularly to feminine emotion that characterizes the masculine plot of differentiation from the mother and from the feminized sphere of the domestic. The typological form, then, enables the painting to present and to reconcile two contradictory impulses within early Victorian masculinity. The Child Jesus is set within a normative model of bourgeois manhood, an idealized family as economic unit and center of affective life. And yet, the prefigurative form suggests, but does not depict, the trajectory of Jesus' life in rejecting this bourgeois construction of masculinity, leaving mother and family for a celibate life bound to male disciples in a communal all-male quest.

This same inability to incorporate Jesus within the hegemonic Victorian construction of manliness is exemplified by Hunt's notorious difficulty in fixing the gender of Jesus in one of the few Pre-Raphaelite representations of the adult Jesus, *The Light of the World* (1853) (plate 5). Hunt appeared eager to incorporate into his representation both feminine and masculine qualities. For Christ, he used a virginal female model: "Appreciating the gravity and sweetness of expression possessed by Miss Christina Rossetti, I felt she might make a valuable sitter for the painting of the head... She kindly agreed" (Hunt *Pre-Raphaelitism* 1: 347). He also seems to have employed male models, but intent on foregrounding the feminine qualities, he tried to keep that practice secret. In a late letter Hunt acknowledges that he had also employed "a variety of male sitters" including Millais and "in person, furtively... Carlyle" to secure "the male character in the head" (Maas *Hunt* 41). The painting itself does convey a desire to move Jesus outside the hegemonic category of the manly. The physical body of Jesus is not shown. The male body, the musculature of the adult Jesus is masked, although there is a suggestion of breasts, by a loose gown of rich, almost satin texture, a costume suitable to a female yet acceptable for Christ within historicist visual conventions. But the face with its full beard carries little of the uncertainty about gender definition that Hunt displayed in his use of models. The modeling of the face "furtively from

Carlyle" inscribes a less muscular form of artistic manliness, the Carlylean artist as prophet that served as the model for Hunt's self-fashioning in his post-Brotherhood period.[10]

In representing the adult Jesus, Rossetti, as one might expect, dwells on that which both Millais and Hunt are at such pains to suppress, the erotic energy that flows from the adult male body of the incarnate Jesus. In a drawing of *Mary Magdalene at the Door of Simon the Pharisee* (1858) (plate 6) and the accompanying poem Rossetti enters, as in his occupation with Dante, one of his favorite territories, the boundary area where religious longing and sexual desire flow together. This fusion appears, for example, in his design for "Mariana in the South" for the Moxon Tennyson, where the kneeling Mariana passionately kisses the foot of Jesus on the crucifix in her room with the same intensity with which Emma Bovary presses her lips to the crucifix in the last moments of her life.

In Rossetti's biblical drawing, Mary Magdalene turns from the carnival of the street toward Jesus. As in other Pre-Raphaelite work, the adult body of Jesus is hidden; a wall blocks out the torso and we see only the head. The halo about this young and virile head indicates the same mix of sacred with sexual energy signified by the more secularized halo around the head of Chiaro, the exemplary virile artist described in "Hand and Soul": "Women loved Chiaro ... he was well-favoured and very manly in his walking; and, seeing his face in front, there was a glory upon it, as upon the face of one who feels a light round his hair" (*Poems* 159). The eyes of Jesus and Mary Magdalene meet in the traditional representation of deep sexual attraction. The poem makes the erotic fascination of the adult Jesus more than explicit, makes visible the sexual subtext of the New Testament in the mode of such late-century works as Wilde's *Salomé*:

> See'st thou not my Bridegroom's face
> That draws me to Him? For His feet my kiss,
> My hair, my tears He craves to-day: – and oh!
> What words can tell what other day and place
> Shall see me clasp those blood-stained feet of His?
> He needs me, calls me, loves me: let me go!   (lines 9–14)

But for all its suggestions of a transgressive eroticism, the typological form here, as in other Pre-Raphaelite works, allows Rossetti that doubleness, even the covertness employed by Browning,

Plate 6 D. G. Rossetti, *Mary Magdalene at the Door of Simon the Pharisee.*

in reconciling the urgency of sexuality with religious art practice. The figural sense of the spiritual incarnated in the body enables Rossetti to present, as in such early representations of the Virgin as *Ecce Ancilla Domini!* (1850) and the poem "Ave," a fusion of the erotic and the spiritual.[11] In the intimate confrontation of male and female in *Ecce Ancilla* the Angel Gabriel appears as a powerful physical embodiment of male sexuality, with the lily transformed into a phallic instrument directed at the Virgin cowering on her bed. At the same time, the male figure of the Angel appears androgynous and except for the muscular arm, the male body is covered and loses any clear outline. As in *The Light of the World*, within Rossetti's Annunciation the erotic force of the sacred male body is contained, and this containment, the quality of reserve in the representation marks Gabriel as a manly figure.

In *Mary Magdalene at the Door of Simon the Pharisee*, the disruptive eruption of erotic longing, as in the Menadic women of Carlyle's *French Revolution*, is projected into the female who is here set amidst the flood of dancers in the carnivalesque outburst of desire.[12] In Mary Magdalene, Rossetti depicts erotic longing. The figural form enables him to reconcile this eroticism with religion by suggesting the future conversion from prostitute to saint. Furthermore, for all its potentially transgressive sense of the erotic attractiveness of the adult Jesus, the work still confirms His bourgeois manliness. This drawing is sharply divided between the serpentine flow of uncontrolled energy associated with the female and the solid rectilinear brick house, the Carlylean body armor that defines Jesus' manly reserve. In the companion poem, sexual overflow is spoken through the female voice. In keeping with the male poetic, the truly manly man remains silent. The adult male sexuality of Jesus, then, is not erased, but rather transmuted into sacred purpose through self-discipline. Paradoxically, in this most erotically charged of Pre-Raphaelite representations of Jesus, celibacy and manliness are reconciled. In manifesting self-control rather than the absence of male desire, Jesus exemplifies manliness as divine virtuoso of the Victorian ideal of masculinity as reserve.

THE AURA OF UNMANLINESS

If the style of *The Carpenter's Shop* in its mastery of mimetic skill and historical accuracy testified to diligent labor in a sacred calling and thus signaled the manliness of the artist, and if its representation of Jesus as worker within a diligent family attested to the manliness of Christ, then how are we to account for the fevered, if not hysterical, response by the early critics and particularly for the original perception of the work as unmanly? In part, the answer lies in the lability of the monastic at mid-century in figuring the anxiety and contradictions of male identity.

The PRB adopted monasticism to represent their own artistic manliness as an exclusively male communitarianism that valorizes the bonding of the male sphere, the production of masculine knowledge, the displacement of male energy into hard work, and the sublimation of desire into a moralized calling. The meaning of the mysterious initials having been revealed before the painting was exhibited, the name of the all-male band evoked in Dickens and other critics another set of associations in which monastic discourse evokes not the manly, but the unmanly. Within this configuration, the term "Pre-Raphaelite" suggests Catholicism. "Brotherhood" implies Romanist monasticism and, with a fear heightened by the revival of Tractarian religious communities both male and female at midcentury, suggests the dangers of male celibacy and male sexual repression in general.

For Dickens and early Victorian art critics, as for Browning and indeed for the Brothers themselves, art history is assumed to be the history of male sexuality. The evaluation of contemporary art becomes then a process of recognizing in the art work the proper or improper management of male potency in the artist. All share the same sense of the psychology and of the pathology of male creative life. As the artist-poems of Browning indicate, within this psycho-sexual writing of art history medieval Catholic art created by celibate monks demonstrates that repression of male sexual energy inevitably causes sexual neuraesthenia, a distortion of the male psyche that inevitably leads to the loss of artistic power, particularly the ability to represent the male body. The art of the celibate or of the sexually repressed man necessarily becomes the opposite of manly, thus falling within the category of the "effeminate," a term that mixes feminization with the nascent homophobia directed at the Tractarians. Kingsley's comment on early Italian painter-monks is, again, representative: "They were prone to despise all by which *man* is brought in contact with this earth – the beauties of sex, of strength, of activity, of grandeur of form; all, that is, in which Greek art excels: their ideal of beauty was altogether *effeminate* ... [having] that ascetic and *emasculate* tone, which was peculiar to themselves" ("Sacred and Legendary Art" 217, emphasis added).

The equation of sexual and artistic impotence that informs Kingsley's rejection of early Italian painting, an idea central to his masculine aesthetic, shapes the initial critical anxiety about *The Carpenter's Shop*. The first viewers saw the work though the grid of a monastic discourse evoked by the association Brotherhood/ monasticism in which the mental deformation created by celibacy must surely be manifested in formal deformation, an inability to value and to represent the body, particularly the male body. It is this connection of monasticism or Brotherhood with sexual repression, combined with the assumption that suppressing the flesh destroys the ability to represent the flesh that accounts for the occupation of the first reviewers with the painter's misshaping of the body, with unnatural bodily dislocations that modern viewers are hard-pressed to find. The *Art-Journal* sees the painting as the result of sexual "asceticism" and thus as a contemporary revival of the false pictorial values created by the practice of medieval celibacy, a modern reenactment of the "time when Art was employed in mortification of the flesh" ("Review" 175). Such unmanly repression is manifested in the painting in mimetic inaccuracy, errors that are charged for the *Art-Journal* reviewer, as for Dickens, with the Victorian male fantasy of horror as abjection, as anxiety about the dissolution of the boundaries of the male body in death: "Joseph is a semi-nude figure, that is, the limbs are uncovered; and in these are scrupulously imitated all the foibles of the early Italian school; in short, in colour and in the attenuation of the limbs, the impersonation of Joseph seems to have been realised from a subject after having served a course of study in a dissecting-room." The consequence of male impotence is mimetic impotence, an inability to portray the human body that repeats the "vulgar errors of men whose ignorance never raised them beyond the coarsest representation of humanity – who would wring the soul by distorting the body" (175).[13]

The Athenæum also links "the very title which they adopt, – that of pre-Raffaellite" with "visible deformity" ("Review" 590). The connection of male celibacy to mimetic error is suggested in the occupation of the reviewer with the recreation of a medieval monastic band, an anxiety that resonates with the contemporary uneasiness about the Puseyite reestablishment of celibate monastic communities: "The idea of an association of artists whose objects are the following out of their art in a spirit of improved *purity* – making sentiment and expression the great ends, and subordinating to these all technical considerations – is not new" (590, emphasis added). And while describing the falling-off of these modern Pre-Raphaelites from the beauties of Giotto and Fra Angelico, the *Athenæum* reviewer of *The Carpenter's Shop*, like the critic of *The Art-Journal*, himself loses manly control. He exhibits the same revulsion at the actuality of the "loathsome" male body, the same upsurge of abjection in the coming to consciousness of the inherent "putridity" of the male flesh that erupts in Carlyle's prose and in the last moments of Browning's Bishop: "In all these painters [Giotto, Fra Angelico] the absence of structural knowledge never resulted in positive deformity. The disgusting incidents of unwashed bodies were not presented in loathsome reality; and flesh with its accidents of putridity was not made the affected medium of religious sentiment in tasteless revelation" (590).

Dickens also perceives the figures as physically deformed, mimetically distorted. To him the work is "odious, repulsive, and revolting" because Jesus is "hideous, *wry-necked*." Mary, too, is "horrible in her ugliness... with that *dislocated throat*... a Monster" ("Old Lamps" 265, emphasis added). For Dickens, actualized rather than idealized male bodies rouse male fantasies of abjection, of the inherent morbidity and sickness of the "undressed" male body as his consciousness, like that of the *Art-Journal* reviewer, turns to the hospital: "Such men as the carpenters might be undressed in any hospital where dirty drunkards, in a high state of varicose veins, are received" (266). In a typically Dickensian literalization of this sense of horror as abjection, the male body decomposes into separate but still living parts: "Their very toes have walked out of Saint Giles's" (266).

The title of Dickens' indictment, "Old Lamps for New Ones," musters yet another count of unmanliness by the contingent association of "Pre-Raphaelite" with an unprogressive medievalism. To Dickens the work "is the sign and emblem" of "the great retrogressive principle" (266). The attack of *The Athenæum* on the Brotherhood for its repudiation of progress within the arts also resonates with imputations of effeminacy, coded, as in Carlyle, as pretension and intellectuality: "It is difficult in the present day of improved taste and information to apprehend any large worship of an Art-idol set up with visible deformity as its attribute; but it is always well to guard against the influence of ostentatious example and the fascination of paradox" ("Review" 590). Such failure to join the march of mind is for the early Victorians consistently figured in the trope of the monastery by withdrawal from the forward movement of men engaged in war or commerce, as in "Pictor Ignotus" and "Stanzas from the Grand Chartreuse." Albeit in comic form, this same figure for the emasculation of the artist governs Dickens' meditation on other possible forms of contemporary Brotherhood, all deeply "retrogressive." He speaks of a "Pre-Perspective Brotherhood," a "Pre-Newtonian Brotherhood," a "P.G.A.P.C.B., or Pre-Gower and Pre-Chaucer-Brotherhood" all devoted to "cancelling all the advances of nearly four hundred years" ("Old Lamps" 266–67).

Associated by their first critics with the aura of unmanliness that with the establishment of Puseyite religious communities had become linked to the idea of an all-male community, perceived as effeminate within an artistic economy of male desire that equates sexual with artistic potency, formal skill in representing the body with bodily desire itself, formal prowess with virility, and artistic manliness with the regulated flow rather than the repression of male sexuality, these young men turned from religious to literary painting to register their own artistic manhood.

Brotherhood literary paintings, like the contemporaneous poems of Browning, employ the trope of imprisonment and escape to represent the problem of the feminization and the effeminization of the male artist. But, in contrast to the artist-poems of Browning, the Brotherhood's cloistered subject is female. The Brotherhood work of Hunt and Millais is occupied with the cloistered woman, either a nun, as in Collins' *Convent Thoughts* (1851) (plate 9) and Millais' *St. Agnes Eve* of 1854 or imprisoned near-nuns such as *Mariana* (1851) (plate 7). Like the occupation with the monastery, the concern with the convent drew upon anxieties about the reestablishment of religious communities in England in which the formation of religious orders for women preceded the establishment of such organized communities for men. By 1851 there were six communities of nuns within the Church of England, with the first Puseyite sisterhood started in 1845. Of these, one was contemplative, the others devoted to public service. One group of sisters attended the same church as the Rossetti family.[14]

The cloistered women of Brotherhood art function as female surrogates that express the Brothers' sense that the male artist cannot inhabit sexless space, that participation in heterosexuality and the male sphere, although dangerous, is necessary for a manly art.[15] This representation of the issues of male artists through female figures in early Victorian art and literature, in the high-born maidens of Tennyson and the cloistered women of Brotherhood art, follows the underlying emotional logic of a masculine aesthetic. Just as within a masculine plot, manhood must be achieved by leaving the female sphere, so in the movement toward artistic manhood the female elements must be separated from essentially male qualities. Browning uses a female muse in "Fra Lippo Lippi" to embody the qualities of emotive softness that are distinct from the essential male self. For Hunt and Millais, too, the qualities of passivity and isolation must be depicted within a female rather than a male body so as to maintain the defining essentialist quality of a masculine poetic, that creativity flows from a form of internal energy specific to the male.

In *Mariana* (plate 7), his painting after Tennyson, Millais follows the poet in displacing onto the immured female concerns about the feminization of the artist. Although Mariana is not a nun within the poem, she is presented by Millais within the visual convention of the cloistered nun, the limit case of virginity. He introduces a complex of Christian iconography not present in Tennyson's text, in particular the Annunciation in the stained glass window and the High Church altar at the right that indicate her imprisonment within the ideas of female chastity. As in the critical response to *The Carpenter's Shop*, sexual suppression and bodily distortion are conflated. In setting the full-bodied female, whose foregrounded buttocks are the focus of Victorian eroticism, against the icons of Christian virginity, the painting represents sexual constraint as generating physical deformation. Her upper body takes an awkward pose while the lower body pushes forward as a sign of repressed sexual desire.

The painting captures the occupation of Tennyson's text with the distortions of the inner life, with the delirium created by sexual repression. Sexual deprivation and isolation distort mental processes, creating the hallucinatory state that is the opposite of the clear-minded visual acuity and objectivity that marks a masculine aesthetic. Here, the preternaturally vivid and intensely detailed objects evoke a brittle mind withering from sexual want, a displacement onto the female of a nineteenth-century male hysteria marked by the symptom of hyperaesthesia. Unmanly madness as the eruption of the chaotic inner life from rigid control is seen in Millais' representation of the mouse, moved from behind the wainscot to scurry across the floor, whose squeaking is heard with such intense clarity by Tennyson's Mariana as to become a shriek (lines 63–64). The autumn leaves blown through the open window evoke the decay entering the interior space of the "dreamy house" (line 61) that is her

134 Victorian masculinities

Plate 7 J. E. Millais, *Mariana*.

mind. Within the binary represented in both Tennyson's and Millais' *Mariana*, as in Carlyle, the opposite of manliness is madness, male hysteria.

Millais, then, could not accept the Carlylean belief that the sexually repressed life figured by the cloister could bring order and health to the psyche. His early *Disentombment of Queen Matilda* (1849) (plate 8) serves as a reply to the disentombment of St. Edmund in *Past*

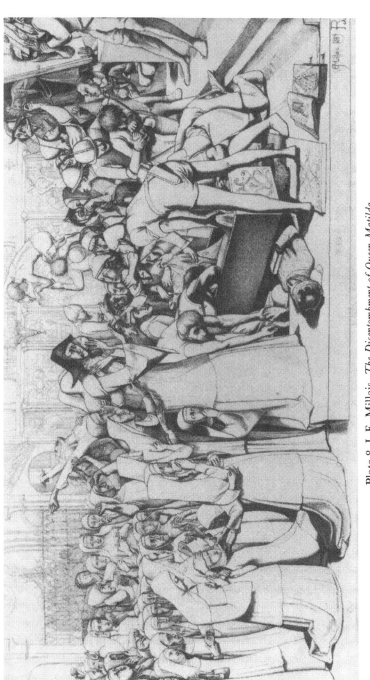

Plate 8 J. E. Millais, *The Disentombment of Queen Matilda*.

Plate 9 Holman Hunt, *Claudio and Isabella*.

and Present. Rather than bringing communal health, opening the casket releases the sealed energy of the nuns, who erupt in delirium, disrupting the orderliness of their ranks. The mental disorder ranges from mild agitation, to fear, to fainting, to the fusion of spiritual and sexual ecstasy, reminiscent of the conventional figure of St. Theresa, shown by the elevated nun at the left-center of the composition.

The fantasy of the immured woman awaiting the liberating penetration of male sexual desire accounts for the appeal to these young men of *Measure for Measure*, a play that in moving between the extremes of sexual control and sexual license appeared to the Brothers to engage the central problematic of Victorian masculinity, the regulation of sexuality. Millais' *Mariana* sets the Christian virtue of chastity against the sexualized female body. Hunt's *Claudio and Isabella* (1853) (plate 9) turns upon the failure of male sexual self-discipline. In this painting, the unmanliness of Claudio lies in the obsessive quality of his love, a failure to attain manly reserve that is registered in the fevered gleam in his eyes as he turns from the light. Although Hunt intended a sharp moral contrast between Claudio and his sister, this moralistic opposition is subverted. Within monastic discourse, the female as nun presents an equally debilitating extreme of sexual management, total sexual abstinence. And the painting presents not the clear contrast between good and evil, but the unresolved problematics of managing desire.[16]

Collins' *Convent Thoughts* (plate 10) also presents the Brotherhood trope of imprisoned virgin as surrogate for the young male artist in a scene that inscribes specific issues of early Victorian artistic manhood. Characteristically, the chaste figure conflates the sexual and the artistic. The nun has turned from contemplating the lily, the sign of virginity, to the daisy, the flower of love. The wall against which she is set is the courtship wall, associated with erotic fulfillment that she will never enjoy. As allegorical figure for the artist, the nun turns from the illuminated missal to contemplate the details of the natural world present even in her enclosed garden, much as Lippo turns from stylized medieval iconography to the details of the material world and the Brothers from idealized Raphaelite art to close observation of natural fact. Like the Unknown Painter as feminized artist, the female celibate figures erotic longing conflated with artistic longing. Desire that cannot be satisfied, impotence in art and in life is here inscribed on the female rather than the male body.

As much as the Pre-Raphaelites identified with the captive woman,

Plate 10 Charles Collins, *Convent Thoughts*.

Artistic manhood

they also adopted the subject position of the male rescuer. If the trope of imprisonment expressed the Brothers' fear of feminization through isolation from sexuality and from the male sphere, the narrative of rescue, the traditional masculine fantasy that differentiates the rescuer from the rescued, the dominant male from the vulnerable female, figured artistic manliness in its positive form. In the Brotherhood period, Hunt painted *The flight of Madeline and Porphyro during the drunkenness attending the revelry* (*Eve of St. Agnes*) (1848) and *Valentine rescuing Sylvia from Proteus* (1851). Millais' *The Rescue* (1855) (plate 12) marks his post-Brotherhood move toward representing in art the values of normative Victorian manliness. And even Rossetti took on this theme in *Found* (begun in 1853) in which the stalwart youth literally and metaphorically lifts the fallen female.

But it was Rossetti, in keeping with his complex relation to hegemonic Victorian masculinity, who alone among the Brotherhood employed the feminine as a positive icon for the male artist, who sought to show not the danger of feminization, but rather the need to incorporate into artistic manhood those qualities the age marked as female. As early as the essay "Hand and Soul" in *The Germ*, Rossetti looked to an ideal of the artist more androgynous than masculine. Chiaro dell' Erma is virile if not downright macho, "well-favoured and very manly in his walking; and, seeing his face in front, there was a glory upon it, as upon the face of one who feels a light round his hair" (159). But if Browning provides the equally sexy Lippo with a muse in Lucy to dissociate female qualities from the masculine artist, Rossetti bestows upon his ideal masculine artist the vision of a female who is "an image, Chiaro, of thine own soul within thee" (166), "the fair woman, that was his soul" (167). If the wisdom that this female figure passes on is to "work from thine own heart" (168), the heart is female. Her guidance is "paint me thus, as I am, to know me" (168). Chiaro's painting of his own self, of the essence of the male artist, is as "the figure of a woman, clad to the hands and feet with a green and gray raiment, chaste and early in its fashion... her hands are held together lightly, and her eyes set earnestly open" (170).

That Rossetti did not paint this figure, but only represented it through language is unfortunate. Such a figure would have been a striking exception to the visual iconography of early Victorian male artists and poets for whom the female figure as sign of the male artist signified not calmness, moral endeavor, stability, but rather the feminine qualities of powerlessness, isolation, madness that, as the later life of Rossetti suggests, threatened the male who withdrew from the sphere of aggressive commercial life and rational masculine knowledge for the career of poet or artist.

GENTLEMAN, PROPHET, BOHEMIAN: STYLES OF ARTISTIC MANHOOD

Within the master narrative of the masculine poetic, the Brotherhood period takes its shape as a time of passage during which these young men worked toward achieving artistic manhood. And the art of these years inscribes this process of masculinization – creating a visual style that incorporates the values of entrepreneurial manliness, reconciling ascetic Christianity with bourgeois manhood in the representation of a celibate Jesus, finding a mode of managing male desire that ensures creative potency and artistic productivity.

If in their youth the Brothers exhibited a diversity of attitudes in their practice, particularly in regard to the "female," in their adult lives, that is, in post-Brotherhood times, these differences intensified. Indeed, the differences in practice, style, and career path of the Brothers after the dissolution of the Brotherhood demonstrate again that rather than any single socially defined model there existed a range of competing possibilities for constructing a manly life as an artist in Victorian England. And yet, for all this diversity, the drive to be manly, to define the artistic endeavor in gendered terms, to differentiate the male self from the female and from the effeminate powers these disparate self-fashionings. The post-Brotherhood work of each artist inscribes this drive toward manliness as well as the losses and gains, the psychic tensions, the unresolved contradictions within each distinct formation of artistic manhood.

The crucial historical fact, of course, is that after five years the Brotherhood disbanded. This dissolution is overdetermined, and the multiple causes of what appears in retrospect an inevitable event point to specific issues of male artistic identity in these decades.

The Pre-Raphaelite Brotherhood exemplifies the attraction, the centrality, the necessity of the homosocial group in early Victorian artistic practice. Certainly, the bonded group provided intense male–male affective ties. William Michael Rossetti speaks of the "intimate friendly relations necessary bet[ween] all P.R.B.s" (Fredeman *P.R.B. Journal* 78) and his journals show the force of these male–male bonds played out in the intense concern with inclusion and exclusion, with who will be admitted and who rejected from the mysterious all-male circle. Such masculine bonds were crucial in providing emotional support for those engaged in a career whose very nature excluded them from the male sphere. This community of male artists, a "Priesthood" in Carlyle's terms (*Heroes* 385), becomes both oppositional to the hegemonic male sphere and yet its very image through the occupation with communicating masculine wisdom, excluding the female, and bonding through shared labor.

The need for such artistic communities fashioned on the monastic model of deeply bonded men and devoted to the new religion of art remained strong through the century, as seen in the continued revival of the homosocial pattern of the Brotherhood. When as Oxford undergraduates William Morris and Edward Burne-Jones sought an artistic career, a decision that for each meant rejecting socially accepted paths toward manhood, a career in commerce or the Church respectively, they saw themselves as entering a secular monastic order devoted to art. At college, they formed an intense homosocial if not homoerotic attachment to the stronger, older male, Rossetti, then at work on the Oxford murals. The attraction was strengthened by Rossetti's reciprocal longing to recreate the intense male–male ties of the first Brotherhood in bonding in a second Brotherhood with Morris and Burne-Jones. For Rossetti, who contemporary critics too easily see only in terms of a heterosexual desire signified in his objectification of the female,[17] such masculine bonding was crucial to his identity and a restrained homoeroticism central to his personality. Burne-Jones became the model for the head of the erotically attractive Jesus in *Mary Magdalene at the Door of Simon the Pharisee* (plate 6). The later relations between Rossetti and Morris form an erotic triangle where the central dynamic is less heterosexual desire acted out through marital infidelity than the intense attraction between the two men continued through the body of Jane Morris.[18]

The homosocial life of Rossetti, in the first and second Brotherhoods and in the later circle that included Swinburne, did move into the troubled boundary area with the homoerotic, and this tension is manifested in his art. In his post-Brotherhood stained-glass design of "St. George and the Dragon" (1861–62) (plate 11), the scene of the male hero locked in battle with the dragon, with Angelica set at the periphery, enacts the homoerotic triangle of two males joining over the passive body of the woman. Here, the male figures of dragon and hero displaced into the world of heroic legend suggest the proscribed

Plate 11 D. G. Rossetti, *The Story of St. George and the Dragon: St. George and the Dragon*.

realm of same-sex erotics. We might recall that in "Goblin Market" Christina Rossetti registered same-sex female desire in an equally fantastic world. St. George thrusts his phallic spear into the dragon's throat and pushes his arm into the orifice of the dragon's mouth. The dragon is equally phallic, its tail locked around St. George in a fierce embrace, with its barbed end suggestively enclosing the genitals of the male hero.[19]

Although to Dickens and other early critics, communal male life registered under the sign of monasticism appeared effeminate through its contingent association with the celibate monasticism of the Tractarians, the primary object of nascent homophobia at mid-century, the Brotherhood followed traditional modes of regulating male–male affection so as not to step over the line into homosexuality. In clear distinction to the Tractarians, the Brotherhood solidified its homosocial ties through trade in the bodies of women. In a fashion strikingly similar to the relation of Tennyson to Hallam, Rossetti offered James Collinson his sister in marriage in order to strengthen the masculine ties of the band. William Michael recalled that when

Collinson, "about the time of the formation of the P.R.B., was introduced to Christina, then aged seventeen, in our family circle, and he immediately fell in love with her ... [Collinson] explained his feelings to Dante Gabriel, who ... represented the matter to Christina and advocated Collinson's cause." But even William Michael, noting that his sister was "in breeding and tone of mind, not to speak of actual genius or advantages of person ... markedly [Collinson's] superior" observed that this sacrifice of a sister was proposed "with perhaps too headlong a wish to serve the interests of a 'Præraphaelite Brother'" (*Some Reminiscences* 1: 72).[20]

Yet, by the mid-nineteenth century, the very notion of a Brotherhood, of an unmarried group of men engaged in communal work, acceptable at other historical moments, especially when displaced into the monastic society of the middle ages, became within the gender anxieties of the time extremely problematic and the difficulty of sustaining such a structure in Victorian England overwhelming. Primarily, such secular Brotherhoods modeled as artistic monastic orders could not be maintained into adult life in the mid-nineteenth century because such formations violate the script for achieving bourgeois manhood. To become a man, the male must move from the homosocial, diffusely homoerotic world of adolescence into the adult world of compulsory heterosexuality, which for the Victorians meant marrying and assuming the role of breadwinner. In literature, this problematic of bourgeois masculinity is played out in the conflict between the masculine plot and the marriage plot, in the ambiguity in Marryat between a vigorous life at sea and a land-locked life in marriage, in the contradiction between Carlylean industrial manhood within a male community and the pressure to marry for the Captains of Industry of *North and South* and *Hard Times*, in the antithesis between artistic potency and marriage in Browning's artist-poems, and, to take another example, the tension in the closure of *In Memoriam* between the vision of a male marriage in heaven and an epithalamium for a heterosexual marriage on earth.

In their lives as men as in their art, the Brothers play out this same opposition between the masculine plot and the marriage plot. For Millais, Hunt, and Rossetti, the dissolution of the Brotherhood becomes the rite of passage to artistic manhood as the Brothers leave behind the masculine bonding of youth. But, if this disbanding becomes their moment of initiation, society offers no single clear model of artistic manhood to replace the earlier homosocial formation. And yet, although they vary in the ways they renounce or revive the youthful homosocial world, the all-male communal life of the Brotherhood, that moment in the past continues as the emotional center of their lives, an all-male Eden from which they have been forever excluded.

Millais has exemplified for his own age and for those who came after the strategy of achieving artistic manhood by rejecting youthful homosociality and an oppositional art for the total merging or submerging of self into the hegemonic formation of middle-class masculinity defined by marriage and commercial success. By 1855, two years after the Brotherhood dissolved, Millais had established himself as artist within the classic pattern of bourgeois manhood. He had married, had his first child, and created an establishment consisting of homes in Scotland and London as well as a studio, a workplace as male sphere separate from the home. This pattern was to continue with a grand mansion built in Kensington, a grand hunting and fishing lodge in Scotland, and seven more children, all supported by his work as a painter.

The Rescue (1855) (plate 12), painted soon after the dissolution of the Brotherhood, is continuous with the masculine rescue fantasies of Hunt and Rossetti. But Millais here rejects an historical or literary subject for a modern subject as if to signify his passage to manhood as his movement from youthful dreaming to valorizing manly activities in the real world of the present day. Yet Millais' heroic exemplar of contemporary manliness emerges not from the entrepreneurial, but from the warrior construction of masculinity. He said of his intention for this painting, "Soldiers and sailors have been praised on canvas a thousand times. My next picture will be of a fireman" (John Guile Millais *Life and Letters* 1: 248). And this purpose was noted in the reviewers' admiration of *The Rescue* for its Carlylean transmutation of this pre-industrial formation of masculinity into the heroism of modern-day life: "A figure booted and helmeted is descending a staircase, laden with a rich prize – none of your knights of chivalry, none of your free lances, but a hero of this nineteenth century – a soldier of the fire brigade" (Codell "Sentiment"). The composition reinforces a patriarchal order justified by male muscularity and courage. The square-jawed fireman's bulk dominates the foreground as he receives the gratitude of the passive kneeling female.

But the bravery and physical strength heroicized here is identified not with the masculinity of the professional or commercial classes, but

Artistic manhood

Plate 12 J. E. Millais, *The Rescue*.

with the working-class. Victorian firemen were mostly former Thames watermen (Cooper "Millais's *The Rescue*" 478). *The Rescue*, then, represents the same formation of working-class manliness as physicality that is admired and envied from a distance and across the divide of class in Brown's *Work* and in the celebration of physical labor in Carlyle and Ruskin. The Victorian idealization of muscular work and bodily courage exemplified here is a class-bound male fantasy of masculinity addressed to a predominantly middle-class audience imaginatively experiencing a form of manly muscularity and warrior courage denied them in their work lives within a commercial society and to which they respond with the vicarious delight of contemporary American men watching professional football on Sunday afternoon.

Although set in the home rather than the factory, the painting also provides a personification of the early Victorian formation of industrial manhood. Throughout Carlyle and in Pater's "Conclusion" the new industrial man is a "fire-man" as the industrial management of potentially destructive fire is metaphorically equated with the self-control of potentially destructive male energy. In the essay, "The Fire Brigade of London" in *Household Words* of 1850, Richard Horne praises the "fireman" through the Carlylean paradox of "fire, the chief friend of man in creations of nature and industrial art, yet the most potent of all enemies of destruction ... the most frightful and appalling when once it obtains dominion over man and man's abodes" (Cooper 478). *The Athenæum* reviewer of *The Rescue* imaginatively connects manly self-discipline with the harnessing of fire to the productive work of the English iron and coal economy. The fireman is "thoroughly English, cool, determined and self-reliant ... resolute, manly, strong as iron, like one accustomed to pass through fire" (Cooper 479).

Fire is also a recurrent Victorian trope for sexualized male desire in its many manifestations, as in Browning's "blue spurt of a lighted match" ("Meeting at Night") and Pater's "hard gem-like flame." Rescue as a dream of bourgeois manliness resonates with the erotic fantasies of Victorian men. More specifically, the Victorian rescue plot includes an element of sadism, of violence against women that is contained by the implied final deliverance of the female by the male.[21] Here the narrative indicates the mental torture of the woman scantily clad in her nightgown, a pain that is a necessary part of the eroticized climax as the woman kneels before the sexually powerful

Artistic manhood 147

Plate 13 J. E. Millais, *The Knight Errant*.

male. This male fantasy of female suffering as intensifying female sexuality was shared by the male viewers. One critic, noting that "it is a sorry sight to see that filthy hose trailing over the woven flowers of the carpet," described the woman within traditional visual conventions of female orgasm to contrast the feminine flood of feeling to the manly reserve of the hero: "The thin lip tightly pressed against the half-shown teeth, the hectic crimson of the cheek, the wild eye, show that in her breast, the agony of maternal terror has just changed into the ecstasy of joy over her rescued darlings" (Codell "Sentiment"). Another critic wrote of the woman as being "wild with tenderness" and William Michael Rossetti described her as expressing "an ecstatic joy that floods every pulse of her being – parts her panting lips, and lights up her azure eyes like cressets" (Cooper "Millais's *The Rescue*" 479).

This same mix of sexualized violence and manly control informs a later rescue fantasy by Millais, *The Knight Errant* of 1870 (plate 13). Here the heroic knight, having killed the naked woman's captor, cuts the ropes that bind her to the tree. Although to the modern viewer, this painting appears as a weakly moralized male fantasy of sadism, to the Victorians the scene exemplifies manliness achieved as the self-regulation of sexuality. As in "Childe Roland," the physical action of battle is suggested rather than portrayed in order to internalize the drama of manliness. The blood-stained sword of the knight limns his own desire to deflower the bound woman, but his manliness as self-discipline is signified by his turning the sword, the sign of phallic male energy, to the moralized purpose of freeing the female. The iron body armor of the knight as opposed to the bare flesh of the female nicely literalizes the need, proclaimed by Carlyle, for psychic armor to protect the male from the sexual contagion of the female and to contain the powerful, potentially destructive force of male sexuality.[22]

For all Millais' legendary status of Victorian artist as entrepreneurial man, his post-Brotherhood work inscribes an anxiety and an uncertainty about reconciling bourgeois manliness with artistic manhood. Given the pervasiveness of the trope of escape from imprisonment within the masculine aesthetic, the liberation from jail in *The Order of Release*, 1746 (1853) (plate 14), particularly given the autobiographical context of his love for Effie Gray, the model for the wife, indicates his own achievement of artistic manhood. Painted in the year the Brotherhood disbanded, the painting marks Millais' renunciation of his homosocial youth and his entry into a bourgeois manhood signified by supportive wife, lovely child, and loyal dog.

And yet the painting also suggests the same uneasiness about marriage and the breadwinner role that appears in Carlyle and Browning. In 1856, Millais wrote to Hunt, "I have more than my

Artistic manhood

Plate 14 J. E. Millais, *The Order of Release, 1746*.

own mouth to fill now, and I work, when otherwise [as a bachelor] I never should have thought of it" (Pointon "Matrimony" 104). The masculine pattern of *The Rescue* and of other Brotherhood fantasies of rescue are here inverted. In this painting, an heroic woman liberates a weakened male. Rather than escaping into virility, as does Lippo, in reuniting with his family the man becomes feminized and, as the bandaged right arm suggests, emasculated. His head bowed, he leans for support on the wife's shoulder. That his face is partly hidden, his eyes wholly in shadow suggests that for the Victorians a man expressing intense emotion was so inconsistent with the norm of manly reserve as to be non-narratable, outside visual conventions. The crying man, the figure so central to debates about masculinity in our own time, is here suggested, but hidden in darkness. Although by the mid-nineteenth century the kilt had become associated with Highlander warrior heroism within the newly invented tradition of the tartan, in this historical allegory of male liberation as entry into married life, the man also wears a skirt.

The ambivalence about marriage, the sense of domestic life as a new form of imprisonment deadly to the male that runs through early Victorian masculine discourse is also present in Millais' work of the Brotherhood period.[23] In *Lorenzo and Isabella* (1849) (plate 15) the domestic unit, the family sitting at table appears "as the inverse of the family conviviality of hearth and home" (Pointon "Matrimony" 113), as uncaring and as murderous. Romantic love is set in opposition to marriage.

Lorenzo and Isabella also suggests, like the contemporaneous "Fra Lippo Lippi," the dilemma of the Victorian male artist within a commercial society – the masculine world of commerce is based on a ruthless acquisitiveness hostile to art and yet repudiation of the male sphere feminizes the artist.[24] Like the Medici palace, this house, as Keats' "Isabella," the source of the painting, makes clear, is the analogue of the nineteenth-century commercial world in being built on the exploitation of industrial workers. The original painting was accompanied by a passage from the poem describing the brothers' plan to use Lorenzo as "the servant of their trade designs" and their ambition to use Isabella as an instrument for commercial gain, "'twas their plan to coax her by degrees/ To some high noble, and his olive trees." Given the valorization in Millais' later work, such as *The North-West Passage* (1874), of the Victorian association of industry and empire with manliness, it is noteworthy that this Brotherhood

Plate 15 J. E. Millais, *Lorenzo and Isabella*.

work illustrates a poem in which evil is figured in the exploitation of both factory workers, "for them many a weary hand did swelt/ In torched mines and noisy factories" (lines 159–60), and of colonized peoples:

> For them the Ceylon diver held his breath,
> And went all naked to the hungry shark;
> For them his ears gush'd blood.   (lines 165–67)

Millais here associates commercial and imperial activities with ruthless masculinist values, with an aggressiveness limned in the foregrounded leg kicking the dog and the harsh cracking of the nut, with the antipathy of the brothers to the loving couple. In contrast to the modeled muscularity of the outstretched leg and the bearded face of the brother in the left foreground, Lorenzo's figure is feminized, his body concealed, his face smooth. Lorenzo's activity is emotive, relational, sexualized, as opposed to the calculating mercantile cruelty of the brothers. And his face is modeled on that of Keats (Codell "Dilemma" 55–56), the early Victorian exemplar of the feminization of the artist within a hostile commercial world.[25]

In its resonance with the Victorian construction of Keats as the exemplary feminized poet, the painting represents the familiar dilemma of the early Victorian male artist. A man may reject the rapaciousness of the male sphere, but within a severely binary discourse of gender, such isolation from manly activities brings softness, feminization. For Millais at the time of the painting, this dilemma was particularly acute as he was trying to attain artistic manhood by moving beyond economic dependence on his parents, a problem that is here displaced into the economic situation of Lorenzo. Furthermore, his Oedipal hostility toward his father and to the patriarchal system exemplified in the Royal Academy is displaced from the father to the brothers. But if the painting as narrative follows the masculine plot in representing the movement toward artistic manhood as freedom from family, the contradictions facing the artist are not here reconciled. As in "The Lady of Shalott," the choice between the emotionally destructive commerce of the male sphere and a feminized isolation marked by unfulfilled sexual desire cannot be resolved. As in Tennyson's early poetry, the resolution is achieved only in the death of an artist removed from the male sphere. In Hunt's later illustration of this poem, *Isabella and the Pot of Basil* (1868), the buried head of the murdered Lorenzo, like the dead body of the Lady of Shalott, continues to disturb the palace of commerce.

In his post-Brotherhood career, Millais refuted the possibilities of feminization and artistic vitiation through the careful fashioning of his public persona. The creation of such a persona, the manufacture of what we now call a media image, was crucial to the career of the Victorian artist. The Brotherhood itself was a form of "open secret." Then as now self-advertising through a putative secrecy intensified public interest. In later life, too, the Brothers continued to devote a good deal of effort to shaping themselves as celebrities, even transforming their oppositional qualities into the form of the commodity, as did Oscar Wilde at the end of the century.[26] In post-Brotherhood years, it often became impossible to distinguish between the commercial value of the product and of the artist. One spoke of buying a "Rossetti," a "Millais," or a "Holman Hunt."

Millais' post-Brotherhood public image has taken shape as that of the artist as entrepreneurial man, the independent producer of commodities for sale on the art market. The appropriation of *Bubbles* as the Pears soap emblem has come to exemplify the commodification of visual art in Victorian England, particularly for the supposed lowering of high art by incorporation into the base world of advertising. The opposition between such mercantile practice and an authentic, that is, oppositional art career is encapsulated in the modern phrase so easily applied to Millais, "selling out." But rather than seeing Millais as seller of commodities, it is more accurate to see him, like contemporary writers such as Dickens, as attempting to incorporate art production into a new, highly valorized construction of masculinity in the nineteenth century, the professional man.

For the doctor or lawyer, as for the novelist and painter, the social formation of professional man resolved specific contradictions of nineteenth-century manhood by reconciling the demand to follow a morally valued calling with the imperative of achieving the financial success that defined bourgeois manliness.[27] For the visual artist particularly, professionalization addressed the problematic that so troubled Smiles, the opposition between painting as the outpouring of natural genius and painting as a form of diligent labor validated by commercial success. Setting the achievement of artistic manhood within the formation of professional man enabled the artist to maintain the sense that he is not painting solely for money but following the demands of a calling, while also allowing him to attain bourgeois manliness marked by wealth and social position, specifically the class position of gentleman. Feltes notes, "These two

Plate 16 J. E. Millais at Dalguise, Scotland.

dimensions, the antithetical ideological structures of labor monopoly and vocational commitment, fuse in the professional project to form 'the specifically bourgeois economic ethic,' generating tensions not only for the profession as a whole but for the individual professional" (*Modes of Production* 43). In the Royal Academy, the exemplar of such monopolization in the arts and an institution of which Millais was elected President, as well as in later nineteenth-century professional societies of artists this tension was addressed through a division of labor in which a secretary, but never the artist, handled the commercial transactions.[28]

The merging of the artist as professional with the artist as gentleman generated yet another set of contradictions, familiar to readers of Victorian novels. The ideal of gentleman revives the gentry model, the idle aristocracy in Carlyle's typology of Victorian manhood that equates manliness with transcending the need to work. The contradiction in the construction of the Victorian gentleman as a man who is simultaneously bound by the work ethic and yet aspires to rise above a life of labor informs the literature of the period. We can think here of Pip and the Finches of the Grove. The visual artist as gentleman publicly rejects the Smilesean aesthetic of hard work that powered the Brotherhood because such work, although laudable in working-class men digging a ditch in Hampstead, is not compatible with the class position of gentleman.

As artistic celebrity, Millais presented himself as both professional and as gentleman, quite forcefully adopting the gentry model of manhood in his public persona. In the carefully controlled self-representation set in Scotland (plate 16), he poses as county gentry, as hunter/fisherman rather than as brain-worker, and certainly not as art-worker. He sits by a phallic column, several long staffs in his lap, a large salmon at his feet. Such trophies testify to his male energy and imply sexual potency, but such potency is manifested in this self-presentation in the traditional pre-bourgeois life of man as hunter, rather than associated with the practice of art, which by its erasure is associated with the feminine.

Even posed in his studio in Palace Gate (plate 17) at the scene of artistic labor, Millais has not removed the deerstalker worn on the moors as if to equate his hunting prowess with his artistic prowess by bringing into the studio the traditional pre-industrial sign of virility. And yet what remains erased in Millais' very individual construction of artist manhood, notable by its absence, is any connection of such virility with artistic work. This is not a representation of the painter painting. There is no reference to the labor of the artist. The photo has a studied indeterminacy. We do not know whether it represents the professional artist resting from his labors or a gentleman with his collection resting after a bracing walk outdoors. Millais sits on one

156 Victorian masculinities

Plate 17 J. E. Millais in his studio at Palace Gate.

side of the room reading. On the other side are easels prominently displaying, among other paintings, *Bubbles*. In the background are an ornate mantel and fireplace decorated with expensive vases, signifiers of the fusion of wealth with artistic taste. The artist as producer and the artist as consumer are here conflated. The vacant space at the center signifies the unbridged gulf in Millais' artistic manhood between gentlemanly respectability and the practice of art. Within the commodity fetishism of the age, the work of art becomes valuable as a signifier of wealth while the labor that produces the object remains repressed.

In this self-presentation, the prominent placement of *Bubbles* testifies to Millais' fusion of the artist as gentleman with the artist as professional man. *Bubbles* exemplifies the transformation of a painting into what has come to be termed in Victorian publishing a "commodity-text," a mode of artistic production inextricably linked to the formation of the writer and of the artist as professional man.[29] Within the nineteenth-century art market, the value of the painting as "commodity-text" lies not in its worth as a material object for sale, but rather in the rights to the painting, the copyright that Millais sold not only for reproductions but also, quite famously, for a soap advertisement. That the painting as physical object remains within his studio signifies Millais' manly control over his own work, the absence of the alienation from the products of his own labor that Browning represents as emasculating Lippo as emergent capitalist artist. Millais' ownership of *Bubbles* signals his distance from the merely entrepreneurial, the petty bourgeois economic activity of selling objects that occupies a low position within bourgeois life.

As fervently as Hunt fashioned the role of artist as Carlylean prophet, he also treated his paintings as commodity-texts. In post-Brotherhood years he was less occupied with the sale of his works as individual commodities than with the more lucrative sale of the rights to reproduce as well as to view such paintings as *The Light of the World*.[30] Only Rossetti, whose later practice veered the most sharply from bourgeois masculinity, did not participate in the practice of treating his paintings as commodity-texts. Instead, as if imitating a pre-capitalist mode of production, he treated his works as hand-crafted material commodities, readily painting new versions himself as in the case of *The Blessed Damozel*, rather than adopting the more professional mode of selling to others the right to mechanical reproduction.

For Millais, then, artistic manhood as professional manhood is manifested in control over one's artistic labor and in effacing the artistic labor itself by fashioning the self within the traditional model of non-working gentry. Artistic manhood achieved as professional man turned hunting and fishing country gentleman avoids the anxiety about the feminization of the artist represented in *Lorenzo and Isabella*. But Millais' later construction of artistic manhood does carry a cost. As for any successful Victorian businessman refashioned as country squire, the source of wealth in labor, in Millais' case the practice of art, remains an open secret, unspoken, out of sight, suppressed and thereby devalued.

With the growth of the art market in the 1840s, painting had been established as a career track along which men could travel upward to the status of gentleman.[31] Encouraged by others who recognized the boy's precocious talents, Millais' well-to-do parents had determinedly set him on this path along which he moved, except for the byway of the Brotherhood, with stunning speed and exemplary success.

They provided early schooling in art, traveled with him to London to supervise his advanced art training there, pulled strings to gain their son's early admission to the Royal Academy.

In contrast, Hunt's early career might have provided an illustration for Smiles' gallery of the artist as self-made man. His father, a warehouse manager, opposed his son's artistic efforts, forcing the young Hunt into the petty bourgeois business world. Through the strength of his own will, in his teens Hunt rejected the clerk's stool for the artist's easel. While a clerk, Hunt exhibited that same diligent labor Smiles attributed to Leonardo and Michelangelo. Largely self-taught, though assisted by classes taken after work, Hunt industriously developed his technical skill, finally providing proof of his acquired technical expertise with a portrait of 1843 called *Old Hannah*. As in the Smilesean narrative, this demonstration of artistic competence persuaded his father to free him from the warehouse to pursue his career as an artist. In the Brotherhood, Hunt found in intimate bonding with other males that support for the manliness of his self-chosen career as artist that he could find neither in his family nor in the larger society.

With the dissolving of the Brotherhood, Hunt had no wish to return to the mercantile world he had renounced nor to embrace the role of professional man with its deep involvement in the world of commerce. Alone of the Brothers, Hunt continued what he saw as the sacralized vocation of the Brotherhood as monastic order. Like Browning, he sought to fashion a forceful manly religious art for his own age. In this post-Brotherhood quest, Hunt adopted another powerful form of artistic manhood available to the mid-century artist/poet, the public role of prophet, a formation exemplified for him by Carlyle. In describing his own carte-de-visite (plate 18), Hunt self-consciously noted that it "is unfortunate in its plagiarism of the Carlyle pose" (plate 19) (Maas, *Art World* 103). In his post-Brotherhood career Hunt develops "the Carlyle pose" to become the Hero as Man of Art. Situating artistic practice in the zone of the sacred separates such labor from the male sphere of commerce and from middle-class respectability. And yet the formation of artist as prophet avoids imputations of feminization and of effeminacy by locating an art career within a preserve closed to women. Furthermore, in the post-Brotherhood years, Hunt accentuated the manliness of this role as prophet in several ways – by continuing the manly visual style of a mimetic accuracy achieved through the hard

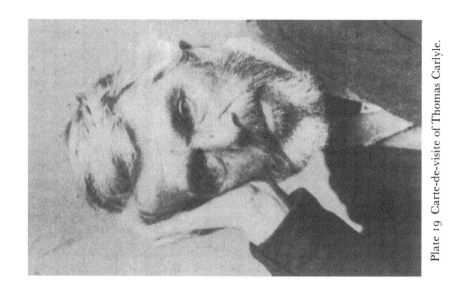

Plate 19 Carte-de-visite of Thomas Carlyle.

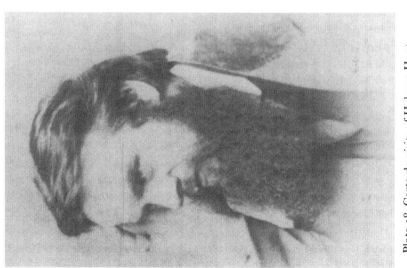

Plate 18 Carte-de-visite of Holman Hunt.

work of diligent observation, by engaging in a very public performance of braving physical danger at the outposts of empire in order to produce sacred art, by selling the rights to sacred paintings for large sums of money.

The Light of the World (plate 5), painted during the dissolution of the Brotherhood, like Millais' *The Order of Release*, inscribes the passage to artistic manhood as the renunciation of youthful homosocial society. Here, Hunt inscribes his adult role of artist as solitary prophet. Carrying the lantern of truth as He knocks on the closed door of Victorian religious sensibilities, this Christ becomes the emblem of Hunt's vision of his own artistic manhood as constructed within the Carlylean notion of the hero as manly artist. As in Carlyle's theorizing of the masculine aesthetic, the manliness of the artist is represented within a typological sense of the modern male hero fulfilling in his own age the masculine heroism figured in the biblical narrative, more specifically for Hunt in the Life of Christ. Unlike Rossetti's Christ, whose eye-beams are entangled with those of Mary Magdalene, or even Millais' Christ as boy within the domestic sphere, Hunt's Christ, like Hunt himself in his later years, evokes the manliness of the adventurer who, having rejected family and hearth, moves on a dangerous journey at the margins of the bourgeois world.

Although conceived to valorize his own artistic mission, this representation of the Carlylean heroism of the artist-priest is vitiated by the gender instability that, as his difficulty in selecting models indicates, vexed Hunt's conception of the adult Jesus. In a letter to *The Times* in 1854, Ruskin, feeling the uncertain gendering of the work, described "the light which proceeds from the head of the figure" as "full of softness... yet so powerful" (Maas *Hunt* 63). Even Carlyle, Hunt's exemplar, on visiting the artist's studio saw in the painting only its divergence from a manliness of style identified with facticity and historical accuracy. In the same fevered tone of Dickens, Kingsley, and *The Athenæum* describing symptoms of unmanliness in contemporary religious art, his anti-Catholicism overriding his usual valorization of the artist as priest, Carlyle draws on the psycho-sexual theory of mimesis to link priestly celibacy with distorted perception of the male body:

It is a poor *misshaped presentation* of the noblest, the *brotherliest*, and the most heroic-minded Being that ever walked God's earth... You should think frankly of His antique heroic soul, if you realised His character at all you wouldn't try to make people go back and worship the *image that the priests have invented of Him*, to keep men's silly souls in meshes of slavery and darkness... this is only empty make-believe, mere pretended fancy, to do the like of *which is the worst of occupations for a man to take to*. (Hunt *Pre-Raphaelitism* 1: 355–56, emphasis added)

Like his Brotherhood colleagues, unable successfully to represent the figure of Christ as a visual icon of artistic manhood, Hunt turned instead to acting-out sacralized artistic manliness in his practice through a very public form of Victorian performance art imitating the Life of Christ. In 1854 Hunt embarked on the first of four trips to the Holy Land, where he was to paint such works as *The Scapegoat* (1856) and *The Finding of the Saviour in the Temple* (1860). As acts of painting, these journeys replicate or fulfill in modern time the dangerous quests of the biblical prophets and of Jesus into the wilderness in the search for spiritual truth. But rather than shaping these acts of artist as prophet and as imitator of Christ in opposition to the dominant Victorian discourse of manliness, Hunt gives this practice a particularly manly inflection. Hunt fashioned his own form of artistic manhood within the typological construction of artist as modern prophet, but he defined the contemporary artist as prophet within the masculine ethos of nineteenth-century imperialism and the perceptual model of Orientalism. Not for Hunt the asceticism and spirituality associated with the Tractarians, nor the early Christian practices as fasting and prayer associated with the unmanly revival of monasticism in Victorian England. In the Holy Land, Hunt adopted the same manly qualities of enterprise and courage celebrated in Millais' representations of Empire. As his adventures painting *The Scapegoat* by the Dead Sea illustrate, Hunt embraced decidedly muscular activities, braving the hostile landscape and subduing the natives by force of character and the threat of advanced weaponry. His account of the act of painting might have stepped out of any Victorian narrative of manly imperial questing:

I suspended my painting and looked from beneath my umbrella, until suddenly the *deeshman* emerged from behind the mountain within half a furlong of me where they all halted. The horsemen had their faces covered with black *kufeyiahs*, and carried long spears, while the footmen carried guns, swords, and clubs. They stood stock-still some minutes, pointing at my umbrella, and then turned out of the beaten way direct to me, clattering at a measured pace among the large and loose stones. I continued placidly conveying my paint from palette to canvas, steadying my touch by resting the hand on my double-barrelled gun. I knew that my whole chance depended upon the exhibition of utter unconcern, and I continued as steadily as if in my studio at home. (Hunt *Pre-Raphaelitism* 1: 490–91)

In his journey to the Dead Sea, the wildest and most primitive area of the Holy Land, in order to paint *The Scapegoat*, Hunt acts out in his own life a masculine plot, specifically the late nineteenth-century imperial quest romance as journey into the self exemplified in H. Rider Haggard's *She* and *King Solomon's Mines*. In search of wisdom, Hunt as male imperialist quester leaves a corrupted commercial England for what he perceives within the Orientalist discourse of his age as a timeless unmodernized land. There, freed from the danger of the female, Hunt formed an intimate although chaste relation to his faithful Arab companion that re-creates the masculine bonds of the Brotherhood and that moves to the very limits of the homosocial. Hunt's account of bonding with Soleiman, who accompanied him to the Dead Sea, places him within the line of such Englishmen as Richard Burton in the nineteenth century and T. E. Lawrence in the twentieth, who found in the "Orient" a wild zone beyond the compulsory heterosexuality of bourgeois masculinity:

We mounted and turned towards Oosdoom...As I rode ahead a young Arab of about twenty came up and kissed my hand, saying that he hoped I was not angry with him. I could not recognise him as an offender; his appeal, with an affectation of unblemished guilelessness, made me feel favourably towards him, and I asked his name. It was "Soleiman." Would I let him be my son? he asked. I agreed, although I was only seven years his senior. My prejudice did not prevent me from seeing that he had a pleasant face, and I could not retain my scowl when he asked my name. (Hunt *Pre-Raphaelitism* 1: 471–72)

Accompanied by this young man with "a pleasant face," meeting tests of courage, the manly artist finally reaches the source of wisdom, described by Hunt as a physical heart of darkness, as "black" liquidity. His account of this psychologized landscape resonates with Victorian male fantasies of the fluid, unclean interior of the male self, with seminal emission "in the hand slimy, and smarting as a sting":

The Sea is heaven's own blue like a diamond more lovely in a king's diadem than in the mines of the Indies, but as it gushes up through the broken ice – like salt on the beach, it is black, full of asphalt ocum – and in the hand slimy, and smarting as a sting. No one can stand and say it is not accursed of God. If in all there are sensible figures of men's secret deeds and thoughts, then is this the horrible figure of Sin – a vanished deceit – earth's joys at hand but Hell gaping behind, a stealthy, terrible enemy for ever. (Staley *Pre-Raphaelite Landscape* 68)

In this journey into the primal self, it is this knowledge of the chthonic male interior that the Carlylean artist as prophet brings back to his male audience in an art that by its shaping form demonstrates the artist's control over this innate maleness.

The practices of hard work, physical danger and masculine bonding exemplified in the painting of *The Scapegoat* were wholly consistent with the Brotherhood's artistic program of fashioning a masculine style, a program to which Hunt alone remained faithful. When applied in these Middle-Eastern expeditions to native customs such as the lighting of the sacred fire, to native fauna such as the goat by the Dead Sea, and to the geological features of the Dead Sea shore, the Brotherhood style of scientific accuracy achieved through manly labor and clear-eyed observation identifies the painter with the imperial project of explorers, ethnologists, naturalists, and geologists, firmly situating Hunt's artistic practice within the male sphere. Such painting creates a particularly masculine form of knowledge, knowledge of the material world, whose purpose is circulation among men. Ruskin noted that *The Scapegoat* provides documentary record of a "scene of which it might seem most desirable to give a perfect idea to those who cannot see it for themselves; it is that also which fewest travellers are able to see" (*Works* XIV: 62).

Hunt's artistic practice, then, reconciles the artist as prophet-hero with the script of imperial manliness. Like many Victorian imperialists, Hunt saw his time in the Orient as a form of investment.[32] In his autobiography Hunt tells of saying to Thackeray in conversation:

I must not allow you to assume that I have suddenly become a wealthy adventurer... Painting subject pictures... is an expensive profession, and after my experience of going to the East on a small capital, I feel obliged to postpone returning there for further work until I have a little money invested to bring me an income that will save me from daily fear that my means will be absorbed before my canvas has been turned into a picture. (*Pre-Raphaelitism* II: 194)

A letter to William Michael Rossetti of 1855 about painting *The Scapegoat* encapsulates Hunt's program of what might be called in Carlylean terms a religio-imperialist art. Here Hunt calls for a new, more manly mission for the Brotherhood in language that, like Hunt's enterprise itself, conflates the artistic, religious, colonial, scientific, and economic:

I have a notion that painters should go out, two by two, like *merchants* of nature, and bring home precious merchandize in faithful pictures of scenes interesting from historical consideration, or from the strangeness of the subject itself... it must be done by every painter and this *most religiously*, in fact, with something like *the spirit of the Apostles* fearing nothing... and every thing must be painted even the pebbles of the foreground from the place itself... I think this must be the next stage of PRB indoctrination... It has been this conviction which brought me out here, and which keeps me away in patience until the experiment has been fairly tried. (Bronkhurst "'An interesting series of adventures'" 123, emphasis added)

These journeys to the Holy Land, especially the act of painting in the remote desert, emerge as a particularly Victorian form of performance art. In reenacting in the nineteenth century the actions of Christ and the prophets, Hunt is attesting to the fusion of the masculine and the sacred in his mission as artist. As in contemporary performance art, the paintings, like the record of the act of production in his autobiography *Pre-Raphaelitism and the Pre-Raphaelite Brotherhood*, achieve significance as documentation of the act of creation. Much of the value and the meaning of the finished work would be lost without knowledge of the courage exhibited by the artist in its making. The representation of a doleful goat cannot be detached from knowledge of the hazards endured by the artist. Millais erases the work of art production to maintain his status as gentleman. Hunt documents the act of creation since the record of his practice testifies to the fusion of normative masculinity and religious purpose shown by the painter and manifested in the painting. As Rossetti's late paintings of women signify the sexual potency of the artist, Hunt's *Scapegoat* signifies a very different form of artistic manliness, a form that, like the activity of Abbot Samson and Lippo, fuses physicality and courage with patient attentiveness to the details of the material world in channeling male energy to sacred purpose.

The use of painting to testify to the manliness of the artist participates in the nineteenth-century fashioning of self into celebrity. Like his contemporary, Oscar Wilde, Hunt in his later years carefully shaped his ostensible difference from bourgeois manliness into a source of monetary value. His artistic personality became a commodity that enhanced the material worth of his art. Toward the end of his life Hunt figured this sense of himself as prophet/imperialist, as exotic yet manly religious artist in a wonderful photograph taken not in the Holy Land, but in his own London backyard (plate 20). The photograph is part of Hunt's increased interest in these last years in

Artistic manhood 165

Plate 20 Holman Hunt reenacting the painting of *The Scapegoat*.

asserting for posterity the manliness of his art, an enterprise whose chief monument is his autobiography, *Pre-Raphaelitism and the Pre-Raphaelite Brotherhood*. For this apologia, Hunt reworked his journals to exclude such unmanly journal entries as "Heaven help me to escape from despair of the worth of my vocation" (Bronkhurst "'An interesting series of adventures'" 112) as well as to suppress his account of his disturbed dreams both before and during the expedition, so that the published work would, in Bronkhurst's words, "emphasize the artist's fearlessness in the face of the very real dangers he was to encounter on his expedition to the Dead Sea" (112).

If Millais' pose at his hunting lodge erases the source of his wealth and devalues the act of art production, Hunt's *œuvre* – paintings, autobiography, photographs – documents the Carlylean heroism of his practice. Here Hunt reenacts the incident recorded in his autobiography (quoted 161–62) in which with unflappable courage he continues to paint *The Scapegoat*, gun at the ready, when confronted by hostile Arabs. Hunt looks directly at the spectator in keeping with his own theatricalization and befitting his sense of himself as celebrity. His is an aggressive rather than contemplative pose, since such masculinized painting requires more courage than spiritual vision. His Middle-Eastern gown draped over the easel, head shielded from the burning sun of the Holy Land, watchful of hostile natives, brush in one hand, gun in the other, Hunt shapes himself into an emblem of his own manly fusion of sacred purpose, artistic energy and imperialist machismo. As Millais posed beside a large column, hands on crotch, several large staffs resting on the chair, so Hunt's pose with brush in one hand, long-barrel rifle hanging from the middle of his body suggests, as do the narratives of Abbot Samson and Lippo, the necessary fusion within a masculine aesthetic of artistic power and religious aspiration with phallic virility.

And yet this self-representation also embodies the unreconciled contradictions within Hunt's individual construction of artistic manhood. Of necessity a masculine poetic displaces manly action beyond the boundaries of industrial England, locating alternatives to bourgeois masculinity on shipboard, in medieval England, and in early Renaissance Florence. Hunt's life-long drive to return to the Middle East also suggests that his particular form of artistic manhood, the fusion of physical courage, scientific accuracy, and religious faith could be achieved only beyond the boundaries of bourgeois society. For only in the East imagined within the self-contradictions of Orientalism as transcending commerce and as the source of valuable commodities for extraction could Hunt reconcile the role of religious artist with the manly pursuits of exploration and exploitation. As his sense of the impossibility of maintaining this role of artist as manly prophet in Victorian Britain drove him obsessively back to the East throughout his later career, it also led him on his return to England into such male fantasies as recreating the Orient within his London garden.

It was Dante Gabriel Rossetti, however, who established in nineteenth-century England the mode of reconciling manliness and art practice that has become one of the most powerful models for resolving male gender anxiety about the artistic life – the Bohemian construction of artistic manhood (plate 21). It is because this avant-garde model has come to dominate our thinking about male artists, along with the gay discourse that emerged at the end of the century, that to us, though certainly not to the Victorians, Millais' quest for the respectability of a professional man and the status of a gentleman can be dismissed as selling out and Hunt's quest for artistic manliness in the Palestinian desert diminished as simply bizarre.

Plate 21 D. G. Rossetti.

The Bohemian formation of artistic manhood exemplified by Rossetti defines itself overtly by opposition to the bourgeois construction of masculinity. Rossetti renounced middle-class respectability by seeming to renounce middle-class status itself. He symbolically allied himself with the working class by living in a working-class district, associating with working-class women, and finally marrying below his class, as did both Brown and Morris. In his youth, Hunt, too, had considered marrying Annie Miller, a model well beneath him in social class. Such downward mobility challenges the bourgeois equation of manhood with monetary success and respectability, yet for Rossetti, as for Hunt, the relation of a non-hegemonic formation of artistic manliness to the bourgeois model is less oppositional than dialectical. As even the most cursory look at Rossetti's career indicates, he devoted a good deal of his energy to getting the best possible price for his art products. Just as the value of Hunt's paintings was enhanced as documentation of the artist's exoticism, so the value of Rossetti's canvases was increased by the well-publicized notoriety of his anti-bourgeois life style. After all, the Midlands industrialist was buying a "Rossetti."

Yet Rossetti's post-Brotherhood formation of artistic manhood does oppose hegemonic Victorian manhood in crucial ways. From the 1860s his visual art rejects that form of knowing his age characterized as masculine and with which he himself dallied during the Brotherhood time – detailed scientific observation of the material world, historical accuracy in representing the past whether of the Bible or Dante's Florence. Nor does his later art celebrate the masculine engagement with the world of England and of the Empire through narratives of quest and rescue. Indeed, this work rejects narrative form altogether. His painting of the 1860s and 1870s inscribes his turn inward. In his rejection of the new world of gallery exhibitions for a small homosocial circle Rossetti re-creates not only the male world of the Brotherhood, but also that isolation from the male sphere, the internalization of desire that earlier Victorians associated with the feminine.

Rossetti's later career demonstrates an erosion of earlier gendered criteria based on a rigid binary of masculine/feminine. As much as his later work hovers at the boundary of the feminine, the art of these years also aggressively affirms its virility. Like the other Brothers, he forges an artistic manhood that, for all its oppositional quality, is devoted to asserting its manliness. To do so, again like Millais and

Hunt, he appropriates elements of the hegemonic Victorian discourse of manhood and from the competing styles of masculinity at mid-century he cobbles together an artistic manhood designed to avoid the twin perils of feminization and effeminacy.

Although the Rossetti circle remained a distinctly homosocial society, there was no hint of the male celibacy whose distorting artistic effects were so feared by the Brotherhood and its critics. Within Bohemia the male artist avoids the aura of unmanliness associated with the unmarried state by a strenuous and public heterosexual life outside of marriage. Taking up with models, or prostitutes since the two were identified for the Victorians, becomes for Rossetti, as for Lippo, a sign of sexual and therefore of artistic potency. But the association with the prostitute also signified for Rossetti, as for Browning, the male artist's own sense of himself as prostitute in bourgeois society, selling his own self to the highest bidder. Rossetti's important statement to Ford Madox Brown of 1873 suggests not only his sense of painting as the objectification of sexualized male desire, but also the deformation of this desire by the demands of the art market: "I have often said that to be an artist is just the same thing as to be a whore, as far as dependence on the whims and fancies of individuals is concerned" (*Letters* III: 1175).

Rossetti's paintings of female models/prostitutes, such as *The Beloved* (1865) (plate 22) or the series of the 1860s and 1870s including such works as *Regina Cordium* and *Veronica Veronese* (1872) for which Alexa Wilding sat as model are best read not as portraits or even celebrations of female beauty,[33] but rather within the Victorian masculine poetic as signs of male potency and therefore of male creativity. Rossetti's personal life may resemble that of the Lady of Shalott immured in a tower, but as artist he is more like "bold Sir Lancelot" (line 77); his paint brush or "helmet-feather/ Burned like one burning flame together" (lines 93–94). His post-Brotherhood representations of the female, including his innumerable portraits of Jane Morris such as *Water Willow* (1871), represent, finally, not the models, but the erotic power of the male gaze. As Christina Rossetti observes in "In an Artist's Studio," the female body becomes a screen on which Dante Gabriel projects sexualized male desire:

> every canvas means,
> The same one meaning, neither more nor less.
> ...
> Not as she is, but as she fills his dream.

Plate 22 D. G. Rossetti, *The Beloved*.

Like Hunt's documentation of his adventures at the Dead Sea, Rossetti's late paintings gain their primary value in attesting to a specific formation of artistic manhood.

These late paintings, then, are continuous with the early Victorian masculine aesthetic in their equation of artistic with sexual potency. They differ in striking a new position within the central problematic of Victorian male identity, the regulation of male desire. The Carlylean Hero as Man of Letters teaches other men to sublimate desire into productive work. Browning, albeit with some strain, seeks a practice through which male desire is channeled into the creation of sacred art. Hunt is given to story paintings such as *The Hireling Shepherd* or *The Awakening Conscience* in which Eros is represented, yet contained within a narrative of salvation.[34] The crucial turn of the earlier masculine aesthetic in these late works of Rossetti is to reject this bourgeois belief in the productive transformation of erotic energy by making erotic pleasure an end in itself and employing the work of art to intensify such pleasure. Although assigned mythological or literary names such as Lady Lilith, Pandora, or Penelope, Rossetti's painted women function primarily as a screen on which the viewer can project his own desire. These works are designed to stimulate a sexualized psychic flow in the male viewer that replicates the reverie depicted in the dreaming women. The enclosed space of the painting turns desire inward. Imprisonment signifies a sexual repression that, as in the contemporaneous theorizing of Pater, becomes valorized as intensifying erotic feeling.

To the present-day viewer, Rossetti's late paintings of women quite rightly appear thoroughly masculinist in privileging the male gaze, in reducing the female subject to the signifier of male creativity, and in equating sexual and artistic potency within a discourse of male creativity.[35] But definitions of masculinity change over time. For the Victorians the life and work of the later Rossetti appeared not aggressively masculinist, but deeply unmanly. Writing in his Preface to *Praeraphaelite Diaries and Letters* of 1900, William Michael sought to rescue his brother's reputation not by refuting the charges pressed at the end of the twentieth century, but by asserting Dante Gabriel's "masculine traits" against the association of his brother with the homoerotic construction of aestheticism. William Michael's terms call up the criteria of the masculine poetic developed earlier in the century. Rather than a "dreamer," an exemplar of that easy dreamful flow of inward emotion marked as feminine, Dante Gabriel becomes an outgoing "genial" personality. Instead of languishing in pallid and "anaemic" enervation, the artist radiates masculine energy, "full of vigour and buoyancy." William Michael is worth quoting, for his attempt to rescue Dante Gabriel for hearty manliness and heterosexuality demonstrates shifts in the definition of artistic manliness from the late nineteenth century to our own time:

> I have more than once had an occasion to confute a current misconception that Dante Rossetti could be adequately described as a sentimentalist, a dreamer, a mystic, an aesthete, and the like, without allowance being made

for a considerable counterbalance of attributes of a very opposite character ... But it was not the less true that he was full of vigour and buoyancy, full of *elan*, well alive to the main chance, capable of enjoying the queer as well as the grave aspects of life, by no means behind hand in contributing his quota to the cause of high spirits – and generally a man equally natural and genial ... People who take an interest in him may depend upon it that the more they learn about him – of an authentic kind – the more will the masculine traits of his character appear in evidence, and the less will room be left for the notion of a pallid and anaemic "aesthete," a candidate for the sunflowers of a DuMaurier design. (3–4)

For all his brother's assertions of Dante Gabriel's artistic manhood, the paintings of dreaming women do register Rossetti's rejection of what the Brotherhood had developed as a manly style. His turn from history and fact to myth and fantasy, from patient scientific observation to fluent reverie, from sexual constraint to sexual flood inscribes how his own formation of artistic manhood differs from manliness as defined earlier in the period. Rossetti's even partial divergence from hegemonic Victorian manliness, his self-imposed isolation from the male sphere, "from the masculine world of commerce, academic philosophical discussion, scientific thought or its technological adaptation" (Gelpi "Feminization" 111) created in his later years an unbearable psychic strain, a strain that runs against the easy reading of Rossetti as masculinist artist. The unresolved psychic issues generated by his isolation from the male sphere, the instability of the relation between his own form of artistic manhood and the earlier Victorian definitions of the feminine, emerged, as in the similar lives of late Victorian women, in somatic symptoms, in hypochondria, drug dependence, and agoraphobia, in the shape of male hysteria.

With Rossetti's work of the 1860s and 1870s, the sharp definitions and valuations of art along the binaries of male/female, manly/unmanly developed earlier in the century dissolve. In the later work of Rossetti what was earlier seen as the unmanly comes now to mark a new form of manliness, a process that appears also in the refashioning of artistic manliness under the sign of monasticism in the contemporaneous critical writing of Walter Pater.

CHAPTER 4

Masculinity transformed: appropriation in Walter Pater's early writing

My conclusion to this study of Victorian masculinities will consider the appropriation and the transformation of early Victorian masculine poetics and technologies of the male self within the emerging poetics of the "aesthetic" and within the construction of the homosexual in the later nineteenth century. My focus will be Pater's essays of the 1860s – "Diaphaneitè" (1864) and particularly "Poems by William Morris" published in *The Westminster Review* in 1868 and republished with extensive revision as "Aesthetic Poetry" in *Appreciations* in 1889. "Poems by William Morris" is a particularly important essay since it includes the text that Pater later used in 1873 with some revision as the "Conclusion" to *The Renaissance*.[1]

These early writings demonstrate Pater's dialectical relation to earlier discourses of masculinity, particularly his intense struggle with the chief early Victorian prophets of a masculine poetic, Carlyle and Browning. The relation of Pater's work of the 1860s and, more generally, of certain elements of modernism and of gay discourse to the masculine poetics and to the formations as well as the fantasies of the male psyche developed earlier in the nineteenth century is best described not in simple terms of rejection, but as a complex process of absorption and revaluation.[2] Indeed, Pater's transformation in the 1860s of earlier Victorian masculinities is best described within Pater's own model of "aesthetic historicism."[3] Pater sees all artists as containing within them all the cultural moments, all the figures that have come before, a richness of absorption exemplified in Pater's description of the *Mona Lisa*. For Pater, this burden of history is transmuted by the unique temperament of an artist such as Leonardo interacting with the spirit of his own age to forge a new, historically specific art form.

If "the composite experience of all the ages is part of each one of us" ("Morris" 146), these essays of the 1860s show how intensely

Pater absorbed the "experience" of early Victorian masculinity – its fantasies and its contradictions, its poetics and its metaphorics, its occupation with male desire and with male madness, and particularly its definition of manhood as a hard-won form of sanity defined as control of this desire, as the achievement of a willed psychic equilibrium. As Morris in Pater's view has absorbed and transformed medieval monasticism as mediated by his own temperament and culture into a "profounder medievalism" ("Morris" 144), so Pater himself appropriated the male fantasies and masculine poetics of his time and through his own temperament as mediated by the spirit of his age, particularly through his own homoeroticism and the emerging homoerotic discourse of 1860s Oxford,[4] transformed the views of his male predecessors into a "profounder" masculinity and masculine poetic.

"Diaphaneitè" and "Poems by William Morris" (including the "Conclusion") share that sense of the power and the pathology of the male psyche that appears in Carlyle and that runs through masculine poetry and art of the 1840s and 1850s. Pater's poetic is grounded in earlier fantasies of the male body and the male psyche. Here are the same metaphorics of the psychic interior – the fluidity of male desire, the movement of the inner life as formless flow, the fear of dissolution countered by figures of restraint and containment. For Pater, as for his predecessors, these figures register his engagement with the central problematic of Victorian masculinity, the regulation of male desire. But Pater's discipline of the self takes a particular inflection and a particular resolution since desire takes the form of a forbidden homoeroticism. Following the received mode of masculine theorizing, Pater defines his own poetic by defining a particular technology for controlling this flux of male desire. And it is this practice of the self, this particular method of regulating male–male desire that Pater terms the "aesthetic." Like the earlier Victorians, then, Pater writes the history of art as the history of male sexuality, although this historical method is turned to the history of a homoerotic sexuality. While continuing to see masculine art as well as male identity within the binaries of order/disorder, sanity/madness, health/disease, he radically reverses the value assigned within these oppositions.

Furthermore, if Pater appropriates the forms, but revalues the terms of Victorian masculine theorizing, he does so within the historicist method of Victorian critical debate, specifically within monastic discourse. The crucial metaphor and the limit case for the technology of the male self continues to be monastic celibacy, and the crucial limit case for the relations between men the all-male world of the monastery. Pater takes up and alters the master historical narrative of the masculine poetic, the tale of the imprisoned monk. Like Carlyle, Browning, and the Pre-Raphaelites, Pater presents the ideal contemporary artist as modern-day monk. But to the labile figure of the monk, Pater provides his own valence, a valorization of celibacy that in stressing the withholding of desire to create a highly eroticized interior life and thus an erotically charged poetry praises in coded form a homoerotic masculine poetic and a homoerotic masculine criticism.

THE AESTHETIC AS A SEXUAL DISCIPLINE

Although the term "aesthetic" has come to describe an art practice in which self-contained formal qualities are privileged over social and ethical signification, when Pater gave to the much-revised "Poems by William Morris" the title "Aesthetic Poetry," he applied the term "aesthetic" only secondarily to stylistic features of the poetry. Its primary reference is to a particular discipline of male desire that for Pater appears here, as it appears throughout history. And the stylistic features of the poetry gain importance as manifestations of that practice of the self.[5] "Poems by William Morris," then, continues the practice of early Victorian masculine theorizing by showing the history of style as grounded in the history of male sexuality. Pater's judgments are based in the analysis of form as sign of a particular sexual regimen. The aesthetic as a psychic and bodily discipline remains his primary occupation.

For Pater, as for Carlyle and Browning, historical criticism narrates the history of managing male desire and the preeminent test case within this history is the medieval monk. Pater defines the mental discipline he terms the "aesthetic" by reworking the nineteenth-century discourse of monasticism into an historicized technology of the male self that provides a model for the management of male–male desire in his own time. Within this Victorian history of mentalities, Pater, like his predecessors, employs monasticism in a wholly secular psycho-sexual sense as the limit case of conditions of male emotional life that cluster about sexual repression. Along a continuum of control, monastic celibacy continues to be the coded term for complete sexual abstinence. But for Pater, in contrast to earlier writers, the figure encodes abstinence from homosexual actions. The life of the monk or "the religious life" ("Diaphaneitè" 217), the life of the "saint" ("Diaphaneitè" 215) becomes for Pater the virtuoso form of containing and thus intensifying male–male desire.

For Pater, the aesthetic practice of the self exemplified in monastic celibacy exists through history in a way that he models as typological.[6] As in Carlyle, applying typological thinking to issues of manliness negotiates a crucial contradiction in the Victorian theorizing of masculinity, the opposition between the essentialist and the constructionist definitions of masculinity. The figural form of *Past and Present* enables Carlyle to reconcile the malleability of masculinity through history implicit in his call for new forms of heroic manliness with his belief that male domination is transhistorical, divinely ordained. Pater's secularized typology operates in a similar fashion by enabling him to present the aesthetic as a transhistorical configuration of the male psyche, a natural law of male consciousness, while arguing that since the shape of masculinity and of the aesthetic has varied through time the formation of masculinity and of a masculine poetic can and will be transformed in the future.

In theorizing masculinity, Pater's rhetoric typically moves between the historically specific and the transhistorical. The "mood of the cloister" ("Morris" 144) is simultaneously particular to the middle ages and a type of a general psychological law. Of medieval monasticism Pater writes, "That whole religion of the middle age was but a beautiful disease or disorder of the senses; and a religion which is a disorder of the senses must always be subject to illusions" ("Morris" 145). The passage moves from history, the past tense "was" to the present tense "is," from an historically specific "religion of the middle age" to "a religion" as the general form of a psychological law stable over time that "must always" apply. The "whole religion of the middle age" becomes one historical manifestation of the aesthetic, the recurring form of male mental discipline whose defining quality in all ages, in the monastery, in Provençal poetry, in the eighteenth century, and in Morris is "a disorder of the senses."

Pater's stance in "Poems by William Morris" as a critic tracing the natural laws of the male psyche through history has several other rhetorical effects. This method implicitly equates his work as critic with the work of the scientist and the scientific historian, an identification that, as in the association with science for Carlyle and the Pre-Raphaelites, diffuses an aura of manly labor over his project. Then, too, the strategy of presenting the formal qualities of *The Defence of Guenevere* as manifestations of psychological laws operating through history distances his valorization of these qualities and of the author from any association with a specific contemporary group, particularly with the homosexual circles emerging at Oxford. The intensities of male–male desire are shown to have marked great literature through the ages.[7]

Pater's sexualized discourse of male art continues the representations of the male psyche elaborated in early Victorian masculine poetics. His early essays deploy the same configuration of images that structure the male fantasies of Carlyle. As in *Past and Present*, in "Poems by William Morris" the primary metaphorics for the male psyche are hydraulic. Male desire is limned as fluid. All mental sensations take liquid form. The psychic management Pater terms the aesthetic is envisaged as the containment and transformation of a fluid, seminal desire: "A passion of which the outlets are sealed, begets a tension of nerve, in which the sensible world comes to one with a reinforced brilliance and relief – all redness is turned into blood, all water into tears" (145).

In describing "a passion of which the outlets are sealed," in representing the psychic and the artistic consequences of closing the valves on the flow of homoerotic desire, Pater follows the model of male pathology that informs earlier Victorian theorizing of masculine art-production. As the limit case, monastic celibacy demonstrates how sexual repression brings about a specific form of madness in men. For Pater in the 1860s, as for poets and artists in the 1840s, constraining male sexuality necessarily and inevitably causes psychic deformation, described here as a "disorder of the senses," a "tension of nerve," an hallucinatory state in which "all redness is turned into blood, all water into tears" (145). These Paterian monks embody the same "delirium" (145), the same restlessness as hysteria figured earlier in the century by such female surrogates for the male artist as the Lady of Shalott, the Soul wandering the Palace of Art, the immured Mariana waiting for her lover. For Pater, the virginal female surrogate appears here as a Mariana of Provençal poetry who longs for the sexually unattainable, feels "the love ... for the chevalier who never comes" (144).

Furthermore, for Pater as for earlier male writers, this psychic destabilization is limned in figures of physical illness, an association that continues the Victorian sense of a physical corruption at the dark heart of maleness: "That whole religion of the middle age was but a beautiful disease or disorder of the senses" (145). Turned upon itself within the aesthetic discipline, the male mind takes sick in "a fever dream" (144). In the poetry of Morris, the modern exemplar of the aesthetic, the "influence of summer is like a poison in one's blood, with a sudden bewildered sickening of life and all things" (145).

In thus appropriating terms of the earlier Victorian discourse of masculinity, Pater's strategy is not that of disavowal, but of transformation through revaluation. With a mordant humor Pater seizes upon paradoxes already present within the received models of normative manliness and of masculine poetics, takes up the subordinated, devalued term in that opposition and assigns to that term a positive value, thus transforming the earlier discourse.

For example, Pater's discipline of the aesthetic is grounded in the Victorian binary that male sexuality is healthy when properly sublimated, unhealthy when too strongly constrained. Working within this system of pathology, Pater represents the practice of sexual repression as creating "disease or disorder of the senses" (145). His crucial turn is presenting this disruption of the equilibrium of manliness not as a condition to be overcome but as a condition to be desired. For Pater sealing the valves of desire creates a disease, but this is a "*beautiful* disease" (145, emphasis added). Turning desire inward generates for Pater as for Browning physical debility in men, But for Pater men that are "frail" are men of an "unaccustomed beauty" (145).

Similarly, Pater picks up another tension within normative Victorian manliness, that sexual constraint moves toward the pleasures of being dominated, that the attraction of discipline merges into the attractions of sado-masochism. In his drive toward psychic stability as the total command of desire, Carlyle turns to the fantasy of subservience to a stronger male, the complete submersion of the individual ego into that of the male hero figured in the ecstatic "brass-collar" obedience of Gurth. Browning may valorize in Lippo the escape of the artist from sexual repression, but he realizes in his portraits of the "failed" painters the psychic pleasure of passivity. The unknown painter draws satisfaction in the bondage of repetition as he continues to paint "the same series, Virgin, Babe, and Saint" (line 60). Andrea del Sarto gains a similar satisfaction in his submission to the economic demands of his wife.[8]

It is the strain of sado-masochism underlying the Victorian call for manly self-mastery that Swinburne so gleefully takes up in his poetry. In "Hymn to Proserpine," he slyly points to the homoerotic sado-masochism implicit in the Christian occupation with the tortured male body: "O lips that the live blood faints in, the leavings of racks and rods!/ O ghastly glories of saints, dead limbs of gibbeted gods!" (lines 43–44). In "Laus Veneris" he ironically figures the displacement of male–male desire into a sexual economy of pain that informs the Victorian idealization of Christian chivalry:

> The fair pure sword smites out in subtle ways,
> Sounds and long lights are shed between the rows
>
> Of beautiful mailed men; the edgèd light slips,
> Most like a snake that takes short breath and dips
>   Sharp from the beautifully bending head,
> With all its gracious body lithe as lips
>
> That curl in touching you.   (lines 215–21)

Like Swinburne, Pater turns the ideals of normative Victorian manliness against themselves. Recognizing in his male predecessors this suppressed longing for domination, even for physical pain in religious devotion and in erotic life, Pater transforms this desire for submission and passivity into a sign of value: "Provençal love is full of the very forms of vassalage. To be the servant of love, to have offended, to taste the subtle luxury of chastisement, of reconciliation – the religious spirit, too, knows that, and meets just there, as in Rousseau, the delicacies of the earthly love" (144–45).

This transformation through revaluing emerges clearly in Pater's appropriation of the Victorian psycho-sexual theory of mimesis. Browning, Kingsley, and Dickens employed monastic painting as a test case demonstrating that sexual repression deforms the male psyche, thus distorting perception of the external world, particularly of the male figure, and thereby producing a mimetically inaccurate art characterized by misshapen bodies. This same assumption about the effect of sexual repression upon perception and mimesis informs Pater's analysis: "Of the things of nature the mediæval mind had a deep sense; but its sense of them was not objective, no real escape to the world without one" (145). For Pater, as for Samuel Smiles, as well as for the Pre-Raphaelites and their critics, a "sense" of the external world that is "objective," the unemotive, scientific way of knowing marked as masculine and exemplified in the manly realist style of the Pre-Raphaelite Brotherhood is unavailable to the man who, within the psychic metaphor of imprisonment, has "no real escape to the world without."

Pater's account of "The Defence of Guenevere" and, more generally, his doctrine of the aesthetic, as much as Dickens' attack on *The Carpenter's Shop*, depends upon this discourse in which deformation of the sexually repressed male mind is inevitably translated into mimetic deformation in the painting. The crucial difference in Pater as critic is that he comes not to blame but to praise in Morris the formal manifestations of this inward turn of desire – the energized dislocation, the orgasmic twisting of the body and of nature itself: "The poem which gives its name to the volume is a thing tormented and awry with passion, like the body of Guenevere defending herself from the charge of adultery" (144). For Pater there is "a wild, convulsed sensuousness in the poetry of the middle age, in which the things of nature begin to play a strange delirious part" (145). The aesthetic as the "mood of the cloister" is deeply attractive to Pater's sensibility in loosing the psyche from manly reserve so that it transforms the material world through the power of the individual temperament: "The strangest creations of sleep seem here, by some appalling license, to cross the limit of the dawn" (145). In valorizing what appeared to earlier critics as outward signs of inward divergence from normative masculinity, Pater is challenging normative masculinity itself.

In praising in Morris what had been feared as male hysteria, Pater is focusing on a contradiction within masculine aesthetics that troubled his male predecessors – that only through the disruption of the hegemonic definition of manliness as psychic control could the artist intensify perception, only by shattering the reserve of manhood could the artist achieve an emotionally vivid art. For the Pre-Raphaelites, the intense scientific concentration marked as masculine turns into its opposite, into the surreal. For Browning's Bishop, sensual acuity is transformed into male madness. Pater picks up the ambivalence of earlier Victorians toward this process, so attractive yet so unmanly, so vivifying yet so diseased. Pater celebrates the clear-eyed realism so valued by Browning and by the Pre-Raphaelite Brotherhood as the central positive term of the masculine poetic only when such attention to the external world moves at its extreme into the hyper-realism that had been repudiated within the masculine poetic as hysteria. For Pater, the aesthetic regimen of mind becomes valuable as a self-conscious mental technique for shattering manly control of the self so as to carry realism to its limit case of hyperaesthesia. Renouncing the ordered scientific knowledge of nature conventionally designated as masculine brings a compensating access of power in another form, in the intensification of mental perception. For Pater, sealing the "outlets" of desire through the "aesthetic" discipline "begets... a reinforced brilliance and relief" (145).

It is this equation of repression with mental intensity that Pater figures in the medieval monk as the "mood of the cloister" and sees as reshaped by the spirit of his own age into the "profounder medievalism" (144) manifested by Morris. It is this vividness of the material world as transformed through the sexually suppressed male psyche that Pater here praises: "The English poet too has learned the secret. He has diffused through *King Arthur's Tomb* the maddening white glare of the sun ... the sorcerer's moon, large and feverish. The colouring is intricate and delirious, as of 'scarlet lilies'... It is in the *Blue Closet* that this delirium reaches its height with a singular beauty" (145).

This same revaluation of realism, the formal quality most clearly marked as manly by the Victorians, appears also in Pater's later essay "Dante Gabriel Rossetti" (1883). In praising Rossetti as another contemporary exemplar of the aesthetic, Pater again values poetic form that manifests inward qualities of tension and stress: "To Rossetti... life is a crisis at every moment" (90). Rossetti's temperament is set within the Victorian terms of "*mania*" (89), male hysteria registered as physical disease. His poems show "a certain feverishness of soul in the moods they present" (89). Here Pater points to fissures in the Brotherhood's manly style, when, as in "My Sister's Sleep" and "The Woodspurge," the psychic armor of the male mind is fractured by extremities of feeling and observation intensifies until it morphoses into male hysteria. In praising Rossetti, Pater subverts earlier masculine poetics in a single brilliant phrase, the "insanity of realism" (89).

Pater's psycho-sexual analysis of art, then, continues the earlier Victorian narrative in which the history of art *is* the history of male practices of sexual self-discipline. Within the historicist discourse that Pater appropriates, monasticism is conceived not as a religious practice, but as an institutionalized technology for regulating the energy of male sexuality. What Pater does in "Poems by William Morris" is to make quite explicit the linkage of cloister and Eros implicit in male theorizing through the 1840s and 1850s. Like St. Edmundsbury, Pater's monastic world is a highly sexualized place. With a glance back at such decorous theorizing Pater plainly asserts, "That religion shades into sensuous love, and sensuous love into religion, has been often seen" (144).

Again picking up what had been suppressed in earlier discourse, most crucially the barely controlled homoeroticism that pervades Carlyle's monastic ideal, Pater clearly equates the "sensuous love" of monastic Christianity with masculine desire: "The Christianity of the middle age made way among a people whose loss was in the life of the senses only by the possession of an idol, the beautiful idol of the Latin hymn-writers, who for one moral or spiritual sentiment have a hundred sensuous images" (144).[9] For Pater the "idol," the unrealizable object of devotion and of desire, is Jesus, more specifically the "fleshly" body of Jesus: "Only by the inflaming influence of such idols [the image of Christ] can any religion compete with the presence of the fleshly lover" (144). Within Pater's sexualized monastic discourse, Jesus becomes the unreachable, since forbidden, object of male sexual desire, the focus of an erotic intensity that, with a barely coded reference to his own life in England of the 1860s, must be internalized since by its nature it is forbidden, never to be consummated. For Pater, then, as for Rossetti and the other Pre-Raphaelites, the adult body of Jesus generates an eroticized attraction that because of linked heterosexist and religious taboos must be defended against. In a daring sentence that he omits from "Aesthetic Poetry" Pater sees the Christian writing of the middle ages as figuring the aesthetic discipline of intensifying desire through repression that can generate a homoerotic literature in his own time: "Who knows whether, when the simple belief in them has faded away, the most cherished sacred writings may not for the first time exercise their highest influence as the most delicate amorous poetry in the world?" (144).

In revising "Poems by William Morris" as "Aesthetic Poetry" Pater mutes the erotic tone of the earlier essay, turning "sensuous love" into the merely "sensuous" and adding the qualifier "dangerously": "Monastic religion at any rate, has its sensuous side, a dangerously sensuous side" ("Aesthetic" 78). This withdrawal from overt statements of a male–male erotics resonates with his note on reprinting the "Conclusion" that he had "conceived it might possibly mislead some of those young men into whose hands it might fall" (*Renaissance* 186). But any model of self-censorship in the face of public pressure fails to recognize Pater's genuine sense of the "danger" of the sensuous, particularly of the male–male desire coded through monastic discourse in "Poems by William Morris." Then as now Pater's critics have seen the aesthetic as a stimulus to homoerotic activity, whereas for Pater the practice of the self he terms the "aesthetic" is exactly the opposite. It is a way of containing male–male desire by turning it inward. As much as Carlyle, Pater fears the eruption, the uncontrolled flood of male desire.

In "Poems by William Morris" Pater offers a sexualized arthistorical narrative that opposes the conflation of sexual and artistic freedom that informs Browning's artist-poems as well as the work of the Pre-Raphaelite Brotherhood. Pater's history of male art is the history of the continuing control of desire within the practice of the aesthetic. Within that history crucial changes occur not as liberation of desire, but rather as contingent shifting in "the object of... devotion" which is always absent and unreachable, "the rejection of one idolatry for the other is never lost sight of" (144).

For Pater, art history becomes the history of object relations writ large. In "Poems by William Morris" the movement from Latin hymns to Provençal poetry to late eighteenth-century romanticism to the "profounder mediævalism" of Morris is not conceived as whiggish liberation, but as the continued practice of the aesthetic as shifting desire from "the life of the senses" to the absent "object of... devotion." For Pater, monasticism exemplifies the form of sexual management that transforms sexual desire into intense passion for an unreachable object of desire, "the art of directing towards an imaginary object sentiments whose natural direction is towards objects of sense" (144). The comparison of Christian practice with that of the Greeks is couched neither as religious progress nor as sexual regression, the standard Victorian narratives, but rather as a juxtaposition of different techniques for displacing otherwise dangerous male desire: "For in that idolatry [of the monastery] the idol was absent or veiled, not limited to one supreme plastic form like Zeus at Olympia or Athena in the Acropolis, but distracted, as in a fever dream, into a thousand symbols and reflections" (144).[10] The monastery for Pater signifies a specific mode of managing male sexuality, a particular practice of containment as intensification of homoerotic desire. The "profounder mediævalism" that he describes in Morris functions as an historicized code for the practice of a homoerotic life and a homoerotic criticism in his own time.

By narrating shifts in sexual object relations over time, Pater suggests the malleability of male sexuality and of masculinity through history, thus subverting any essentialist identification of the heterosexual with the manly. He speaks of Provençal poetry in terms of such fluidity of desire:

> The rejection of one idolatry for the other is never lost sight of. The jealousy of that other lover, for whom these words and images and strange ways of sentiment were first devised, is the secret here of a triumphant colour and heat. It is the mood of the cloister taking a new direction, and winning so a later space of life it never anticipated ... Hereon, as before in the cloister, so now in the chateau, the reign of reverie set in. (144)

In the later middles ages, then, erotic desire moves from Jesus to the absent and unreachable object that can be either male or female, the "chevalier" or "the Lady of Tripoli" (144). If configurations of masculinity and of art take a new form in the poetry of Morris in the modern world, they will as surely take equally different forms in the future. "A later space of life ... never anticipated" (144) will see the emergence of a homoerotic manhood as well as a homoerotic poetry, visual art, and critical practice. It is this new construction of masculinity and this transformed masculine poetic that are the true subjects of "Poems by William Morris."

To describe this transfigured masculinity of the future Pater again zooms in on points of stress within normative manliness that have been reconciled through monastic discourse. Victorian men felt a deep unease in being compelled to move from a masculine bonding that exists on the boundary of the homosocial/homoerotic to a heterosexual bonding within marriage, the central institution of normative bourgeois life. This ambivalence about marriage emerges in the imaginative appeal to a wide male readership of the Carlylean community of self-engendering men in *Past and Present*, in the persistent pull of a secular Brotherhood to the Pre-Raphaelites throughout their lives, and in Browning's equation of the failed artist with the married artist. Thus, in describing the new masculinity as characterized by "the love which is incompatible with marriage" (144), Pater is drawing upon a barely concealed strain, on what is already present, or one might say latent, within the received discourse of bourgeois masculinity.

In revaluing this opposition to marriage, Pater is also pointing to the repressed homoeroticism within earlier male writers. As Swinburne in "Laus Veneris" points to the homoeroticism at the heart of the Victorian ideal of Christian chivalry,[11] so Pater is suggesting that the hearty all-male life of St. Edmundsbury and the diligent communal art practice of the Pre-Raphaelite Brothers is grounded upon the constraint of homoerotic desire. Pater's praise of "the love which is incompatible with marriage" exemplifies his strategy of not disavowing earlier masculine poetics, but rather of making overt what was earlier covert, of extending what was already present in earlier male writers. In this case he picks up the continuing uneasiness about heterosexuality registered in the ongoing idealization of masculine bonding as well as in the pull of the homoerotic within masculine theorizing. Given the intense sense of the unmanliness of all-male groups that emerges in the late 1840s in the sharp attacks on the Pre-Raphaelite Brotherhood, chaste masculine bonding based on the repression of the homoerotic, a crucial element of earlier masculine poetics, could easily be turned to become the central figure of a new homoerotic masculine poetic.

In representing this transformed masculinity, Pater sees the discipline of the mind written on the body within the received typology of the male body that appears as early as *Past and Present*, the contrast of the hearty heterosexual, the "almost stupid Man of Practice" to the frail effeminate male, the "light adroit Man of Theory" (160). Throughout history, whether in the cloister, in Provence, or in the writings of Rousseau, the aesthetic practice of the self generates specific physical forms of manhood: "Under this strange complex of conditions, as in some medicated air, exotic flowers of sentiment expand, among people of a remote and unaccustomed beauty, somnambulistic, frail, and androgynous, the light almost shining through them, as the flame of a little taper shows through the Host" (145).[12] Again, Pater appropriates the conventions of masculine discourse, but revalues the pejorative, seeing as "unaccustomed beauty" the muscular frailty that filled Carlyle and Kingsley with such apprehension.

Furthermore, in speaking of a "strange complex of conditions" from which emerge a new "people" Pater anticipates the new metaphorics of masculinity that will dominate the last decades of the century. Carlyle, Browning, and the Pre-Raphaelites represent their ambivalent feelings about the malleability of masculinity over time through an historicist method. In Pater's conceptualizing of masculinities this historicism becomes mixed with the new discourse of evolution to suggest a biological basis for the homoerotic.[13] Here Pater suggests virtually a new species or "people" whose sexual difference is inscribed in materialist terms on their bodies, "a remote and unaccustomed beauty, somnambulistic, frail, androgynous, the light almost shining through them" (145). For Pater this bodily transformation of males into the "frail, and androgynous" in the past is seen as an evolutionary mutation prefiguring in Darwinian rather than in typological terms the embodied masculinity of the future.

With the shift from an historicist to a Darwinian vocabulary that appears in the early Pater, late nineteenth-century thinking about masculinities takes several new emphases. The Darwinian figures continue the pervasive earlier Victorian sense that masculinity is inherently unstable, subject to change over historical time. Within the biological discourse of Darwin, masculinity becomes as subject to change as any other organic phenomenon, but the materialism of this discourse shifts the figuration from the mind to the body, to the primacy of physical change. The transformation of typological historical thinking into Darwinism also shifts attention from past to future, to the concern that, as with other species, organic evolution of the human species will not end in the present, but continue irresistibly and with a fearful uncertainty into future time. Carlyle had in *Past and Present* moved to a vision of the future that in typological terms expressed his faith that heroic manliness would be manifested in historically new and beneficent ways in the coming Captain of Industry. Pater's language anticipates late nineteenth-century evolutionary fictions occupied with masculinity in terms that look to transformation not only of the spiritual and psychological, but also of the biological basis of manliness. Such fictions continue in evolutionary figures the early Victorian anxiety about the destabilization of a heterosexual masculinity defined as sexual potency. Hardy's Angel Clare, Jude, and especially Father Time are imagined as precursors of a new biological species of male too "frail," even too "androgynous," to live in this world. H. G. Wells' Eloi, "the frail, androgynous" new species breathing "medicated air" and surrounded by "exotic flowers," figure in Huxleyan terms the effeminization feared by men throughout the Victorian period.

REWRITING THE MASCULINE PLOT

Although it anticipates evolutionary future fictions of masculine anxiety, "Poems by William Morris" remains within the Victorian historicist coding of the debate about the condition of manliness. Pater's narrative of the history of art as the history of male sexuality takes as its central example the monk escaping from the walled prison of the monastery. But typically Pater appropriates this masculine plot only to rewrite it, reshaping the narrative as a repudiation of the central idea of earlier masculine poetics, the identification of male creativity with the liberation of heterosexual desire.

In "Poems by William Morris" Pater represents Morris' move from *The Defence of Guenevere* to *The Life and Death of Jason* and *The Earthly Paradise* as a manifestation in historical time of transhistorical laws. Morris' stylistic development, "this simplification interests us, not merely for the sake of an individual poet – full of charm as he is – but chiefly because it explains through him a transition which, under many forms, is one law of the life of the human spirit, and of which what we call the Renaissance is only a supreme instance" (146). Morris recapitulates in the nineteenth century the passage from the middle ages to the Renaissance, the crucial moment within the Victorian art-historical narrative that Pater, like Browning, figures within a secularized typology through the narrative of the monk's escape from the imprisoning monastery: "Just so the monk in his cloister, through the 'open vision,' open only to the spirit, divined, aspired to, and at last apprehended, a better daylight, but earthly, open only to the senses" (146).

Personal as well as cultural transformation are registered as transformations in the management of male desire. Pater represents the "transition which ... is one law of the life of the human spirit" by the changed perception of a monk looking out through a figurative breach in the wall, a barrier that in Pater's metaphorics, as in the reference in the "Conclusion" to the "thick wall of personality" that encloses the "narrow chamber of the individual mind," represents the boundary of the psyche. In looking out through the walls of the psychic "cloister" into "daylight" the celibate male transfers desire outward to the "earthly." The figure again depends upon the Victorian psycho-sexual model of mimesis. Turning outward leads to that clear-eyed mimetic objectivity marked as masculine, as opposed to the "delirium" generated by sexual repression and marked as feminine: "Here there is no delirium or illusion, no experiences of mere soul while the body and the bodily senses sleep, or wake with convulsed intensity at the prompting of imaginative love; but rather the great primary passions under broad daylight as of the pagan Veronese" (146).

But Pater employs this historicized narrative of masculinity only to illuminate its implicit contradictions and revalue its devalued elements. Here he rewrites the masculine poetic by rewriting the artist-poems of Browning, the apparent prophet of hearty heterosexuality whom Pater was later rather slyly to praise as a "tender, manly poet" ("Browning" 46), a phrase that valorizes the psychic tensions of masculinity that Browning was at such pains to cover over. Within Browning's artist-poems, liberation from monasticism is contradicted by the fall of the artist into new forms of imprisonment, particularly the reification of heterosexual desire within capitalist art-production. In his own equally sexualized rewriting of this masculine plot Pater, too, represents the liberation from monasticism in the Renaissance, the "return from the overwrought spiritualities of the middle age to the earlier, more ancient life of the senses" (147), as an unfortunate fall not because the artist encounters new bonds on heterosexuality, but because the rejection of celibacy represents rejection of that continuing repression of homoerotic desire that is for Pater the crucial psychic practice of the male artist. In Pater's hands, the liberationist Victorian tale of the escaped monk takes a new form:

For us the most attractive form of classical story is the monk's conception of it, when he escapes from the sombre legend of his cloister to that true light. The fruits of this mood, which, divining more than it understands, infuses into the figures of the Christian legend some subtle reminiscence of older gods, or into the story of Cupid and Psyche that passionate stress of spirit which the world owes to Christianity, have still to be gathered up when the time comes. (147)

In this revaluation of the escaped monk, Pater reworks "Fra Lippo Lippi" through Carlyle since, as much as Carlyle, Pater fears opening the floodgates of male sexuality. He carries on the Carlylean fear of fluids. If Victorian theorists coded the ideal male artist along a spectrum of imagined monks, in this imaginary portrait in miniature, resonant with his own desire to reconcile homoeroticism with Christian practice, Pater pictures the ideal artist-monk as closer to Pictor Ignotus than to Lippo. What Pater here celebrates is not the ebullience and guiltless heterosexuality of Lippo. Pater's unknown painter remains within the monastery, escaping "from the sombre legend of his cloister" only in an imagination that eroticizes the "figures of the Christian legend" and, conversely, "infuses" into overtly sexual pagan material such as "Cupid and Psyche" the internalized sexual restraint that characterizes Christianity. Rather than valuing the man who, like Lippo, acts out his erotic desire, Pater values the artist as monk who exemplifies the repression of homoerotic desire that generates a "mood" which, in characteristically oxymoronic rhetoric, Pater calls "that passionate stress of spirit." Within this monastic figuring of the aesthetic, it is only through "stress" that the inner life becomes "passionate," because male–male desire is not acted out, but displaced onto an unattainable object, the "older gods" or the "figures of Christian legend" rather than fleshly male bodies.

Again, Pater appropriates to subvert. He picks up the occupation of the early Victorian discourse of masculinity with the internalization of erotic life, with eroticized fantasies that are represented as debilitating to the psychic life of men. But rather than seeing this internalization of male sexuality as the mark of the failed painter exemplified in Pictor Ignotus, Pater revalues Browning by marking this transmutation of male sexuality into the "passionate stress" of unrealizable desire as the sign of artistic success. Pater's tale of the escaped monk ends with the rhetorical turn to the present that characterizes monastic discourse. But unlike Browning and the Pre-Raphaelites, Pater is not covertly calling for increased male sexual freedom, but rather for a new "mood of the cloister" as a repressed and thus intensified homoeroticism. Pater transforms the monastic cell into the closet, the space in which is hidden and thus heightened the male–male desire forbidden expression within society.[14] It is from this practice of unacted homoeroticism coded in the medieval monk that for Pater a new art and a new literature will emerge: "The fruits of this mood ... have still to be gathered up when the time comes" (147).

Typically, the wholly psycho-sexual ground of Pater's analysis, his representation of Christianity not as revelation but as a fiction justifying a particular management of male desire, so overt in the *Westminster* text is softened in the revision for *Appreciations*. In "Poems by William Morris" the monk escapes from the cloister to "true light"; in "Aesthetic Poetry" this becomes "natural light." In the

Westminster the erotic feelings of paganism are transferred to "Christian legend," in *Appreciations* to the "figures of Christian history." "Aesthetic Poetry" does not call for the application of this "mood of the cloister" in the present. There is, instead, only the dry historical statement that the "passionate stress of spirit" created by the sexual repression of Christianity "constitutes a peculiar vein of interest in the art of the fifteenth century" (82).

In "Diaphaneitè" Pater also recasts the Browningesque figure of the sexually liberated monk as ideal artist by instead equating "the saint" with "the artist" (216). Reversing the heterosexist basis of earlier masculine poetics coded within the received monastic discourse, Pater represents the ideal quality of the artist, "the repose of perfect intellectual culture" (217), as the contemporary equivalent of monastic celibacy, the historicist form that figures for Pater the intensifying internalization of male–male desire. Pater sees the exemplary male artist not in the model of Fra Lippo Lippi, as endowed by nature with a heterosexual energy unfortunately constrained by social and religious inhibitions, but rather as having through a "happy ... accident of birth or constitution" a deliverance from heterosexual desire, a definition wholly at odds with the normative Victorian definition of maleness as innate heterosexual energy:

Like the religious life, it [perfect intellectual culture] is a paradox in the world, denying the first conditions of man's ordinary existence, cutting obliquely the spontaneous order of things. But the character we have before us is a kind of prophecy of this repose and simplicity, coming as it were in the order of grace, not of nature, by some happy gift, or accident of birth or constitution, showing that it is indeed within the limits of man's destiny. (217)

Even the curious passage in "Diaphaneitè" on "Greek statues" which moves the figure of celibacy back in time subverts the Victorian equation of heterosexual and artistic potency: "The beauty of the Greek statues was a sexless beauty; the statues of the gods had the least traces of sex. Here there is a moral sexlessness, a kind of impotence, an ineffectual wholeness of nature, yet with a divine beauty and significance of its own" (220). As first applied to Athenian sculpture, the term "sexless" means androgynous. But the meaning of this resonant term shifts radically within the passage. From "sexless" as androgyny, the dissolving of gender differences, Pater moves to "moral sexlessness," a phrase repudiating the high-minded ideological aggressiveness valued within hegemonic Victorian masculinity. This "sexlessness" as a "moral" category is then turned back to the body as "a kind of impotence, an ineffectual wholeness of nature" that assumes, again within earlier Victorian discourse, that forms of moral and literary behavior are essentially grounded on qualities of male sexuality. But Pater breaks with the essentialist heterosexist basis of that earlier masculine discourse by imagining men who are by "birth or constitution" born without heterosexual desire. Celibacy as "sexlessness" or "a kind of impotence" is turned to code an innate homoeroticism in some few men, men who form an artistic and cultural elite. And it is this elite of homoerotic men, celibate in the double sense of lacking by their nature heterosexual desire and of internalizing rather than acting out this homoeroticism, who are valorized, sacralized as having "a divine beauty and significance" (220).

In this effort to link the renunciation of heterosexuality represented through the coded figure of monastic celibacy with the intensified interiority of a repressed homoeroticism, Pater displays his anxiety of influence about the Victorian prophet of celibacy as the central discipline of manliness, Thomas Carlyle.[15] Pater's need to engage Carlyle in this very early essay comes from the necessity of distancing his own repudiation of heterosexual desire from the Carlylean celibacy that argues for such repudiation as socially productive in channeling heterosexual energy into strenuous activity within the world, for a "moral sexiness" in contrast to Pater's "moral sexlessness." To do so, Pater creatively misreads Carlyle by identifying the Carlylean practice of sexual management with those socially disruptive, violent political activists that Carlyle is attracted to yet condemns within his histories. Pater links Carlylean masculinity to figures of *The French Revolution* such as Danton, "the type Carlyle has made too popular for the true interest of art" (219), and, most interestingly, Charlotte Corday. In imaginative sympathy with the Carlyle of *Past and Present* as well as of *The French Revolution*, Pater focuses on the "half-dæmonic" female as the exemplar of disorder, as surrogate for the disruptive rush of male desire: "'What,' says Carlyle, of Charlotte Corday, 'What if she had emerged from her secluded stillness, suddenly like a star; cruel-lovely, with half-angelic, half-dæmonic splendour; to gleam for a moment, and in a moment be extinguished; to be held in memory, so bright complete was she, through long centuries!'" (221).

Through this productive misreading that identifies Carlyle with the disruptive sexualized activity he denounces, Pater carves out his own space as theorist of masculinity. He transforms the Carlylean heroism of celibacy as the sublimation of desire into energetic work in the world into a Paterian heroism of celibacy as withdrawal from male sphere so as to turn erotic energy into an intensified inner life. It is this new incarnation of the celibate monk as the sexually inactive male, the virtuoso of sexual constraint who can check his homoerotic desire, that Pater presents as the new celibate Hero as Man of Letters: "Over and over again the world has been surprised by the *heroism*, the insight, the passion, of this clear crystal nature" (220, emphasis added).

In appropriating and transforming a central binary of Victorian masculine poetics, the opposition of the celibate to the sexually liberated even libertine male, Pater reshapes the monk to model his own reshaping of the vocation of the male artist/critic. Pater's monk in the monastic cell as closet figures the practice of the male artist living a rigorously self-disciplined psychic life within a male community. This practice resonates with Pater's own situation within a community of celibate men and with his own practice of sexual self-discipline as internalization of a socially forbidden male–male desire that generates a productive internal tension or "passionate stress of spirit" ("Morris" 147). The turning inward that had been dismissed in the masculine poetics of Browning and the Pre-Raphaelites as male hysteria marked by distorted erotic fantasizing becomes revalued by Pater as the most productive form of critical and artistic discipline. For Pater, this psychic tension, an extreme form of the quality of reserve that defines Victorian manliness, provides the critic access to similar withholdings of desire in others and to the inscription of this practice in their art, a critical activity exemplified in his own tracing of the "delirium" of the aesthetic from Latin hymns through Provençal poetry to the poems of William Morris.

In his appropriation of the figure of the celibate monk in these early essays, then, Pater transforms prior Victorian masculine poetics in order to announce in characteristically evasive historicist form his own future project. In *The Renaissance* Pater will continue the early Victorian practice of writing the history of art as the history of male sexuality, but will represent the past not as the history of heterosexual liberation, but, in his reading of such figures as Leonardo, Michelangelo, and Winckelmann as the history of the aesthetic as the management through inwardness and through coded inscription in art of unrealizable male–male desire.

CONTINUITY AND CHANGE: MASCULINITY AS A "HARD GEM-LIKE FLAME"

The conclusion to this study will consider Pater's "Conclusion" as a separate and distinct work so as to foreground the dialectical relation of this most famous and most influential of his writings to earlier Victorian masculinities and to earlier Victorian masculine poetics. Given Pater's appropriation of his predecessors' theorizing of masculinity and their formulations of the male self, I will emphasize the continuity of the "Conclusion" with this masculine discourse. Given Pater's transformations of this earlier discourse, I will be attentive to the ways that the "Conclusion" transforms the received discourse of masculinity so as to enable Pater as a strong critic to distinguish himself from his male predecessors, particularly Carlyle.[16]

That the "Conclusion" is set within the frame of earlier masculine poetics is shown by the relation of the paragraphs that have come to be called the "Conclusion" to the two different texts they conclude. In both cases, these intense concentrated paragraphs close a series of observations about the temperament of specific artists and poets as manifested in their work. And yet the "Conclusion" says little or nothing about the contemporary poetry of Morris nor about the art of the Renaissance. Instead, as indicated by the ease of their transferability, these famous words are wholly self-contained, a call not for a particular formal program but for a particular practice of regulating male desire. Rather than an essay on style, the "Conclusion" is a sermon on manhood. The movement in both "Poems by William Morris" and *The Renaissance* from discussion of specific poems and paintings to generalizations about the management of male sexuality points not only to Pater's continued grounding of artistic analysis in the analysis of managing male desire, but also to his continuation of earlier masculine theorizing that sees such analysis of artistic form acquiring significance as leading to "conclusions" about the proper discipline of male mental life. As much as Carlyle in the 1840s, Pater in the later decades of the century undertakes a critical practice whose manliness lies in facilitating and exemplifying the arduous achievement of manhood.

Not only the goals, but also the language of the "Conclusion" emerges or flows from the earlier Victorian fantasizing of the male psyche within a hydraulics of male desire. As much as the celebrated figures of the "Conclusion" point ahead to crucial modernist tropes, such as the stream of consciousness, they arise from the metaphorics of early Victorian masculine discourse. Like Carlyle speaking of the "free-flowing channel" that may be torn "through the sour mud-swamp of one's existence (*Past* 197), Pater imagines the interior of the male psyche, the "inward world of thought and feeling" (148), in figures of fluidity, as the flow of "water" (148). Furthermore, Pater's figures continue the pervasive earlier Victorian anxiety about the destructive power of male energy imagined in fluid, seminal terms. Pater imagines the energies of the psyche as the rush and flood of untamed, uncontrolled waters. Beneath the facade of manly reserve, the "water" is only "in apparent rest." The male psyche is a "whirlpool ... still more rapid," "the race of the midstream," "a drift of momentary acts of sight and passion and thought. At first sight experience seems ... a flood of external objects" (148).

In contrast to Carlyle, however, in the "Conclusion" Pater does not fantasize the inner fluidity of maleness as inherently diseased. He excises the pervasive early Victorian identification of male sexuality with pollution. Instead, in the rush of waters Pater limns his fear of the dissolution of male identity into the mercurial fluidity of its own interior self. His anxiety clusters about such terms as "dissipated," "suspended," "loosed," "melts." "Objects ... are dissipated"; "the cohesive force is suspended"; "each object is loosed into a group of impressions"; "all melts under our feet" (148). In this occupation with the male self as inherently unstable, the "Conclusion" continues the earlier Victorian occupation with a breakdown of rigid psychic control imagined by Carlyle as the liquefaction of the "iron energy" (*Past* 95) that defines manhood, as the morphosis of rock into the lava of "volcanoism" (*Past* 96).

Sharing the anxieties about mental stability common to other Victorian men, equally aware of the difficulty in achieving and sustaining the psychic equilibrium of manhood, Pater shapes the "Conclusion," his own manifesto about the formation of the male self, along the trajectory of the masculine plot. The "Conclusion" internalizes the quest for manhood, shapes in metaphors of the mind the movement from the feminine to the manly.

Pater's psychologized masculine plot begins with the conventional early Victorian trope of male imprisonment. The male self, the implied unnamed protagonist, is described as immured within "the narrow chamber of the individual mind," set behind "that thick wall of personality through which no real voice has ever pierced on its way to us, or from us" (148). These celebrated carceral images continue a series of confined unmanned men – the monks who in the *Westminster* essay prefigure the "profounder" nineteenth-century medievalism of Morris, the "enchanted" feminized workers at St. Ives, Pictor Ignotus lost in erotic fantasy, Lippo locked within the Medici palace, the Highlander of *The Order of Release*. The images call up, too, the line of imprisoned female surrogates for the unmanly who figure surrender to the uncontrolled flux of mental sensation – the soul wandering the Palace of Art, the Lady of Shalott, the Mariana of Tennyson and Millais, the nun of *Convent Thoughts*.

Pater's evocation of male mental confinement – the "individual in his isolation, each mind keeping as a solitary prisoner its own dream of a world" – achieves a particularly tangible form in resonating with the actual methods of the late nineteenth-century penitentiary, particularly in its reference to "solitary" confinement, a form of mental torture to be suffered some years later by Oscar Wilde. As in Carlyle and in Tennyson, the force of the term "isolation" also suggests a life lived as a solitary on the model of the romantic poet, apart from other men, removed from the bonded activity of the male sphere. The "Conclusion" continues the strand, or strain, in masculine discourse, exemplified in "Stanzas from the Grande Chartreuse," that associates such separation from the world of masculine work with the loss of virile power, with impotence. In this stage within the masculine plot of isolation from the male sphere, here limned as physical imprisonment, the male protagonist becomes emasculated, "dwindles down," as well as feminized, "a tremulous whisp" (148).

For Pater, "Analysis goes a step further still" (148). The "Conclusion" presses the representation of unmanning beyond the metaphors of the cloister and the prison, plunging into the fluidity that defines the essence of maleness itself. The downward, inward trajectory of the loss of manliness that lies at the center of the masculine plot moves here toward its linguistic limits, the point at which the ceaseless motion and liquidness of male energy moves finally beyond the structuring power of language, the point at which in its formlessness the flux of maleness becomes non-narratable: "It is with the movement, the passage and dissolution of impressions, images, sensations, that analysis leaves off, that continual vanishing away, that strange perpetual weaving and unweaving of ourselves" (148).

The trajectory of unmanning continues from the figure of "unweaving" downward to the "dissolution" of male "personality" as death itself. At the center of this text in its first publication in "Poems by William Morris" is the figure of death by drowning, or death as drowning, the extreme representation of the continuing Victorian male sense of abjection as fear of the breakdown of any containment of the fluid self and the dissolving of the fragile structure of manhood into the essential flux of maleness. In a passage that calls to mind Tennyson's similar vision of death as dissolution in "Crossing the Bar," but absent from Tennyson's religious faith, Pater writes in the *Westminster Review*:

Such thoughts seem desolate at first; at times all the bitterness of life seems concentrated in them. They bring the image of one washed out beyond the bar in a sea at ebb, losing even his personality, as the elements of which he is composed pass into new combinations. Struggling, as he must, to save himself, it is himself that he loses at every moment. (148)

Pater here sees the self in the conventional model of energies, "the elements of which he is composed," held together briefly and with difficulty in the tense equilibrium of manliness. Pater's central fear, like that of other Victorian men, is that this temporary configuration of masculine identity, what Pater calls "himself," will not hold, will ultimately dissolve into the primal liquid of male being, return to the flux and eventually "pass into new combinations."

Strikingly, this paragraph was omitted when the "Conclusion" was transferred to *The Renaissance*. The elimination of this morbid image is in keeping with the general softening of the *Westminster* material in its later revised forms. With characteristic secretiveness Pater withheld public expression of his personal fears about the instability of personality. With equally characteristic sensitivity to the response to his work, he may well have been apprehensive about expressing male anxieties he felt that his readers might share. And most importantly, the implied death at the mid-point of the narrative attenuates the force of the "Conclusion" as an assertion of the need for and the possibility of achieving the discipline of manhood.

Like Browning's Unnamed Painter or the nameless speaker of Locksley Hall, Pater's "he," the unnamed male protagonist who personifies the male psyche, has fallen into male madness as the loss of psychic control, limned here through "the image of one washed out beyond the bar in a sea at ebb, losing even his personality." Having surrendered control so as to dissolve into the flux of sensation and desire, the state marked at this historical moment as feminine and effeminate, the implied male protagonist, like other protagonists within the masculine plot and like participants in nineteenth-century initiation rituals, must now remasculinize himself. He must repudiate the feminine by actively restructuring his psyche through the discipline of containment, fixing the overwhelming psychic flux into "hard" forms.

In emulation of the Carlylean Hero as Man of Letters, Pater undertakes an inward journey, a spiritual quest into the chthonic energy of the male self so as to return and speak prophetically of manhood achieved.[17] The "Conclusion" turns sharply from feminization to masculinization, from figures of dwindling, unweaving, dissolution, drowning to those of structuring, control, agency. From the sense of being "washed out beyond the bar in a sea at ebb" the "Conclusion" moves to the heroic actions of man "struggling, as he must, to save himself" (148).

This crucial turn is registered linguistically as a shift from passive to active voice that dramatizes the turn to mental control as well as the masculinity of imposing form upon the formlessness traditionally marked as feminine. The language moves from the passive and receptive, from "a counted number of pulses only is given to us" to the active voice, the analogue of manly activism, "How can we pass most swiftly from point to point?" From being buried "under a flood" while "all melts under our feet" the male must now "catch at any exquisite passion," "discriminate" among the flux of sensations (148).

In the masculine plot, closure comes with the achievement of manhood. In Pater's internalized representation of masculinity attained, manhood is figured not by a physical action, but by a psychic practice defined in metaphor, the most familiar of Paterian words: "To burn always with this hard gem-like flame, to maintain this ecstasy, is success in life" (148). As a figure of manhood, this celebrated metaphor exemplifies the embeddedness of Pater's writing in earlier figurations of masculinity as well as his subversion of the models he appropriates. As oxymoron the figure shows Pater's own, ultimately futile effort to reconcile the contradictions and the tensions of this Victorian discourse of manhood by shaping his own vision of masculinity transformed.

The figure continues the earlier Victorian paradox of masculinity – male energy powers the male psyche, yet it must be contained and controlled lest it endanger the stability of the self and of the male-dominated social order. Pater's metaphorics emphasizes not the diseased quality, but rather the power of the formlessness beyond language lying at the heart of maleness. For Pater as for his predecessors, the crucial act in achieving manhood lies in imposing order on this inner flux, setting and continuing to set a containing form on the formlessness of male desire by a virile act of will. For Pater, too, maleness is an essence, manliness a process, a continuing activity of maintaining a hard-won regulation of inward flux. Thus Pater represents manhood not with nouns, that is, not as a stable entity, but with infinitives denoting ongoing action – "To burn ... to maintain."

This ceaseless effort to contain the seething energy within is marked and masked by the public demeanor of reserve. In Carlyle, the Victorian metaphorics of manhood as reserve turns to fantasies of the male body as inner formlessness beneath a body armor or carapace, and to manliness achieved as energy bound within this rigid exterior, as "hard energy" (*Past* 207) or "iron energy," (*Past* 95).

The "Conclusion" continues this metaphorics of masculinity. Like Carlyle's "hard energy," Pater's "hard gem-like flame" offers a normative representation of manliness as reserve, as tight control of the internal current of male potency.[18] Like "the race of the midstream," a "flame" is a continuous flow of energy, a process rather than a stable object. Crucially the "flame" as inward male energy becomes a figure for manhood only when bounded, given the "hard" edge of a "gem." The "hard gem-like flame," then, is not only Pater's but his age's vision of manliness as contained power. "Gem-like" emphasizes the fitting of a boundary to the flow of energy, setting a limit to the danger of this seminal force. Furthermore, "gem-like" suggests the quintessential activity of manliness as struggle, forging a "hard" form out of primal energies much as a gem or diamond is forged from primordial fire within the earth. And, as the case of Abbot Samson illustrates, manly reserve is the more admirable the more powerful the sexual flame that must be contained.

Pater's hopes for the stable equilibrium of manhood are, however, characteristically qualified. The "hard... flame" of manhood is not a "gem" but only "gem-like," only a simulacrum of the diamond. Echoing Carlyle's metaphor of manhood as "crystallised" energy (*Past* 61), "gem-like" suggests both rigidity and fragility in the formation of masculinity. For Pater, the reserve of the Victorian gentleman, although appearing to have the firmness of a gem, is brittle. Like an imitation diamond, it is easily shattered. This continuing anxious sense of manhood as fragile construction rather than as solid structure, as barely controlled flux rather than indestructible essence, appears sharply in comparison with the use of the figure of the male self as flame and as gem in the work of Pater's one-time pupil, Gerard Manley Hopkins.

Hopkins' own meditation on masculinity as flame, "That Nature is a Heraclitean Fire and of the Comfort of the Resurrection" (1888), also moves along the trajectory of the masculine plot. The poem figures male identity as energy set into individuated form, and at its center also imagines the extinction of the self as the dissolution of personality, as momentarily bound energies falling back into the undifferentiated flux: "But quench her bonniest, dearest to her, her clearest-selvèd spark/ Man, how fast his firedint, his mark on mind, is gone!" (lines. 10–11). As in the "Conclusion," the poem moves from this vision of the death of men as the dissipation of formed or "selvèd" energies to the achievement of manhood as the transmutation of formless fire into the "hard" form of the gem: "This Jack, joke, poor potsherd, patch, matchwood, immortal diamond/ Is immortal diamond" (lines 22–23). For Hopkins manliness is not "gem-like" but a gem, "Is immortal diamond." The perfected male self stands within the fire of mental life as an enduring entity with the hardness of diamond, a portion of the changeless essence of the divine that remains steady within the flux of mental energies.[19] In Pater's figure of the psyche, the "hard" resides only in the boundary, the floodgate holding in check the formless flow of male desire.

In the "Conclusion" the early Victorian rhetoric of strenuous yet tenuous control over the energies of an inherently decentered self takes on a specific sexual valence. The metaphors of psychic containment continue to take on phallic resonance. As Carlyle praises "hard energy" (*Past* 207), Pater limns the male ideal as a "hard gem-like flame." Both Carlyle and Pater seek to transform celibacy into the highest form of phallic virility, but in the

"Conclusion" Pater continues to repudiate the Carlylean technology of sublimating male desire into productive labor. Like "Diaphaneitè," the "Conclusion" moves away from the earlier Victorian valuing of a tempered release of male desire and toward valorizing the totalizing containment of that sexual energy. The ideal becomes complete withholding as a means of intensifying a male–male desire forbidden physical fulfillment. For Pater, the ideal mental state becomes tumescence, the ability to "burn always," to "maintain" this rigid, "hard...flame." Pater sees the orgasmic, the release or spending of seminal energy, the sudden flaring of the flame, Browning's "blue spurt of a lighted match," as collapsing the "hard" and "gem-like," disrupting the constant and continuous pleasurability that is the aim of aesthetic self-discipline.

Pater's "hard gem-like flame" also continues the early Victorian equation of the technology of the male self with the technology of the male sphere. In the "Conclusion," as in *Past and Present*, taming the natural energies of the male psyche is equated with taming the forces of nature, managing male desire with the industrialization of nineteenth-century England, a process represented in the metaphorics of Pater as of Carlyle as harnessing the natural power of water and fire. As Carlyle figures a new masculine heroism in the streams of England harnessed to power the "Undershot" water-wheels, so Pater limns mental discipline as channeling the circular unproductive "whirlpool" of the mind, as transforming the "race of the midstream" into a millrace. As the fiery male energy within Abbot Samson is transmuted by virile psychic restraint into a "noble central heat, fruitful, strong, beneficent" (*Past* 96) that prefigures the controlled fire of Manchester, so Pater's "flame" as focused containment of male energy equates aesthetic mental discipline with the productive concentration of fire in the disciplined flame of the forge, with the transmutation of the fierce natural energy of fire into the steam that powers England's industrial supremacy and creates the "hard" commodities of Victorian England, "gem-like" in their commercial value.[20]

In implicitly connecting the mental discipline of the aesthetic with the work of industry, Pater, like his predecessors, deploys a rhetoric that brings his activity as "brain-worker," his practice as critic and even as detached connoisseur of pleasurable sensation within the orbit of normative bourgeois manliness. The difficulty, if not the desperation, of such linkage becomes evident in Pater's description of aesthetic manhood as "success in life," a phrase used within the vocabulary of bourgeois manhood to mark the economic rewards and social respectability gained through aggressive competition with other men. That Pater should apply "success," the central value of entrepreneurial masculinity, to his own formation of the masculine that in its interiority and passive receptivity defines itself by its contrast to the bourgeois model points to the deep ambivalence with which Pater in the 1860s, like earlier Victorian men, engaged the bourgeois formation of masculinity, his conflicted desire to contain his own transformation of masculinity within normative definitions of the manly.

And yet, as much as the "Conclusion" demonstrates Pater's effort to keep his model of the male psyche as well as his own practice as a critic within the bounds of the hegemonic discourse of manliness, his early writing challenges prior formations of masculinity and of a masculine poetic in ways that contemporary readers, as well as Pater himself, quite rightly perceived as fundamental and as dangerous. Preceding masculine poetics were occupied with the problematic of disciplining male desire, but for all their variation, the final purpose of such practices of regulation remained solidly bourgeois, firmly in line with the discipline of the male self in the Victorian businessman and industrialist, the artisan and factory worker in being directed toward increasing the output of attractive goods for the market. In early Victorian masculine poetics, the history of literature and of art is set within a narrative of sublimation as a progress that transforms the dangerous force of male desire into productive artistic energy, much as male energy is channeled into hard work in the Smilesean life of the engineer. In Carlyle, in Browning, and in the Pre-Raphaelite Brotherhood the effort to discipline male desire, the problematic that so occupies Pater, takes the form of desexualizing that desire. For Carlyle this energy is channeled into industrial labor figured by a community of celibate males and into productive celibacy as heroism in the Man of Letters. For Lippo, for Hunt, and for Millais, if not for Rossetti, sexual desire is turned to clear-eyed scientific observation and, almost miraculously, transmuted through rigorous artisanal work into mimetically accurate, sacralized visual art – "and for the church/ A pretty picture gained" ("Lippo" lines 388–99).

Although the "Conclusion" appropriates the occupation with the discipline of male energy, Pater wholly reverses the relation between self-discipline and art practice that grounds earlier Victorian masculine poetics by transforming the goals of this practice of the self. Rather than presenting aesthetic self-discipline as the necessary precondition for the production of art, he presents the art product as the necessary instrument for the production of pleasure within the self. In Pater, as in Browning's Bishop, the economy of the male self is transformed from an economics of production to an economics of consumption.[21] The production of art is not mentioned in the words that make up the "Conclusion," nor, surely, is the sublimation of sexual desire into other forms of labor. The "hard gem-like flame" is a figure for the self as process, not for the process of creating art. As in the contemporaneous painting of Rossetti, the work of art becomes an instrument for the intensified eroticizing of male psychic life, for the containment of male desire within the self as a flame is contained by its edge. It is as a refutation of the fundamental and essentially bourgeois principle underlying the varied forms of the Victorian masculine poetic – the necessity of transforming male desire into art production – that Pater's figure of self as flame acquires its most subversive force.

Finally, if the "Conclusion" appropriates the vocabulary of normative Victorian masculinities – of reserve as the "hard" exterior containing the flux of male energy; of manliness as the "hard" or difficult discipline of desire; of the focused "flame" of the disciplined male self as analogue of the controlled flame of the steam engine and the forge; of psychic control as "success in life" similar to the mental discipline needed for victory within the commercial competitiveness of the male arena – Pater subverts this formation by foregrounding the erotics always present within the practice of psychic restraint for earlier Victorians. For Pater the aesthetic discipline of the self becomes a technique to keep male energy sexual and non-productive, a way to "burn always... to maintain this ecstasy." Pater continues the Victorian practice of controlling male sexuality within the body armor of gentlemanly reserve so as not to disrupt self and society, but driven by the imperative of managing homoerotic desire forbidden expression by his society, Pater finds in the practice of celibacy exemplified in the monk a technology of the self that imprisons a desire that may never be consummated within the containment vessel of the "thick wall of personality" so that it may glow more brightly, "burn always with this hard gem-like flame."

Notes

INTRODUCTION

1 In seeing the defining quality of bourgeois masculinity as the control of sexual energy, I differ with the view that, as expressed by Nead in *Myths of Sexuality*, assigns to the Victorians "a code of sexual mores which condones sexual activity in men as a sign of 'masculinity'" (6).
2 In using the term "repression" here and throughout this study I am following Foucault in *The History of Sexuality*, volume 1 and Kucich in *Repression in Victorian Fiction* by employing the word in an early-nineteenth-century rather than a Freudian sense and in emphasizing the varied uses of repression in masculine practices of the self.
3 In this coded anxiety about marriage expressed by male Victorian writers, we see the analogue to the covert attack on marriage that some feminist criticism has identified as specific to the work of female Victorian writers. See especially Gilbert and Gubar, *Madwoman in the Attic*.
4 See "The Monastery and the Clock" in Mumford's *Technics and Civilization* (12–18) and Sussman's *Victorians and the Machine* (ch. 1).
5 See the discussion of this paradox in Mermin's "The Damsel, the Knight, and the Victorian Woman Poet," where, however, the primary concern is with women writers.
6 Awareness of the complexity of this interchange can be seen in Dellamora's *Masculine Desire*, as in his account of "male love" in Pater's *The Renaissance* as "androgynous in character" (153), and is exemplified in the work of Adams on the re-creation of normative forms of Victorian masculinity in Pater, "Gentleman, Dandy, Priest."
7 See Barker-Benfield's "The Spermatic Economy" and Christ's "Victorian Masculinity and the Angel in the House" for discussions of the Victorian definition of masculinity within the metaphorics of energy.
8 See the excellent account of nineteenth-century male initiation by Carnes, *Secret Ritual and Manhood in Victorian America*, and the quite fascinating cross-cultural anthropological survey of male initiation rites by Gilmore, *Manhood in the Making*.
9 A compelling and methodologically exemplary study of this same drive toward masculinization in our own time that deserves mention is

Jeffords' *The Remasculinization of America*. In drawing parallels between our own time and the *Fin de Siècle*, a period outside the scope of this study, Showalter in *Sexual Anarchy* also recognizes the drive toward masculinization as a strategy of men faced with what they perceive to be threats to stable masculine identity. She contextualizes these strategies not merely as a "response to female literary dominance," but more broadly in terms of the effects of "British imperialism and fears of manly decline" (83).

10 In *Sexual Anarchy* Showalter productively employs not only the model of a battle between the sexes, the paradigm employed by Gilbert and Gubar in *No Man's Land*, volume 1, but also that of "a battle *within* the sexes" (9). This theoretical model of conflict among diverse styles of masculinity is employed to stunning effect in Leverenz's study of male writers of the American Renaissance.

1 THE CONDITION OF MANLINESS QUESTION: THOMAS CARLYLE AND INDUSTRIAL MANHOOD

1 My use of the term "male fantasy" follows Theweleit in *Male Fantasies*. I am not seeking a source of fantasy in Carlyle's unconscious mental life nor positing an essential male psychic structure, but rather attempting to map Carlyle's particular mental configurations of the male body, the male psyche, and the female.
2 "Preface to the Second Edition of *Lyrical Ballads*," 737. For a fine discussion of issues of masculinity in Wordsworth see Wolfson, "*Lyrical Ballads* and the Language of (Men) Feeling."
3 See the account of the nineteenth-century American view of masculinity as the management of seminal energy in Barker-Benfield, "The Spermatic Economy." Barker-Benfield cites the work of Carlyle's contemporary in America, the Reverend John Todd, author of the highly popular *The Student's Manual* (1835), for whom the "image for the working of the male body under the stimulus of a properly resolute will was that of a 'fountain' of 'unequaled...unconquerable energy'" (339). In his library Todd had "a covered, five-foot-three-inch high, indoor fountain, self-contained and ever replenished, furnishing the 'waters of life.' Todd proudly explained 'I have only to touch a little brass cock' for the waters to 'leap up' and generate 'pearls dropping into a well, golden balls falling into cups of silver'" (340).

In "*Lyrical Ballads* and the Language of (Men) Feeling," Wolfson discusses the ambivalence of Wordsworth about the manliness of such overflow of strong feelings and his attempt to contain such potentially feminized metaphors of the loss of control by also deploying the nineteenth-century ideal of manly reserve.
4 For discussion of the economic metaphorics of spermatorrhea see Barker-Benfield, "The Spermatic Economy." For an account of the medical discourse see Cohen, *Talk on the Wilde Side*, especially ch. 2, "Taking Sex

in Hand: Inscribing Masturbation and the Construction of Normative Masculinity."
5 The image resembles the fantasy illustrated by Theweleit of male identity as a train on its rigid track passing over the chaos of the waves (*Male Fantasies* 1: xviii).
6 See Poovey's account in *Uneven Developments* of how in *David Copperfield* "contaminating sexuality is rhetorically controlled by being projected onto the woman" (100).
7 For a fine account of the connection of the sexual female with the new language of the sanitation movement see the discussion in Nead's *Myths of Sexuality* of "Filth and Infection: Prostitution and the Language of Disease" (118–34).
8 Many commentators have noted the importance of such misogyny to Carlyle's politics: Dellamora (*Masculine Desire* 65); Hirsch ("History Writing" 227); Spear ("Filaments" 77); Findlay ("'Maternity must forth'" *passim*); Rosenberg (*Carlyle passim*).
9 This essay was originally published in *Fraser's Magazine* in 1849, then republished as a pamphlet in 1853. I quote from the 1853 version.
10 My reading of Carlyle's representation of the Jamaican Black as the projection of male fears about the loss of control over aggressive and sexual energy within the male self differs from Hall's argument in "Competing Masculinities" that "Carlyle's hostility to black men... was linked to his feminization of them" (273).
11 Henry Maudsley, a prominent Victorian psychologist employs this same metaphor of repression as fermentation to describe the origins of masturbatory insanity in puberty:

> The period during which this fermentation is going on is at best a very trying period for a youth; if there be in him any natural instability of nerve element, owing to the curse of a bad descent, or to some other cause, it is easy to perceive that the natural disturbance of the mental equilibrium may pass into the actual destruction of it; that a physiological process in a feeble mental organism may end in pathological results. (quoted in Cohen *Talk on the Wilde Side* 59)

12 See Sussman *Fact into Figure* and Rosenberg *Carlyle and the Burden of History* for discussion of typological patterns in Carlyle's historical writing.
13 In *The Religious Order*, Hill discusses the importance of such "virtuoso" religious practices in nineteenth-century Anglicanism.
14 I am here following the arguments of Kristeva in *Powers of Horror*.
15 I differ here from the argument of Gilbert and Gubar in *Madwoman in the Attic* that occupation with the trope of imprisonment distinguishes the female from the male literary imagination in the nineteenth century.
16 See Hall, "Competing Masculinities," for a fine contextual account of the Eyre controversy employing a different typology of Victorian masculinities than used in this study.

17 The persistence of this idea is discussed throughout Schor's perceptive reading of formal issues through the lens of gender in *Reading in Detail*.
18 In *Uneven Developments* Poovey sees *David Copperfield* as exemplifying a narrative of male life in which desire is "stabilized and its transgressive potential neutralized in the safe harbor of marriage" (90). My concern in this study is with the plots that opposed this bourgeois script for men, with the recurrent masculine anti-marriage plots of the period that register an anxiety that desire may not only be "neutralized" but also neutered in domesticity. Furthermore, Poovey's identification of women with "self-regulation" within the Victorian "system of representation" (114–15) neglects the centrality of self-regulation to the Victorian definition of bourgeois manliness.
19 Excerpts from Carlyle's yet unpublished essay are provided in Kaplan's article "'Phallus-Worship' (1848)." Citations refer to this article.
20 The contestation and eventual masculinization of the role of sage in the early Victorian period is perceptively discussed in Christ, "'The Hero as Man of Letters.'" In "Strenuous Idleness" Clarke offers an astute biographical account of how the contradiction between the masculinity represented by the Calvinist work ethic of his father and that exemplified in the "idleness" of such literary figures as Coleridge drove Carlyle to construct a new "cultural role for aspiring male writers" (40).

In her chapter "*David Copperfield* and the Professional Writer" in *Uneven Developments* Poovey argues that "to enhance the social status of the literary man, Dickens constructed and appropriated a representation of work that rested on and derived its terms from the ideological separations of spheres and from the representation of women's domestic labor as nonalienated labor" (125). While this is an accurate account of the male fantasy registered in this particular novel, a fantasy much at odds with Dickens' own hectic activity within the male sphere, it is an over-generalization to see this novel as exemplifying "that process by which literary discourse became a 'feminized' discourse by the mid-nineteenth century" (125). The project of Carlyle, as well as Browning, the Pre-Raphaelites, and the early Pater exemplify the enterprise of defining literary discourse as masculine by shaping literary and artistic work as a form of labor firmly situated in the male sphere.
21 In *Sexual Anarchy*, Showalter discusses this circulation of wisdom among males in the literature of the 1890s (ch. 5).
22 See the fine article by Lentricchia, "The Resentments of Robert Frost," comparing the subject positions of Wordsworth and Frost as observer and participant respectively in shaping their poetic representation of physical work.
23 I am here following Wolfson's discussion in "*Lyrical Ballads* and the Language of (Men) Feeling" of the problematic of a manly poetic in Wordsworth.
24 See the perceptive discussion of erotics and the afterlife for Tennyson in Craft, "'Descend and Touch and Enter.'"

25 In *Tradition/Counter/Tradition* Boone argues persuasively for such displacements in nineteenth-century American literature as utopian modes of re-imagining manhood rather than as mere fantasies of protracted adolescence.
26 My discussion of the increasingly difficult route to manhood in the industrial age and of nineteenth-century male initiation rituals is throughout indebted to Carnes' brilliant book *Secret Ritual and Manhood in Victorian America*.
27 I am here following the arguments of Carnes (*Secret Ritual* 124) and of Miller in *The Novel and the Police*.
28 Brantlinger in *Rule of Darkness* provides a fine discussion of Marryat's maritime novels in a colonialist context (ch. 2), but his interest is not in issues of masculinity.
29 See the superb account of Emerson's difficulty with "man-making" in Leverenz, *Manhood and the American Renaissance*.
30 The connection of the Anglican Church with the formation of the homosexual is traced in detail in Hilliard, "UnEnglish and Unmanly."
31 Altick discusses this context and notes that the authorship of this poem has not been established (*Past* 120).

2 THE PROBLEMATIC OF A MASCULINE POETIC: ROBERT BROWNING

1 In *Retreat into the Mind*, Faas has demonstrated, in somewhat exhaustive detail, how extensively Browning's early dramatic monologues are grounded in what he terms the "rise of mental science" (4).
2 The early Victorian definition of male madness itself falls within a binary that preserves the distinction male/female. As Nead notes in *Myths of Sexuality*, female deviance is "represented as a consequence of abnormal and excessive sexual feelings; desires which are defined as commonplace in man are treated as a form of madness in woman" (50).
3 See Marcus, *The Other Victorians*, for an influential, if dated, account of Victorian pornography.
4 This adoption of the practice of reserve by the European bourgeoisie in the nineteenth century is discussed in Sennett, *The Fall of Public Man*.
5 Tucker in "Dramatic Monologue and the Overhearing of Lyric" suggestively notes these hesitations in the poem as signs of the dissolution of the self (234–36), but does not relate this observation to Victorian practices of masculinity.
6 Browning's quest for a manly career is treated with depth and perception in Maynard's *Browning's Youth*, the definitive study of Browning's entry into manhood.
7 See the discussion of "entrepreneurial manhood" in Leverenz, *Manhood and the American Renaissance*, ch. 3.
8 This acute statement, however, introduces an essay on "The Damsel, the Knight, and the Victorian Woman Poet," an analysis devoted not to

the problematics of artistic manhood, but rather to the contradictions between being a woman and a poet in the Victorian age.
9 Critical discussion of the disjunction between the bourgeois construction of manhood and masculine poetic practice in the early Victorian period has focused on the opposition of masculine/feminine in Tennyson, as in Stevenson, "'The High-Born Maiden Symbol' in Tennyson," and Sinfield, *Tennyson* (ch. 2). Among recent critics there has been a tendency to valorize the female identification in Tennyson, as in the incisive and influential essay by Elliot L. Gilbert, "The Female King." An exception is Shires' "*Maud*, Masculinity and Poetic Identity," which accurately describes Tennyson's effort to reconcile poetic identity with normative masculinity by investing in the masculine modes of warfare and commerce. Because of the extensive study of gender conflict in the early poetry of Tennyson, I do not devote a section specifically to Tennyson's work, but consider issues of masculinity in his early poetry within discussion of his contemporaries whose conflicts about masculinity have been less fully explored.
10 For an essay that seeks to demonstrate the valorization of the female in Browning see Knoepflmacher, "Projection and the Female Other."
11 For the definitive discussion of the Victorian art-historical controversies including concerns about manliness that form the context for the artist-poems, see DeLaura, "The Context of Browning's Painter Poems."
12 I am thinking here especially of Part One, "We 'Other Victorians,'" and Part Two, "The Repressive Hypothesis" in *The History of Sexuality*, volume 1.
13 See the discussion of Emerson's "man-making" words in Leverenz, *Manhood* (ch. 2).
14 In his fine book *Browning's Dramatic Monologues and the Post-Romantic Subject* Martin examines the relation of capitalist ideology to the form of the dramatic monologue and to Browning's deconstruction of the individual subject. I agree that these artist-poems must be read as a response to a market economy, but am here stressing the connection between this economy and issues of masculinity.
15 For discussion of the Victorian typological aesthetic as reconciling secular realism with transcendentalism see Sussman, *Fact into Figure* and Landow, *Victorian Types, Victorian Shadows*.
16 As Nead points out in *Myths of Sexuality*, the double standard encapsulates the sharp Victorian binarism of male/female, "the differentiation between active male sexuality and passive female sexuality" (6). Nead also notes that the "double standard had particular significance for the regulation of middle-class women; the notion of female chastity was most rigorously applied within the middle classes and was an important aspect of bourgeois ideologies of home and marriage" (6).
17 In *Uneven Developments*, Poovey sees the production of serialized novels in interchangeable parts in the 1840s as exemplifying alienated literary labor in "factorylike conditions of production" (104–5).

18 Discussion of the lyric element in this poem is indebted to Tucker, "Dramatic Monologue and the Overhearing of Lyric" (232–33).
19 Critics have noted the economic language of the poem, but not in the context of gender issues. See Dooly, "Andrea, Raphael, and the Women of 'Andrea del Sarto'" and Martin, *Browning's Dramatic Monologues* (141–45).
20 See the reading of this poem as an ironic criticism of the commodification of sexuality in Harris, "D. G. Rossetti's 'Jenny.'"
21 Although the disjunction between artistic potency and marriage in "Fra Lippo Lippi" and "Andrea del Sarto" invites speculation about the autobiographical element in these poems, such analysis is beyond the scope of this study. There has been lively critical controversy concerning Browning's anxiety about his manhood within his marriage. See Haigwood, "Gender-to-Gender Anxiety and Influence in Robert Browning's *Men and Women*."
22 See Craft, "'Descend and Touch and Enter.'"
23 The varied representation of that myth in male writing is perceptively explored by Munich in *Andromeda's Chains*.
24 The model of the erotic triangle is discussed in Sedgwick, *Between Men*, ch. 1.
25 In "Victorian Poetry/Oedipal Politics" Kramer suggests that Andrea's artistic flaws may be caused not by "his infatuation with his wife," but rather "represent the outcome of homosexual panic" (360). Donald argues in "Coming out of the Canon" that in "Andrea del Sarto" Browning "defines imaginative intensity and achievement in terms of homosexuality" (250). My own view is that Browning associates artistic potency with the containment of homoeroticism within the middle-class configuration of the homosocial that the Victorians marked as masculine.
26 This scene became a literary icon of homosexual desire within the coding of such desire in the later nineteenth century. In *Billy Budd* Melville describes Claggart's conflicted attraction to Billy with the image of "Saul's visage perturbedly brooding on the comely young David" (327). In "The Critic as Artist" Wilde shows his own attraction to the homoerotic feeling in Browning's poem: "There, stands dread Saul with the lordly male-sapphires gleaming in his turban" (57).

3 ARTISTIC MANHOOD: THE PRE-RAPHAELITE BROTHERHOOD

1 As Nead notes, "Respectability meant different things for men and for women; for women, it was defined in terms of their location within the domestic sphere and their consequent sexual respectability" (*Myths of Sexuality* 28).
2 See the fine discussions of male Victorian artists' drive toward professionalization in Gillett, *Worlds of Art* and in Codell, "Spielmann."

See also the excellent account of the analogous professionalization of the novelist in Feltes, *Modes of Production of Victorian Novels* (5–7).
3 I have discussed this issue in "The Pre-Raphaelite Brotherhood and their Circle: The Formation of the Victorian Avant-Garde."
4 For this account of masculine bonding in the Royal Academy, I am grateful to correspondence with Julie Codell. See also the description of homosocial activities of the Royal Academy in Gillett, *Worlds of Art*.
5 See, for example, the discussion of this effect in Christ, *The Finer Optic*.
6 I have discussed in "Rossetti's Changing Style" the connection of this hallucinatory effect with the movement from the sacred to the secular in the consecutive versions of "My Sister's Sleep."
7 Schor brilliantly demonstrates the gendered significance of detail through a number of historical examples in *Reading in Detail*.
8 See, for example, Hughes, *The Manliness of Christ*.
9 See Steinberg, "The Sexuality of Christ in Renaissance Art and in Modern Oblivion."
10 See the interesting discussion in Pointon, "Artist as Ethnographer," of Hunt's *The Shadow of Death* as a projection of his own guilt and anxiety onto the uncovered, distorted body of the adult Jesus.
11 My discussion of this issue is indebted to Munich's account in *Andromeda's Chains* of what she terms Rossetti's "Fleshly Annunciations" (95–103).
12 Interestingly, Nead connects the many representations of Mary Magdalene in the 1850s to the Parliamentary debates about divorce that concluded with the passage of the Matrimonial Causes Act in 1857, legislation that established adultery by the wife as grounds for divorce but not adultery by the husband (*Myths of Sexuality* 52–72). Rossetti's work, completed in 1858, also represents Magdalene as sexual female threatening masculine sexual control situated within a fortress-like domestic interior space.
13 Discussion of the religious context of the response to *The Carpenter's Shop* is indebted to Errington, *Social and Religious Themes in English Art*.
14 See Treuherz, "The Pre-Raphaelites and Medieval Illuminated Manuscripts."
15 I have discussed the differing signification of the nun in Pre-Raphaelite work in "The Pre-Raphaelites and the 'Mood of the Cloister.'"
16 See the fine discussion of Brotherhood illustrations of this play in Hersey, "Hunt, Millais, and *Measure for Measure*."
17 I am thinking here of Pollock's *Vision and Difference* and Pearce's *Woman/Image/Text*.
18 For this perspective on the Morris–Rossetti relationship, I am indebted to conversations with Carole Silver.
19 This reading is indebted to that of Munich in *Andromeda's Chains* (106–7). Her analysis, however, shifts from seeing the work as coding a forbidden physical sexuality between men to reading the dragon as female and the embrace as suggesting heterosexual intercourse.

20 This example of the confusion of personal and professional relationships within the Brotherhood was suggested by Sharon Smulders in her work in progress on Christina Rossetti.
21 See the fine discussion in Munich's *Andromeda's Chains* of the Victorian "Poetics of Rescue" (14–16).
22 Munich perceptively describes this painting as exemplifying the Victorian "Poetics of Rescue" (16–18). My own reading focuses on the work as illustrating problematics of Victorian masculinity.
23 Pointon convincingly argues in "Histories of Matrimony" that Millais' *The Flood* of 1850 links marriage and death by linking the deluge with a marriage feast and sees in the varied reactions of bride, bridegroom and guests an "allegorical project [that] brings together the anxiety, obligation, and fearfulness of marriage as a form of social regulation at a particular historical moment [and] does so from the point of view of a man" (119).
24 See the fine article by Codell, "The Dilemma of the Artist in Millais's *Lorenzo and Isabella.*"
25 This Victorian formation of Keats is described by Wolfson in "Feminizing Keats."
26 See the fine discussion in Gagnier, *Idylls of the Marketplace*, of Wilde's shaping of the "deviant" self into a commodity during the late nineteenth century.
27 Poovey discusses this issue for Dickens in her chapter on "*David Copperfield* and the Professional Writer" in *Uneven Developments*.
28 I am indebted to Julie Codell for this information.
29 This discussion applies to the production of art objects the models developed by Feltes in his significant work on Victorian publishing, *Modes of Production of Victorian Novels*, in which he sees the commodity-text as "produced in the new capitalist mode of production, produced in struggle by the new 'professional' author within the new structures of control over the publishing process" (8).
30 See the fascinating account of the world tour of *The Light of the World* in Maas, *Holman Hunt and The Light of the World*.
31 See the account of the economics and the career opportunities in this period in Gillett, *Worlds of Art* (ch. 2).
32 In "The Artist as Ethnographer," Pointon likens Hunt's work outside of England to "an industrial venture" (37).
33 See the feminist reading of Rossetti's depiction of women in Pollock, *Vision and Difference* (chs. 4 and 5).
34 Pollock discusses this use of moralized narratives to regulate desire in the male viewer in *Vision and Difference* (130–31).
35 Within the feminist rewriting of the Pre-Raphaelites, Rossetti's late paintings of women have come to exemplify masculinist art and are presented, as in Pollock's *Vision and Difference* and Pearce's *Woman/Image/Text*, as a test case for how women might deal with such art.

4 MASCULINITY TRANSFORMED: APPROPRIATION IN WALTER PATER'S EARLY WRITING

1 Citations of "Poems by William Morris" throughout refer to the 1868 *Westminster* version. Citations of the much revised version of this essay as "Aesthetic Poetry" will be so indicated. Although citation of the paragraphs that were later used in somewhat revised form as the "Conclusion" to *The Renaissance* will be from the *Westminster* version, for convenience I shall refer to these familiar words as the "Conclusion." Generally, critics have looked at Pater's early writings only in their later form – "Poems by William Morris" as the much revised, attenuated "Aesthetic Poetry" and the paragraphs we have come to call the "Conclusion" in the context of *The Renaissance*.

2 In adopting a teleological perspective that values Pater's work as participating in the historical movement toward modernism and deconstruction, for example, Loesberg's *Aestheticism and Deconstruction: Pater, Derrida, and de Man*, recent Pater criticism has foregrounded the discontinuity of Pater's work with earlier Victorian ideas of normative masculinity and of manly art. Exceptions to this approach are Adams' essay "Gentleman, Dandy, Priest," which emphasizes Pater's incorporation of normative masculinities, and Morgan's "Reimagining Masculinity," which notes, for example, how "Pater's imaginative construct of diaphanéité remains very much a masculine state" (320).

3 The formulation of "aesthetic historicism" follows Williams' excellent work *Transfigured World: Walter Pater's Aesthetic Historicism*.

4 The homoerotic ambience of Pater's Oxford is described in Dellamora's *Masculine Desire* (ch. 3).

5 See the interesting account of aestheticism as a personal discipline in Hunter, "Aesthetics and Cultural Studies."

6 In *Transfigured World*, Williams discusses Pater's secularized typology, but does not discuss the relation of his typological form to gender issues. For a general discussion of the Victorian secularization of typology see Sussman, *Fact into Figure*.

7 See the compelling discussion of current awareness of the homoerotic quality of much canonical literature in debates on the literary canon in Sedgwick, *Epistemology of the Closet*, 48–59.

8 In "Coming out of the Canon," Donald argues that since Andrea "chooses erotic *failure* by choosing Lucrezia, Andrea's defiant heterosexuality reveals an underlying and pervasive sadomasochism" (250).

9 Such homoerotic resonance is expunged from "Aesthetic Poetry," the later revision of "Poems by William Morris." The description of Jesus as "beautiful idol" is, for example, erased. The attenuated passage reads, "The Christianity of the Middle Ages made way among a people whose loss was in the life of the senses partly by its aesthetic beauty, a thing so

profoundly felt by the Latin hymn-writers, who for one moral or spiritual sentiment have a hundred sensuous images" (78).
10 With characteristic evasiveness, in "Aesthetic Poetry," Pater substitutes for the overtly anti-Christian "idolatry" and "idol" the word "devotion," an ambiguous term that admits of both a religious and a psycho-sexual resonance: "The devotion of the cloister knew that mood, thoroughly, and had sounded all its stops. For the object of this devotion was absent or veiled, not limited to one supreme plastic form like Zeus at Olympia or Athena in the Acropolis, but distracted, as in a fever dream, into a thousand symbols and reflections" (78).
11 See the discussion of the homoerotic element within the Victorian idealization of chivalry in Dellamora's *Masculine Desire* (ch. 8).
12 In keeping with his softening of the wholly secular stance of the early essay, in "Aesthetic Poetry" Pater dropped the words "as the flame of a little taper shows through the Host."
13 Williams in *Transfigured World* (260) notes Pater's use of Darwinian evolution, but not in the context of gender issues.
14 For discussion of this psychic practice, see Sedgwick, *Epistemology of the Closet* (55–57).
15 In *Masculine Desire* (65–66), Dellamora discusses the connection of these passages to Carlyle, but his discussion places a different emphasis.
16 Citations of the "Conclusion" will continue to refer to the original publication as the final paragraphs of "Poems by William Morris" in the *Westminster Review* of 1868. A complete account of changes in these paragraphs when republished in the varied editions of *The Renaissance* appears in Hill's invaluable edition and such changes will be noted where relevant.
17 I agree with Williams in *Transfigured World* (18–26) in seeing Pater as setting up a position in the "Conclusion" in order to reject it, but take a different emphasis in setting Pater's rhetoric within the context of earlier Victorian masculine metaphorics.
18 See the fine discussion in Adams' "Gentleman, Dandy, Priest" of Pater's deployment of the Victorian ideal of manliness as reserve in *Marius the Epicurean*.
19 Hopkins' close connection with Pater suggests that the poem be read intertextually as a response to the "Conclusion" as published in *The Renaissance*.
20 Meisel in *The Absent Father* (54–63) notes the figure of forging with its industrial resonance as important to Pater, but without noting the connection to contemporary formations of masculinity.
21 This connection between Pater's poetics and the shift to an economic theory based on consumption in the late nineteenth century is noted by Gagnier, "On the Insatiability of Human Wants: Economic and Aesthetic Man."

Bibliography

Adams, James Eli. "Gentleman, Dandy, Priest: Manliness and Social Authority in Pater's Aestheticism." *ELH* 59 (1992): 441–66.
Arnold, Matthew. *The Poetical Works of Matthew Arnold.* Oxford University Press, 1961.
Barker-Benfield, Ben. "The Spermatic Economy: A Nineteenth-Century View of Sexuality." In Michael Gordon (ed.), *The American Family in Social-Historical Perspective.* New York: St. Martin's, 1972. 336–72.
Bly, Robert. *Iron John.* New York: Vintage, 1990.
Boone, Joseph. *Tradition/Counter/Tradition: Love and the Form of Fiction.* University of Chicago Press, 1986.
Brantlinger, Patrick. *Rule of Darkness: British Literature and Imperialism, 1830–1914.* Ithaca: Cornell University Press, 1988.
Bronkhurst, Judith. "'An interesting series of adventures to look back upon': William Holman Hunt's Visit to the Dead Sea in November 1854." In Parris (ed.), *Pre-Raphaelite Papers.* 111–25.
Browning, Elizabeth Barrett. *Poetical Works of Elizabeth Barrett Browning.* Boston: Houghton Mifflin, 1974.
Browning, Robert. *Robert Browning: The Poems.* 2 vols. Ed. John Pettigrew. New Haven: Yale University Press, 1981.
  Robert Browning's Poetry. Ed. James F. Loucks. New York: Norton, 1979.
  Dearest Isa: Robert Browning's Letters to Isabella Blagden. Ed. Edward C. McAleer. Austin: University of Texas Press, 1951.
Carlyle, Thomas. *The French Revolution.* 3 vols. London: Chapman and Hall, 1896.
  On Heroes, Hero Worship, and the Heroic in History. London: Dent, 1956.
  "The Nigger Question." In *English and other Critical Essays.* London: Dent, 1964. 303–33.
  Past and Present. Ed. Richard Altick. Boston: Houghton Mifflin, 1965.
  Sartor Resartus. London: Dent, 1956.
Carnes, Mark C. *Secret Ritual and Manhood in Victorian America.* New Haven: Yale University Press, 1989.
Carter, Angela. "Black Venus." In *Saints and Strangers.* New York: Penguin, 1987. 109–26.
Chitty, Susan. *The Beast and the Monk: A Life of Charles Kingsley.* New York: Mason/Charter, 1975.

Christ, Carol T. *The Finer Optic: The Aesthetic of Particularity in Victorian Poetry*. New Haven: Yale University Press, 1975.
"'The Hero as Man of Letters': Masculinity and Victorian Nonfiction Prose." In Morgan (ed.), *Victorian Sages*. 19–31.
"Victorian Masculinity and the Angel in the House." In Martha Vicinus (ed.), *The Widening Sphere: Changing Roles of Victorian Women*. Bloomington: Indiana University Press, 1977. 146–62.
Clarke, Norma. "Strenuous Idleness: Thomas Carlyle and the Man of Letters as Hero." In Michael Roper and John Tosh (eds.), *Manful Assertions: Masculinities in Britain since 1800*. London: Routledge, 1991. 25–43.
Codell, Julie F. "The Dilemma of the Artist in Millais's *Lorenzo and Isabella*: Phrenology, the Gaze, and the Social Discourse." *Art History* 14 (1991): 51–66.
"Marion Harry Spielmann and the Role of the Press in the Professionalization of Artists." *Victorian Periodicals Review* 22 (1989): 7–15.
"Sentiment, the Highest Attribute of Art: The Socio-Poetics of Feeling." *Dickens Studies Annual* 22 (1992): 233–52.
Cohen, Ed. *Talk on the Wilde Side: Toward a Genealogy of a Discourse on Male Sexualities*. New York: Routledge, 1993.
Cooper, Robyn. "Millais's *The Rescue*: A Painting of a 'Dreadful Interruption of Domestic Peace.'" *Art History* 9 (1986): 471–86.
Craft, Christopher. "'Descend and Touch and Enter': Tennyson's Strange Manner of Address." *Genders* 1 (1988): 83–101.
"'Kiss Me with Those Red Lips': Gender and Inversion in Bram Stoker's *Dracula*." In Showalter (ed.), *Speaking of Gender*. 216–42.
Davidoff, Leonore and Hall, Catherine. *Family Fortunes: Men and Women of the English Middle Class, 1780–1850*. University of Chicago Press, 1987.
DeLaura, David J. "The Context of Browning's Painter Poems: Aesthetics, Polemics, Historics." *PMLA* 95 (1980): 367–88.
"Hopkins and Carlyle: My Hero, My Chevalier." *Hopkins Quarterly* 2 (1975): 67–76.
Dellamora, Richard. *Masculine Desire: The Sexual Politics of Victorian Aestheticism*. Chapel Hill: University of North Carolina Press, 1990.
Dickens, Charles. *Hard Times*. Harmondsworth: Penguin, 1991.
"Old Lamps for New Ones." *Household Words* 1 (1850): 265–67.
The Speeches of Charles Dickens. Ed. K. J. Fielding. Oxford: Clarendon, 1960.
Donald, Adrienne. "Coming out of the Canon: Sadomasochism, Male Homoeroticism, Romanticism." *Yale Journal of Criticism* 3 (1989): 239–52.
Dooly, Allan C. "Andrea, Raphael, and the Women of 'Andrea del Sarto,'" *Modern Philology* 81 (1983): 38–46.
Ehrenreich, Barbara. *The Hearts of Men: American Dreams and the Flight from Commitment*. New York: Anchor, 1983.

Errington, Lindsay. *Social and Religious Themes in English Art, 1840–1860*. New York: Garland, 1984.
Faas, Ekbert. *Retreat into the Mind: Victorian Poetry and the Rise of Psychiatry*. Princeton University Press, 1988.
Feltes, N. N. *Modes of Production of Victorian Novels*. University of Chicago Press, 1986.
Findlay, L. M. "'Maternity must forth': The Poetics and Politics of Gender in Carlyle's *French Revolution*." *Dalhousie Review* 66 (1986): 130–54.
Ford, Ford Madox. *Ford Madox Brown: A Record of his Life and Work*. London: Longmans, 1896.
  Parade's End. New York: Knopf, 1961.
Foucault, Michel. *The History of Sexuality*, volume I: *An Introduction*. New York: Pantheon, 1978.
  The History of Sexuality, volume II: *The Use of Pleasure*. New York: Pantheon, 1985.
Fredeman, William (ed.). *The P.R.B. Journal: William Michael Rossetti's Diary of the Pre-Raphaelite Brotherhood, 1849–1853*. Oxford: Clarendon, 1975.
Gagnier, Reginia. *Idylls of the Marketplace: Oscar Wilde and the Victorian Public*. Stanford University Press, 1986.
  "On the Insatiability of Human Wants: Economic and Aesthetic Man." *Victorian Studies* 36 (1993): 125–53.
Gaskell, Elizabeth. *North and South*. Harmondsworth: Penguin, 1987.
Gelpi, Barbara Charlesworth. "The Feminization of D. G. Rossetti." In Richard A. Levine (ed.), *The Victorian Experience: The Poets*. Athens: Ohio University Press, 1982. 94–114.
Gilbert, Elliot L. "The Female King: Tennyson's Arthurian Apocalypse." *PMLA* 98 (1983): 863–78.
Gilbert, Sandra and Gubar, Susan. *The Madwoman in the Attic: The Nineteenth-Century Female Literary Imagination*. New Haven: Yale University Press, 1979.
  No Man's Land, volume I: *The War of the Words*. New Haven: Yale University Press, 1988.
Gillett, Paula. *Worlds of Art: Painters in Victorian Society*. New Brunswick: Rutgers University Press, 1990.
Gilmore, David D. *Manhood in the Making: Cultural Concepts of Masculinity*. New Haven: Yale University Press, 1990.
Haigwood, Laura. "Gender-to-Gender Anxiety and Influence in Robert Browning's *Men and Women*." *Browning Institute Studies* 14 (1986): 97–118.
Hall, Catherine. "Competing Masculinities: Thomas Carlyle, John Stuart Mill, and the Case of Governor Eyre." *White, Male and Middle-Class: Explorations in Feminism and History*. New York: Routledge, 1992. 255–95.
Harris, Daniel. "D. G. Rossetti's 'Jenny': Sex, Money, and the Interior Monologue." *Victorian Poetry* 22 (1984): 139–59.

Hersey, George. "Hunt, Millais, and *Measure for Measure*." *Journal of Pre-Raphaelite and Aesthetic Studies* 1 (1987): 83–88.
Hill, Michael. *The Religious Order: A Study of Virtuoso Religion and Its Legitimation in the Nineteenth-Century Church of England*. London: Heinemann, 1973.
Hilliard, David. "UnEnglish and Unmanly: Anglo-Catholicism and Homosexuality." *Victorian Studies* 25 (1982): 181–210.
Hirsch, Gordon. "History Writing in Carlyle's *Past and Present*." *Prose Studies* 7 (1984): 225–32.
Hopkins, Gerard Manley. *Gerard Manley Hopkins*. Ed. Catherine Phillips. Oxford University Press, 1986.
Hughes, Thomas. *The Manliness of Christ*. London: Macmillan, 1879.
Hunt, Holman. *Pre-Raphaelitism and the Pre-Raphaelite Brotherhood*. 2 vols. London: Macmillan, 1905.
Hunter, Ian. "Aesthetics and Cultural Studies." In Lawrence Grossberg, Cary Nelson, and Paula A. Treichler (eds.), *Cultural Studies*. New York: Routledge, 1992. 347–66.
Jeffords, Susan. *The Remasculinization of America: Gender and the Vietnam War*. Bloomington: Indiana University Press, 1989.
Kaplan, Fred. "'Phallus-Worship'(1848): Unpublished Manuscripts III – A Response to the Revolution of 1848." *Carlyle Newsletter* 2 (1980): 19–24.
Keats, John, *The Complete Poems of John Keats*. Ed. Jack Stillinger. Cambridge, MA: Harvard University Press, 1978.
King, Roma A., Jr. "Eve and the Virgin: 'Andrea del Sarto.'" In *The Bow and the Lyre: The Art of Robert Browning*. Ann Arbor: University of Michigan Press, 1957. 11–31.
Kingsley, Charles. "The Poetry of Sacred and Legendary Art." *The Works of Charles Kingsley*. London: Macmillan, 1880. Volume xx: 188–226.
Knoepflmacher, U. C. "Projection and the Female Other: Romanticism, Browning, and the Victorian Dramatic Monologue." *Victorian Poetry* 22 (1984): 139–59.
Kramer, Lawrence. "Victorian Poetry/Oedipal Politics: *In Memoriam* and Other Instances." *Victorian Poetry* 29 (1991): 351–64.
Kristeva, Julia. *Powers of Horror: An Essay on Abjection*. New York: Columbia University Press, 1982.
Kucich, John. *Repression in Victorian Fiction: Charlotte Brontë, George Eliot, and Charles Dickens*. Berkeley: University of California Press, 1987.
Landow, George P. *Victorian Types, Victorian Shadows: Biblical Typology in Victorian Literature, Art, and Thought*. London: Routledge, 1980.
Lentricchia, Frank. "The Resentments of Robert Frost." In Laura Claridge and Elizabeth Langland (eds.), *Out of Bounds: Male Writers and Gender[ed] Criticism*. Amherst: University of Massachusetts Press, 1990. 252–67.
Leverenz, David. *Manhood and the American Renaissance*. Ithaca: Cornell University Press, 1989.

Loesberg, Jonathan. *Aestheticism and Deconstruction: Pater, Derrida, and de Man.* Princeton University Press, 1991.
Maas, Jeremy. *Holman Hunt and The Light of the World.* Aldershot: Wildwood House, 1987.
The Victorian Art World in Photographs. London: Barrie and Jenkins, 1984.
Marcus, Stephen. *The Other Victorians: A Study of Sexuality and Pornography in Mid-Nineteenth-Century England.* New York: Basic Books, 1964.
Marryat, Frederick. *Peter Simple.* London: Dent, 1974.
Martin, Loy. *Browning's Dramatic Monologues and the Post-Romantic Subject.* Baltimore: Johns Hopkins University Press, 1985.
Maynard, John. *Browning's Youth.* Cambridge, MA: Harvard University Press, 1977.
Meisel, Perry. *The Absent Father: Virginia Woolf and Walter Pater.* New Haven: Yale University Press, 1980.
Melville, Herman. "Billy Budd." In *Billy Budd, Sailor and Other Stories.* Harmondsworth: Penguin, 1986. 287–385.
"The Paradise of Bachelors and the Tartarus of Maids." In *Billy Budd, Sailor and Other Stories.* Harmondsworth: Penguin, 1986. 259–86.
Mermin, Dorothy. "The Damsel, the Knight, and the Victorian Woman Poet." *Critical Inquiry* 13 (1986): 65–80.
Millais, John Guile. *The Life and Letters of Sir John Everett Millais.* 2 vols. New York: Frederick A. Stokes, 1899.
Miller, D. A. *The Novel and the Police.* Berkeley: University of California Press, 1988.
Morgan, Thaïs E. "Reimagining Masculinity in Victorian Criticism: Swinburne and Pater." *Victorian Studies* 36 (1993): 315–32.
(ed.). *Victorian Sages and Cultural Discourse: Renegotiating Gender and Power.* New Brunswick: Rutgers University Press, 1990.
Mumford, Lewis. *Technics and Civilization.* New York: Harcourt, 1934.
Munich, Adrienne Auslander. *Andromeda's Chains: Gender and Interpretation in Victorian Art and Literature.* New York: Columbia University Press, 1989.
Nead, Lynda. *Myths of Sexuality: Representations of Women in Victorian Britain.* Oxford: Blackwell, 1990.
Parris, Leslie (ed.). *Pre-Raphaelite Papers.* London: Tate Gallery, 1984.
Pater, Walter. "Aesthetic Poetry." In *Selected Writings.* 190–98.
"Browning." In *Essays from "The Guardian."* London: Macmillan, 1910. 41–51.
"Dante Gabriel Rossetti." In *Selected Writings.* 199–208.
"Diaphaneitè." In *Miscellaneous Studies: A Series of Essays.* London: Macmillan, 1905. 215–22.
"Poems by William Morris." *The Westminster Review* (American Edition) 90 (October 1868): 144–49.
The Renaissance: Studies in Art and Poetry. Ed. Donald J. Hill. Berkeley: University of California Press, 1980.
Selected Writings of Walter Pater. Ed. Harold Bloom. New York: Columbia University Press, 1982.

Pearce, Lynne. *Woman/Image/Text: Readings in Pre-Raphaelite Art and Literature.* University of Toronto Press, 1991.
Pointon, Marcia. "The Artist as Ethnographer: Holman Hunt and the Holy Land." In Pointon (ed.), *Pre-Raphaelites Re-viewed.* 22–44.
— "Histories of Matrimony: J. E. Millais." In Pointon (ed.), *Pre-Raphaelites Re-viewed.* 100–22.
— (ed.). *Pre-Raphaelites Re-viewed.* Manchester University Press, 1990.
Pollock, Griselda. *Vision and Difference: Femininity, Feminism and Histories of Art.* London: Routledge, 1988.
Poovey, Mary. *Uneven Developments: The Ideological Work of Gender in Mid-Victorian England.* University of Chicago Press, 1988.
"Puseyism, or the Oxford Tractarian School." *Edinburgh Review* 77 (1843): 501–54.
"Recent Developments of Puseyism." *Edinburgh Review* 80 (1844): 309–68.
"Review of Royal Academy Exhibition." *The Art-Journal* n.s. 2 (1 June 1850): 173–75.
"Review of Royal Academy Exhibition." *The Athenæum* no. 1179 (1 June 1850): 587–90.
Rosenberg, John D. *Carlyle and the Burden of History.* Cambridge, MA: Harvard University Press, 1985.
Rossetti, Christina. *The Complete Poems of Christina Rossetti.* Ed. R. W. Crump. Baton Rouge: Louisiana University Press, 1979–90.
Rossetti, Dante Gabriel. *Dante Gabriel Rossetti: Poems & Translations 1850–1870 Together with the Prose Story "Hand and Soul."* Oxford University Press, 1965.
— *Letters of Dante Gabriel Rossetti.* Ed. Oswald Doughty and John Robert Wahl. 4 vols. Oxford: Clarendon, 1965–67.
Rossetti, William Michael (ed.). *Praeraphaelite Diaries and Letters.* London: Hunt and Blackett, 1900.
— *Some Reminiscences of William Michael Rossetti.* 2 vols. New York: Scribners, 1906.
Ruskin, John. *The Works of John Ruskin.* 39 vols. Ed. E. T. Cook and Alexander Wedderburn. London: George Allen, 1903–12.
Schor, Naomi. *Reading in Detail: Aesthetics and the Feminine.* New York: Methuen, 1978.
Sedgwick, Eve Kosofsky. *Between Men: English Literature and Male Homosocial Desire.* New York: Columbia University Press, 1985.
— *Epistemology of the Closet.* Berkeley: University of California Press, 1990.
Seigel, Jules Paul. *Thomas Carlyle: The Critical Heritage.* New York: Barnes and Noble, 1971.
Sennett, Richard. *The Fall of Public Man.* New York: Vintage, 1978.
Shires, Linda. "*Maud*, Masculinity, and Poetic Identity." *Criticism* 29 (1987): 269–90.
Showalter, Elaine. *Sexual Anarchy: Gender and Culture at the Fin de Siècle.* New York: Viking, 1990.
— (ed.). *Speaking of Gender.* New York: Routledge, 1989.

Sinfield, Alan. *Alfred Tennyson*. New York: Blackwell, 1986.
Smiles, Samuel. *Self-Help; with Illustrations of Character, Conduct and Perseverance*. New York: Harper, 1876.
Spear, Jeffrey L. "Filaments, Females, Families, and Social Fabric: Carlyle's Extension of a Biological Analogy." In James Paradis and Thomas Postlewait (eds.), *Victorian Science and Victorian Values: Literary Perspectives*. New Brunswick: Rutgers University Press, 1985. 69–84.
Staley, Allen. *The Pre-Raphaelite Landscape*. Oxford: Clarendon, 1973.
Stearns, Peter N. *Be a Man! Males in Modern Society*. 2nd edn. New York: Holmes and Meier, 1990.
Steinberg, Leo. "The Sexuality of Christ in Renaissance Art and in Modern Oblivion." *October*, no. 25 (1983): 1–217.
Stevenson, Lionel. "'The High-Born Maiden Symbol' in Tennyson." In John Kilham (ed.), *Critical Essays on the Poetry of Tennyson*. New York: Barnes and Noble, 1960. 126–36.
Surtees, Virginia. *The Paintings and Drawings of Dante Gabriel Rossetti (1828–1882)*. 2 vols. Oxford University Press, 1971.
Sussman, Herbert. *Fact into Figure: Typology in Carlyle, Ruskin, and the Pre-Raphaelite Brotherhood*. Columbus: Ohio State University Press, 1979.
  "The Pre-Raphaelite Brotherhood and their Circle: The Formation of the Victorian Avant-Garde." *Victorian Newsletter* no. 57 (1980): 7–9.
  "The Pre-Raphaelites and the 'Mood of the Cloister.'" *Browning Institute Studies* 8 (1980): 45–56.
  "Rossetti's Changing Style: The Revisions of 'My Sister's Sleep.'" *Victorian Newsletter* no. 41 (1972): 6–9.
  Victorians and the Machine: The Literary Response to Technology. Cambridge, MA: Harvard University Press, 1968.
Swinburne, Algernon Charles. *Selected Poems*. Ed. L. M. Finlay. Manchester: Carcanet, 1987.
Tennyson, Alfred. *The Poems of Tennyson*. 3 vols. Ed. Christopher Ricks. Harlow: Longman, 1987.
Theweleit, Klaus. *Male Fantasies*, volume I: *Women, Floods, Bodies, History*. Minneapolis: University of Minnesota Press, 1987.
  Male Fantasies, volume II. *Male Bodies: Psychoanalyzing the White Terror*. Minneapolis: University of Minnesota Press, 1989.
Treuherz, Julian. "The Pre-Raphaelites and Medieval Illuminated Manuscripts." In Parris (ed.), *Pre-Raphaelite Papers*. 153–69.
Tucker, Herbert F. "Dramatic Monologue and the Overhearing of Lyric." In Chaviva Hosek and Patricia Parker (eds.), *Lyric Poetry: Beyond New Criticism*. Ithaca: Cornell University Press, 1985. 227–43.
Vance, Norman. *The Sinews of the Spirit: The Ideal of Christian Manliness in Victorian Literature and Religious Thought*. Cambridge University Press, 1985.
Wilde, Oscar. "The Critic as Artist." In Richard Aldington and Stanley Weintraub (eds.), *The Portable Oscar Wilde*. New York: Penguin, 1981.

Williams, Carolyn. *Transfigured World: Walter Pater's Aesthetic Historicism.* Ithaca: Cornell University Press, 1989.
Wolfson, Susan. "Feminizing Keats." In Hermione de Almeida (ed.), *Critical Essays on John Keats.* Boston: G. K. Hall, 1970. 317–56.
"*Lyrical Ballads* and the Language of (Men) Feeling: Writing Women's Voices." Unpublished paper.
Woolf, Virginia. *Jacob's Room.* New York: Harcourt 1923.
Wordsworth, William. "Preface to the Second Edition of *Lyrical Ballads.*" In *The Poetical Works of Wordsworth.* Ed. Ernest de Selincourt. Oxford University Press, 1960.
Workman, Gillian. "Thomas Carlyle and the Governor Eyre Controversy: An Account with Some New Material." *Victorian Studies* 18 (1974): 77–102.

Index

abjection, 29, 49, 77, 130–31, 196
aestheticism, 4, 175
   Browning, 74, 77–78, 80
   discipline of self, 77–78
   homoerotic discipline, 182–83, 189, 202
   male sexual pathology, 74, 77–78, 80, 96, 119
   Pater, 119, 175–84, 189, 202
   Rossetti, 96
   see also hysteria, typology
Arnold, Matthew, 70, 84
   "Stanzas from the Grande Chartreuse," 6, 84, 97, 195
artistic manhood, 6–7, 14–15
   avant-garde, 115, 166–68
   Bohemian, 14, 166–68
   Browning, 73–74, 97, 100
   Carlyle, 34, 37–43
   entrepreneurial, 91, 93, 94–97, 116–17, 201
   gentleman, 14, 153–57
   gentry, 155–57
   Hunt, 42, 158–66
   Millais, 153–57
   Pater, 192–93, 201–2
   Pre-Raphaelite Brotherhood, 121
   professional man, 14, 114, 153–57
   prophet, 14, 158–66
   romantic, 82, 85, 115, 195
   sage, 38, 42, 71
   Tennyson, 42

Barthes, Roland, 120
Bly, Robert, 7, 8, 18, 20, 46
bonding, masculine, 4–6, 48, 185
   Browning, 73, 104–10
   Carlyle, 5, 17, 60–63
   Hunt, 158
   Pre-Raphaelite Brotherhood, 5, 111, 140–44
   Rossetti, 141

Royal Academy, 115–16
Brown, Ford Madox, 39–42, 120–21, 168
   Work, 39–41, *40*, 120–21, 146
Browning, Elizabeth Barrett, 99
   "To George Sand," 99
Browning, Robert, 3, 5, 26, 43
   and Carlyle, 35, 57, 73, 88, 93, 100–1, 108
   and Pater, 77, 80, 173, 188–90
   and Pre-Raphaelite Brotherhood, 73, 83, 88
   and Rossetti, 106
   and Tennyson, 75, 84–85
   see also aestheticism, artistic manhood, bonding, celibacy, Christ, manliness of, Christ, sexuality of, communities, energy, homoeroticism, hysteria, imprisonment, initiation, liberationist narrative, madness, marriage, marriage plot, mimetic distortion, monk, plot, poetics, repression, reserve, typology
   "Andrea del Sarto," 45, 93–95, 98–99, 107–8
   "The Bishop Orders His Tomb," 76–78
   "Childe Roland to the Dark Tower Came," 49, 101–4
   "Fra Lippo Lippi," 2, 4, 30, 39, 44–45, 52, 83–84, 87–93, 100–1, 106–7
   "Meeting at Night," 105–6, 146
   "My Last Duchess," 78–80
   "Parting at Morning," 105–6
   "Pictor Ignotus," 2, 4, 6, 31, 52, 85–86
   "Popularity," 100
   "Porphyria's Lover," 74, 80
   "Respectability," 91, 96
   "Saul," 108–10, 122–23, 209 n 26
   "Soliloquy of the Spanish Cloister," 2, 74–76
Burne-Jones, Edward, 141
Burton, Richard, 162

Index

Carlyle, Thomas, 3–6, 117
  and Browning, 35, 57, 73, 88, 93, 100–1, 108
  and Hunt, 126, 158–61
  and Pater, 173, 188–92, 199–200
  carte-de-visite, photograph, *159*
  The French Revolution, 21–22, 24
  "The Hero as Man of Letters," 37–39
  "The Nigger Question," 22–23
  Past and Present, 1, 2, 21–22, 51–55, 61–64, 67–72
  "Phallus-Worship," 36–37, 45, 64, 75
  Sartor Resartus, 1, 28–30, 49–51
  See also artistic manhood, bonding, celibacy, Christ, manliness of, communities, energy, homoeroticism, hysteria, imprisonment, initiation, madness, maleness, marriage, marriage plot, masculinity, monastic discourse, monk, narrative form, plot, poetics, Puseyism, repression, reserve, Tractarians, typology
Carter, Angela, 95
celibacy, 3, 27, 57–58, 66
  Browning, 27, 74, 85
  Carlyle, 17, 21, 27–28, 31–33, 38, 54, 64, 69–72
  Millais, 133–37
  Pater, 27, 175–76, 188–92, 199, 202
  Pre-Raphaelite Brotherhood, 27, 120, 128–37
  Tennyson, 133–34
  see also communities, homoeroticism, madness, mimetic distortion, monk, Puseyism, repression, Tractarians
Christ, manliness of, 120
  Carlyle, 160–61
  Browning, 110
  Hunt, 125–26, 160–61
  Millais, 120–25
  Pre-Raphaelite Brotherhood, 120
  Rossetti, 126–28
  see also Christ, sexuality of
Christ, sexuality of, 110, 121–23
  Browning, 110
  Hunt, 125–26
  Millais, 121–25
  Pater, 182
  Pre-Raphaelite Brotherhood, 121–23
  Rossetti, 126–28
  see also homoeroticism, Christ, manliness of
Collins, Charles, 132, 137
  Convent Thoughts, 2, 132, 137, *138*, 195
communities, male, 1, 2, 65

artistic communities, Victorian, 140–44
  Browning, 101, 104, 106
  Carlyle, 38, 60–61
  celibate religious communities, Victorian, 1, 2, 5, 57–58, 112, 129–30, 132
  Pre-Raphaelite Brotherhood, 112, 117, 129, 140–44, 158
  see also Puseyism, Tractarians
Conrad, Joseph, 39
  Heart of Darkness, 39, 44, 48
Craft, Christopher, 9

Darwin, Charles, 186
Davidoff, Leonore, 12
DeLaura, David, 55
Dickens, Charles, 66, 88, 92
  and *The Carpenter's Shop*, 112, 119, 121, 129–32
  as professional man, 153
  Hard Times, 66, 143
  "Old Lamps for New," 112, 120, 131–32

Ehrenreich, Barbara, 7, 8
Emerson, Ralph Waldo, 7, 18, 19, 56
energy, male, 3, 10–11, 13
  Browning, 73, 84, 93
  Carlyle, 17, 19–28, 34–35, 37, 54–55, 69–70
  commodification of, 90, 93, 95–96, 169
  desexualization of, 4, 6, 37, 42, 54–55, 69, 117, 201–2
  as diseased, 19, 24, 33, 178
  as fire, 10, 13, 105, 146, 198–200
  Pater, 3, 174, 183, 194, 196
  regulation of, 3, 4, 10–11, 17, 25–28, 73, 111, 116, 137
  regulation compared to industrialization, 11, 14, 24, 34–35, 146, 200, 202
  Rossetti, 96, 169, 170–71
evolution and masculinity, 186–87
Eyre, Governor Edward John, 31, 33

Feltes, N. N., 153
Ford, Ford Madox, 44
  Parade's End, 44
figural form, *see* typology
Foucault, Michel, 10–11, 12, 83–84, 90
Freud, Sigmund, 19, 84

Gaskell, Elizabeth, 64–66
  North and South, 64–66, 143

Haggard, H. Rider, 162
Hall, Catherine, 12
Hardy, Thomas, 186

Jude the Obscure, 186
Tess of the d'Urbervilles, 186
homoeroticism, 3, 5, 9–10, 55–56
　boundary with homosocial, 5–6, 9–10, 17, 49, 56–61, 73, 104, 106–7, 141
　Browning, 73, 106–10
　Carlyle, 17, 19, 52–61, 185
　in 1840s, 55–60, 63, 143, 185
　homoerotic poetic, 182–85, 192–93
　Hunt, 162
　monastic discourse, 52, 62–63, 182–84
　Pater, 3, 182–83, 191
　Pre-Raphaelite Brotherhood, 142–3, 185
　Rossetti, 141–42
　see also celibacy
homophobia, 5–6, 9, 58, 142
homosexual, construction of, 59–60
　see also homoeroticism
Hopkins, Gerard Manley, 199
　"That Nature is a Heraclitean Fire," 199
Hunt, William Holman, 125–26
　as artist-prophet, 126, 158–66
　and Carlyle, 126, 158–61
　as celebrity, 164–66
　as imperialist, 161–66
　paintings as commodity-texts, 157
　post-Brotherhood career, 158–66
　see also artistic manhood, bonding, communities, Christ, manliness of, Christ, sexuality of, homoeroticism, maleness, plot, typology, visual style
　The Awakening Conscience, 171
　carte-de-visite, photograph, 158, *159*
　Claudio and Isabella, *136*, 137
　The Finding of the Saviour in the Temple, 123, 161
　The Flight of Madeline and Porphyro, 139
　The Hireling Shepherd, 171
　Isabella and the Pot of Basil, 152
　The Light of the World, *124*, 125–26, 157, 160
　Old Hannah, 158
　Pre-Raphaelitism and the Pre-Raphaelite Brotherhood, 164–65
　reenacting the painting of *The Scapegoat*, photograph, 164–66, *165*
　The Scapegoat, 119, 161–66
　Valentine Rescuing Sylvia, 139
Huxley, Thomas Henry, 186
hysteria, male, 13
　Browning, 76–77
　Carlyle, 68, 72
　as hyperaesthesia, 133, 181
　Pater, 180–81
　Pre-Raphaelite Brotherhood, 119, 133–37, 180–81
　Rossetti, 119, 172, 181
　Tennyson, 133–34
　see also madness

imperialism, 23, 49, 161–66
imprisonment, as trope, 30, 90
　Browning, 30, 85, 90–91
　Carlyle, 29–30
　Millais, 148
　Pater, 177, 180, 187–88, 194–95
　Pre-Raphaelite Brotherhood, 30, 111, 132
　Rossetti, 96
　Tennyson, 30, 133–34
initiation, 46–47, 102, 143, 197
　Browning, 100–4
　Carlyle, 53–55, 102

Jewsbury, Geraldine, 36–37

Keats, John, 152
　as feminized artist, 152
　"Isabella" and Millais' *Lorenzo and Isabella*, 150–52
Kingsley, Charles, 2, 16, 55, 57, 86, 129
Kristeva, Julia, 29

Lawrence, T. E., 162
Leverenz, David, 7, 8, 13
liberationist narrative of masculinity, 4
　Browning, 83–85, 90, 93
　Millais, 148–50
　Pater, 4, 187–89

madness, male, 13
　Browning, 73, 74, 108
　Carlyle, 68–70
　Pater, 119, 177, 197
　Pre-Raphaelite Brotherhood, 119, 133–37
　Rossetti, 119, 139–40
　Tennyson, 48, 133–34
　see also hysteria
maleness, 8, 76, 77
　Carlyle, 24, 25, 68–69
　Hunt, 162–63
　Pater, 195–96, 198
　Victorian definition of, 10, 12–13
　see also manhood, manliness, masculinity
manhood, 8, 13
　as a plot, 13, 45–46, 198
　Victorian definitions of, 10–11, 13, 15
　see also artistic manhood, maleness, manliness, masculinity, reserve

Index

manliness, 13
  Victorian definitions of, 3, 4, 10–11, 13, 25, 27–28
  see also artistic manhood, Christ, manliness of, maleness, masculinity, reserve
marriage, male anxiety about, 4–5, 49, 108, 184
  Browning, 97–98, 104
  Carlyle, 17, 35–36, 45, 61
  Millais, 148–50, 211 n 23
  Pater, 184–85
  Pre-Raphaelite Brotherhood, 115, 143
marriage plot, opposition to, 48, 143–44
  Browning, 97–98, 101
  Carlyle, 17, 35–36, 45, 47, 61, 63–64
  Dickens, 66
  industrial novels, 64–66, 143
Marryat, Frederick, 47–48, 103, 143
  Peter Simple, 47–48, 51
masculinity, 8, 13
  bourgeois, 4–6, 11–13, 19, 34–35, 39, 71
  Christian, 13
  entrepreneurial, 14, 70, 81–82, 201
  gentleman, 153–57
  gentry, 11, 13, 33, 50, 70, 97, 155–57
  homoerotic, 26, 185–86, 202
  imperial, 161–66
  industrial, 4, 13, 16–17, 27, 34–35, 50, 71, 146
  professional man, 114, 153–57
  warrior, 31, 33, 48–49, 64, 144
  working-class, 11–13, 41, 65, 71, 146
  see also artistic manhood, liberationist narrative, maleness, manhood, manliness, reserve, typology
Maynard, John, 81
Melville, Herman, 5, 209 n 26
Mermin, Dorothy, 82
Millais, John Everett, 112
  as gentleman, 155–57
  gentry manhood, 155–57
  paintings as commodity-texts, 156–57
  post-Brotherhood career, 144–57
  as professional man, 153–57
  see also artistic manhood, celibacy, Christ, manliness of, Christ, sexuality of, communities, imprisonment, liberation narrative, marriage, mimetic distortion, plot, rescue plot, typology, visual style
  Bubbles, 156–57
  The Carpenter's Shop (*Christ in the House of His Parents*), *113*, 119–23, 128–32;
    reception of, 112–14, 119, 128–32
  study for *Christ in the House of His Parents*, *123*, 123–25
  at Dalguise, Scotland, photograph, *154*, 155
  The Disentombment of Queen Matilda, 134–37, *135*
  Ferdinand Lured by Ariel, 117
  The Flood, 211 n 23
  The Knight Errant, *147*, 148
  Lorenzo and Isabella, 150–52, *151*
  Mariana, 2, 132–34, *134*, 137, 195
  The North-West Passage, 150
  Ophelia, 119
  The Order of Release, 1746, 148–50, *149*, 160, 195
  The Rescue, 139, 144–48, *145*
  St. Agnes Eve, 132
  in studio, photograph, 155–57, *156*
mimetic distortion, 4, 27, 129–32, 160, 179
  Browning, 3, 86
  Millais, 129–32
  Pater, 179–80, 187–88
  Pre-Raphaelite Brotherhood, 129–32
  psycho-sexual cause, 3, 4, 86, 129–32, 179–80
  Rossetti, 119, 181
  see also celibacy, monk, poetics, repression, visual style
monastery as sign, 3–7
  for affective life between men, 4–6, 55–61, 175–76
  for all-male society, 4, 73
  for artistic community, 115, 158
  for factory, 6, 54–55, 115
monastic discourse, 2–7
  Carlyle, 16–19, 25
  Pater, 174–75, 181–82
  Pre-Raphaelite Brotherhood, 111–12, 115, 128–29, 140–41
monk, 2–7, 16
  artist-monk, 3–7, 38, 83, 86, 129
  Browning, 16, 73, 83
  Carlyle, 16–17, 25–27, 51–55
  as factory worker, 6, 54–55, 115
  and homoerotic life, 3, 16, 57–61, 175, 182, 202
  Pater, 3, 175, 202
  Pre-Raphaelite Brotherhood, 115
  and sexual discipline, 3, 202
  see also celibacy, imprisonment, mimetic distortion, monastery, monastic discourse
Morris, William, 1, 141, 168
Munich, Adrienne, 9

narrative form, masculine, 42–44
　Carlyle, 42–44
　Conrad, 44
　Ford, 44
　Woolf, 44
Newman, John Henry, 57, 58, 59

Pater, Walter, 3, 4, 10, 58
　aesthetic historicism, 173–74
　and Browning, 77, 80, 173, 188–90
　and Carlyle, 173, 188–92, 199–200
　and Rossetti, 181, 202
　sado-masochism, 178–79
　and Swinburne, 179, 185
　see also aestheticism, artistic manhood,
　　celibacy, Christ, sexuality of,
　　community, energy, homoeroticism,
　　hysteria, imprisonment, liberationist
　　narrative, madness, maleness,
　　marriage, mimetic distortion,
　　monastery, monastic discourse, monk,
　　poetics, plot, repression, reserve,
　　typology
　"Aesthetic Poetry," 182–83, 188–90
　"Browning," 188
　"Conclusion," 183, 193–202
　"Dante Gabriel Rossetti," 119, 181
　"Diaphaneitè," 190–92
　"Poems by William Morris," 1, 2,
　　176–81, 183–84, 187–89
　The Renaissance, 192–93
plot, masculine, 13
　Browning, 13, 73, 100–4
　Carlyle, 13, 28–29, 49–55
　definition of, 13, 35–36, 47
　Dickens, 66, 143
　Gaskell, 64–66, 143
　Hunt, 162–63
　as initiation rite, 46–47
　and marriage plot, 35–36, 45, 47
　Millais, 148–50
　model for social reform, 62–63
　Pater, 13, 187–89, 194–98
　Pre-Raphaelite Brotherhood, 13, 133,
　　143–44
　Tennyson, 48–49
　see also manhood, marriage plot, poetics
poetics, masculine, 7, 14, 82, 169, 201–2
　Browning, 82–83
　Carlyle, 17–18, 35–42
　Pater, 175, 188, 193, 201–2
　Pre-Raphaelite Brotherhood, 35, 133
　Tennyson, 43, 48–49, 84
Pre-Raphaelite Brotherhood, 3, 4, 16, 45,
　60

　as avant-garde, 115
　dissolution of, 140–44
　lives governed by masculine plot, 143–44
　see also artistic manhood, bonding,
　　celibacy, Christ, manliness of, Christ,
　　sexuality of, community,
　　homoeroticism, hysteria, imprisonment,
　　madness, marriage, mimetic distortion,
　　monastic discourse, monk, poetics,
　　rescue plot, typology, visual style
Puseyism, 1, 130, 132
　and Carlyle, 57–61
　see also communities, Tractarians

repression, 3, 4, 27–28, 67, 111, 129–30
　Browning, 73, 74
　Carlyle, 23, 27–28, 34, 37, 67, 73
　Pater, 176–78, 182, 189
　Tennyson, 133–34
　see also celibacy, hysteria, imprisonment,
　　madness, mimetic distortion, reserve
rescue plot, 146–47
　Millais, 144–50
　Pre-Raphaelite Brotherhood, 111, 139,
　　144
　Rossetti, 139
reserve, 3, 43, 44, 65, 128
　Carlyle, 28, 29, 34–35, 67
　Browning, 78–79
　Pater, 198–99, 202
　see also manhood, manliness, masculinity,
　　repression
Rossetti, Christina, 142, 169
　"Goblin Market," 142
　"In an Artist's Studio," 169
Rossetti, Dante Gabriel, 95, 118, 119,
　202
　and Morris, 141
　post-Brotherhood career, 166–72
　sexuality of late work, 169–72
　and Swinburne, 141
　see also aestheticism, artistic manhood,
　　bonding, celibacy, Christ, manliness of,
　　Christ, sexuality of, energy,
　　homoeroticism, hysteria, imprisonment,
　　madness, mimetic distortion, rescue
　　plot, typology
　"Ave," 127
　The Beloved, 169, *170*
　The Blessed Damozel, 157
　Ecce Ancilla Domini!, 127–28
　Found, 139
　"Hand and Soul," 126, 139–40
　"Jenny," 95–96, 106
　Mariana in the South, 126

Mary Magdalene at the Door of Simon the Pharisee, 121, 126–28, *127*, 141
"My Sister's Sleep," 119, 181
The Passover in the Holy Family, *122*, 123
portrait, photograph, 166, *167*
Regina Cordium, 169
St. George and the Dragon, 141–42, *142*
Veronica Veronese, 169
Water Willow, 169
"The Woodspurge," 119, 181
Rossetti, William Michael, 142, 148, 171
Ruskin, John, 32, 41, 83, 85, 91, 103, 118, 160, 163

Salome, 90
Sand, George, 36–37
Sedgwick, Eve Kosofsky, 9, 10
Sennett, Richard, 44
Shelley, Percy, 115
Sinfield, Alan, 9
Smiles, Samuel, 116–17, 118, 153, 158
  entrepreneurial aesthetic, 116–17
  Self-Help, 116–17
spermatorrhea, 202
Stearns, Peter, 12, 13
Swinburne, A. C., 179, 185
  and Pater, 179, 185
  and Rossetti, 141
  "Hymn to Proserpine," 179
  "Laus Veneris," 179, 185

Tennyson, Alfred, 43, 75, 84, 85, 142, 152
  "Crossing the Bar," 196
  "The Lady of Shalott," 82, 84, 152, 169, 177, 195
  "Locksley Hall," 44, 48–49, 50–51, 68, 71, 76, 105, 196

"Mariana," 2, 133–34, 177, 195
Maud, 48, 68, 76
In Memoriam, 45, 99, 108, 143
  see also artistic manhood, celibacy, hysteria, imprisonment, madness, plot, poetics, repression
Theweleit, Klaus, 11–12, 33, 52
Tractarians, 1, 2, 112, 120, 129, 161
  and Carlyle, 57–61
  see also communities, Puseyism
typology, 4, 176
  aestheticism, 4, 176
  Browning, 26, 88, 100, 109–10
  Carlyle, 24, 26–27, 29, 31, 37, 52, 60, 71, 176, 186
  Hunt, 161
  masculinity, 125
  Millais, 121, 125
  Pater, 26, 176, 186
  Pre-Raphaelite Brotherhood, 123
  Rossetti, 126–28

Vance, Norman, 12
visual style, masculine, 87–88, 180–81
  Hunt, 163
  Millais, 119–21
  Pre-Raphaelite Brotherhood, 112, 116–19, 140, 172, 180–81
  see also mimetic distortion

Wells, H. G., 186
Wilde, Oscar, 126, 153, 164, 195, 209 n 26
  Salomé, 126
Woolf, Virginia, 44
  Jacob's Room, 44
Wordsworth, William, 18, 39, 43, 115

Printed in Great Britain
by Amazon